CORNISH
MILESTONES

Above: *SX165545 Lanreath*

Front cover main picture: *SX018523 St Austell.*
Front cover secondary picures left to right: *SX057721 B3266 St Mabyn; SW395276 A30 Crows an Wra;*
SX265558 B3253 St Martin; SX064744 B3266 St Tudy; SW916486 A390 Probus.
Back cover main picture: *SW751384 Old Tretheague Bridge road, Stithians*
Back cover left: *SX011463 St Austell.* Right: *SW389340 B3318 St Just*

CORNISH MILESTONES

*The development of Cornwall's Roads
in the eighteenth and nineteenth centuries*

BY

IAN THOMPSON

TWELVEHEADS PRESS

TRURO 2013

CONTENTS

The standard caption format for individual milestones depicted throughout lists:
the Ordnance Survey map reference number; road number (where applicable);
followed by the parish or general location; suffixed by the English Heritage Grade II listing number.
i.e *SW379286 B3306 St Just Airfield 69220*

Units of measurement and money are given in the form concurrent with events described.
Money: £1 = 20 shillings (s) = 240 pence (d)
      1 shilling = 12 pence
      1 guinea = 21 shillings
Distance: 1 mile = 8 furlongs = 80 chains = 1,760 yards = 1.609 kilometres
      1 yard = 3 feet = 36 inches = 0.914 metres
      1 pole = $16\frac{1}{2}$ feet = 5.03 metres

TWELVEHEADS PRESS

First published in 2013 by Twelveheads Press.
Twelveheads Press, 2 Woodside Cottages, Chacewater, Truro, Cornwall TR4 8LP.
ISBN 978 0 906294 78 9
British Library Cataloguing-in-Publication Data.
A catalogue record for this book is available from the British Library.
Typeset in Baskerville
Printed by Tower Print Ltd, South Wales

INTRODUCTION

Cornwall has the best collection of granite milestones in Britain and therefore the world. This is partly due to the relative neglect of Cornwall's road network through much of the 20th Century, but also due to the care of the county's highway workers and the enduring nature of Cornish granite.

The history of Cornish milestones is bound up with the development of the transport system of what was through the 18th and 19th Centuries one of the most industrial counties in Britain. The growth of tin mining and copper mining put ever increasing pressure on a road system which had seen little improvement since the middle ages. The response was funded not by a central government, but by local entrepreneurs in Cornish towns who fought to bring trade and prosperity to their community and themselves by setting up Turnpike Trusts. Their road making efforts are almost invisible today, but the milestones remain.

Train of Mules carrying Copper Ore, from THE MINE BY I. TAYLOR, JOHN HARRIS 1834. CORNISH STUDIES LIBRARY

EARLY ROADS

It is possible to see how roads developed from the earliest occupation of Britain by men following the trail of animals. The earliest settlements would have established paths to grazing land, and as communities developed they would be linked by trading routes taking advantage of dry ground and linking places where rivers could be crossed. Well trodden paths and routes became roads as traffic increased.

The importance of tin in the ancient world put Britain on the map. The Bronze Age needed both tin and copper to make bronze. Heroditus in 430 BC referred to Britain as the Cassiterides, from which he said came tin. Pytheus of Massalia (modern Marseilles) claimed to have circumnavigated the British Isles in about 325 BC He talks of the Cornish mining tin ore, smelting it and working it into pieces the shape of knuckle bones and exporting tin via the island of Ictis. Since Ictis was reached at low tide from the mainland it has sometimes been identified as St Michael's Mount. Pytheus says merchants took thirty days

to reach the River Rhone with pack horses laden with tin. The Rhone could then be used to carry Cornish tin to the Mediterranean and the thriving port of Marseilles. It was much easier to carry heavy goods by water than overland. The best way to reach England from Cornwall was along the coast by boat, but roads were still needed in Cornwall to connect the tin mines to the coast.

Evidence of Roman roads in Cornwall awaits future discovery. Five Roman milestones have been identified in Cornwall. These are described and discussed later in this book. No evidence of the arrow straight paved military roads typical of the Romans has been found in Cornwall. A number of military camps and signal stations have been identified, but it seems the Romans traded with Cornwall rather than conquered it and this required a lower status road network requiring subtle archaeological skills to identify it.

ROADS AND THE CHURCH

After the Romans left there is little evidence of road construction or even road repair for several centuries. River crossings are the key to long

Looe Bridge was built through a series of Indulgences in the fifteenth-century

East Looe and West Looe

distance travel and the repair of bridges was essential. In the Anglo-Saxon period most land was subject to a threefold tax, the Trinoda Necessitas, one part of which was for the repair of bridges. In 960, for example, when King Edgar gave Tywarnhayle (Porthtowan SW694475) to his thegn Eanulf, a condition of the gift was to help in the construction of bridges.[1]

During the middle ages, the courts of the Manor, the Hundred and the Shire were concerned with the maintenance of roads and bridges. In each Manor two way wardens were chosen annually with powers to oblige tenants to give money, materials or labour for the repair of Manorial Bridges. In the Hundred Court, the Sheriff protected the King's Highway and Bridges from encroachment.

When the King's Justices came to Launceston to hold the county court known as an Eyre, the juries summoned from each Hundred were required to report on problems with roads or bridges. In the Eyre of 1283 the Jury of Powder called out the Bishop of Exeter for enclosing a park at Lanner in St Allen, obstructing two common highways to the hurt of all men passing with carts, on horseback or on foot travelling to the market of Truro.[2] The Bishop defended himself by saying that his predecessor had made an alternative road. The Justices were satisfied by a fine and the Bishop kept his park. The lost road can be traced from Lanner Mill (SW830496) through Bishop's Wood to Idless (SW820476) as a green lane today.

There is written evidence of the involvement of the church, especially in the repair of bridges. The keeping of roads in repair came to be considered 'a pious and meritorious work before God, of the same sort as visiting the sick and caring for the poor'.[3] Travellers were regarded as unfortunate people whose progress on their toilsome journeys it was Christian charity to assist. Bridge construction and repair was aided by the system of Indulgences. By doing good work a Christian sinner could reduce his time in Purgatory, usually by a period of forty days, and speed his journey to heaven. Indulgences became increasingly common and reached a peak in the 15th century, which Charles Henderson described as 'the Golden Age of bridge building in Cornwall' when some of the most important bridges in the county were built.

ROADS AND THE TUDORS

When Henry VIII dissolved the monasteries he took away the financial power of the church to repair the roads. The Protestant Reformation poured scorn on the concept of Indulgences as superstitious nonsense and they were abolished. Legislation to fill the void left by church-sponsored repairs was enacted in 1555 in the reign of Queen Mary (2 & 3 Philip & Mary c.VIII). This first Highway Act required constables and churchwardens in each parish to call a meeting in Easter week each year to choose two surveyors who would supervise the repair of any parish highways leading to any market town. The surveyors were authorised to require occupiers of land to attend at Midsummer with wains or carts, and other householders, cottagers and labourers were to work on the roads providing their own tools. Work was to be undertaken on four days of eight hours each.

The Act was renewed in 1562, now with compulsory powers to obtain materials for road repairs and an increase in 'statute labour' from four to six days (5 Eliz. c.XIII). The principle of compulsory labour on the roads was to continue until the General Highway Act of 1835, when it was superseded by highway rates.

The system of statute labour was better than no system, but it was seriously flawed. The surveyors were unpaid local men of modest standing with no training in road maintenance and little power to enforce compliance. Labour was given grudgingly and work was done to the lowest standard that would meet the amateur surveyors' approval. Parishes differed in their attitude to work so a long distance road could vary from good to impassable at a parish boundary. Parishes which contained a major thoroughfare were hard pressed to maintain it as the traffic continued to increase with each passing decade.

THE FIRST TURNPIKE ACT

The Restoration of Charles II after the English Civil War gave an opportunity to rethink how roads should be maintained. As Britain grew more prosperous and trade and travel increased, roads were under ever greater pressure. It might have been acceptable in the Middle Ages that travel should cease during the winter months because the roads were impassable, but in a modern, post-war nation this was not good enough. An old idea was resurrected and redesigned so that the road user would pay for the maintenance of a road. In 1346 tolls had been imposed by the authority of Edward III for the repair of three roads in London.[4]

The first Turnpike Act was passed in 1663 for repairing the Great North Road, to York and Scotland, in the counties of Hertfordshire, Cambridgeshire and Huntingdonshire. There were to be three toll-gates or turnpikes as they were called, one in each county. The surveyors for this first turnpike road were appointed by the Justices in each county and were empowered to call on statute labour as well as the money raised in tolls. Charges were 'for every horse, one penny; for every coach, sixpence; for every wagon, one shilling; for every cart eight pence; for very score of sheep or lambs, one half-penny; for every score of oxen or neat cattle, five pence; for every score of hogs, two pence.' No person returning the same day with the same horse or vehicle or cattle was to pay a second time. The Act was to remain in force for eleven years.

TURNPIKE FEVER

For the next quarter of a century no other Turnpike Acts were sought. A few more were then obtained, but road building was given a different impetus by insurrection and the need to move troops and equipment safely and speedily. Between 1726 and 1737 General Wade constructed 240 miles of what were in effect military roads in Scotland. He employed up to five hundred soldiers on the work each summer and created new garrisons at Fort William, Fort Augustus and Fort George.

Before 1720 there was little turnpike activity in areas remote from London. In the 1740s many new Turnpike Trusts were set up in the north of England including a number of important coal routes. The years of 'Turnpike Mania' began in 1751 and continued to 1772. In those twenty-two years 389 trusts were established, more than in the previous forty years or the succeeding sixty-six years. The peak decade was from 1751 to 1760 and this was when many of the Cornish Turnpike Trusts were set up.[5]

The Turnpike Trusts established under these 18th century Acts differed from the original 1663 turnpike. They were run by a board of trustees who raised loans when the Trust was set up which would fund road improvements from the outset. Money collected in tolls was to be used to pay off the loan, with any surplus being used to pay for further road improvement.

TURNPIKE MILESTONES

The key paragraph for milestones, identical in six Acts for different Cornish trusts studied by the author is quoted here:

And be it further enacted by the Authority aforesaid,

That the said Trustees, or any five or more of them, may, and they are hereby impowered and required, to cause the said Road to be Measured and Milestones or Posts to be fixed or set up on the Sides thereof, with Inscriptions to be made thereon, denoting the Number of Miles, and distances to Places, as they, or any five or more of them, shall think fit.

It is clear from this that the Trustees of a new Turnpike Trust had a legal duty to erect accurately spaced milestones at one mile intervals along their roads. This was the statute mile defined in the reign of Elizabeth I as 1760 yards and put an end to 'long miles' and to local estimates of mileage. When the carriage of goods was paid for by the distance travelled by the carter or waggoner, an accurate distance was essential. Before the establishment of the penny post, the letter rate depended on distance. The

Post Office was keen to promote the erection of milestones. A dispute between the Post Office mileage and the Launceston Turnpike Trust's milestones is mentioned in a later chapter. Distances between milestones were measured using a standard chain, though some Trusts may have used a measuring wheel. The accuracy with which this was done is indicated on several surviving terminus stones at the end of a turnpike road, notably for the Callington Trust and the Saltash Trust, where the distance is recorded to the nearest furlong, pole and yard.

Each Trust had its own design of milestones. While some Trusts stuck to a standard design, many would use an appropriately modern design on later road improvements. Typically, early milestones would be rectangular with an inscription on one face, while by the 1830s a triangular design was more popular with inscriptions on two faces. At the start of the

The Turnpike Trusts of Cornwall

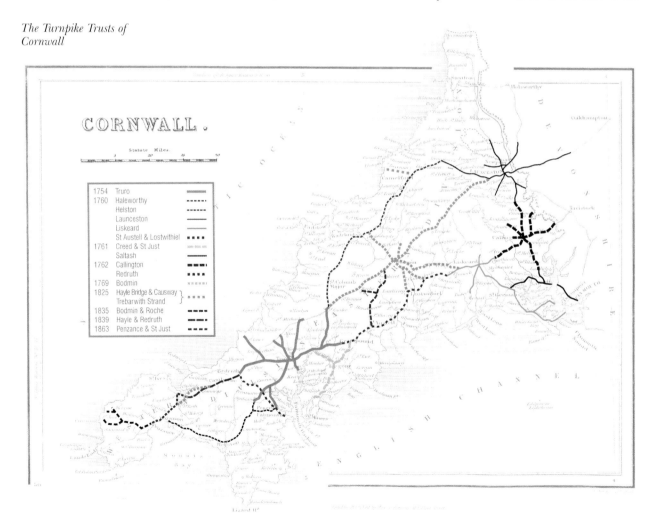

turnpike age, the common number system was changing from Roman numerals to Arabic numerals. A milestone with Roman numerals is usually, though not invariably an early milestone. The unyielding granite used for almost all of Cornwall's milestones does not lend itself to elaborate carving and many milestones carry just a single letter for the principal town and a number for the distance. Gravestones from the 18th and 19th centuries show delicate work, neat spacing and accurate spelling. These are not features typical of milestones from the same period.

It is important to realise that not all milestones were set up by Turnpike Trusts. Some milestones were erected on roads to great houses and a large number of milestones were erected at the end of the 19th century when the County Council was established and took over responsibility for main roads. In comparison to the south-east of England, turnpikes came late to Cornwall. In a number of cases milestones came before turnpikes. Examples of pre-turnpike milestones can be seen in West Penwith, on the road from Mitchell to Hayle and on the original post road to Bodmin from Camelford.

COUNTY BRIDGES

From the 16th century certain bridges were deemed to be of such importance that their maintenance was governed by the County Court. A bridge became a county bridge when the Justices of Quarter Sessions ordered its repair. For example, in 1774 when the Justices were told that the 'ancient and common bridge' now called Buryas Bridge (SW446290) on the boundary between the parishes of Paul and Madron was 'in decay', they ordered 'that the same be rebuilt according to the plan produced to this Court by John Dennis, at the expense of the County and to be for the time to come a County Bridge.' [6]

In West Looe a plaque still marks the end of the old Looe Bridge which was **REPEARED BY THE COUNTY: 1689** (SW253534) and so became a County Bridge.

Records show that the bridge was built in the 15th century by private subscription at the instigation of the church. In 1411 an indulgence of 40 days was granted to all penitent faithful who would contribute towards the cost of the new bridge. Further indulgences were granted in 1415 and 1418.

Usually the county took responsibility for the approach roads to a County Bridge as well as the bridge itself. The limit of the county's responsibility was marked by a 'county bridge

Looe Bridge was repaired by the County in 1689 and so became a County Bridge.

The present Looe Bridge was built in 1853 for £2,980

stone', usually a small round topped stone bearing a carved letter **C** in the 19th century. A considerable number of county bridge stones survive. One on the Haleworthy Trust's turnpike at Knightsmill (SX072806) is Grade II listed as a milestone, the listing surveyor mistaking the **C** for the initial letter of Camelford exactly three miles away.

SCIENTIFIC ROAD MAKING

The Turnpike Trusts raised money for road improvements and they spent money on road repairs, but often the results were unsatisfactory. Repairs were destroyed by winter weather and costs rose. A number of surveyors were learning improved road making skills, but it was one man, John Loudon McAdam who set out the requirements for economic and scientific road construction so clearly and determinedly that his name stands above all others to this day.

McAdam was born in Ayrshire in 1756, two years after Cornwall's first Turnpike Trust was established for roads into Truro. At the age of 14 he went to America to work for his uncle in New York. He became a successful merchant, returning to Scotland in 1783, where he turned his attention to road construction. He became a commissioner for roads in Scotland and travelled extensively in England to study the condition of the roads of the ever expanding turnpike network. In 1811 he presented his *Observations on the Highways of the Kingdom* to a Select Committee set up to consider regulations and improvements to roads.

The focus of attention for decades had been on the effect of the width of wheels on the road surface, the argument being that wide wheels would roll a road flat, but narrow wheels would cut deep ruts. Minimum widths had been specified for wheels on different classes of vehicles and penalties were charged at toll gates for vehicles with very narrow wheels. McAdam dismissed the debate on wheel width as irrelevant and placed his emphasis on the nature of the road surface. He had carried out experiments on the type of material needed for a good road and shared his conclusions with the Committee.

He had found that the key to a successful road was an impermeable crust which prevented water penetrating to the soil beneath. Whatever the nature of the soil, if it was kept dry it would bear any weight likely to be put on it. To achieve an impermeable crust, McAdam recommended that cleaned stones be broken into small uniform pieces no more than 1½ inches each in size and laid on the road in two layers, the first being consolidated before the second was applied. He suggested that material already placed on the road could be cleaned, broken up and re-used, which would save the cost of bringing in new material. He specified a shallow camber of one inch in one yard to allow drainage to ditches at the side of the road. He had found that broken stone would compact under the action of traffic because of its angular nature and form the impermeable crust needed. Unbroken stones would slide over each other and be pushed aside by traffic like the smooth pebbles on a shingle beach and must not be used.[7]

In 1816 McAdam was appointed general surveyor to the Bristol Turnpike Trust where he was able to put his theory into practice. He also turned his attention to the proper training of surveyors, preaching his doctrine of a layer of clean broken stone to all who would listen. John Loudon McAdam produced a dynasty of road surveyors. His three sons became road surveyors as did four of his grandchildren. It was his son, William McAdam who specialised in work on new lines of road in the west of England, with this work being carried on by William's son Christopher. The gentle gradient and sweeping curves of the London Road built by the McAdams for the Truro Trust is described in Chapter 4, together with the special milestones with cast iron plates that are a feature of this road.

GUIDESTONES

Finding the way is a fundamental of any long distance travel. While local people would know which way to turn at a cross roads, a stranger would not. This matter was addressed by central government at the end of the 17th century. In 1697, by Act of Parliament (8 & 9 WIII c.XVI), local Justices of the Peace were authorised to instruct highway surveyors to put up a direction stone or post 'for the better convenience of travelling in such Parts of the Kingdome which are remote from Towns and where several Highways meet.' Further Acts followed and it was normal to include a clause about direction stones or posts in the wording of a Turnpike Act.

While wooden signposts are outside the scope of this book and metal fingerposts are largely to do with the 20th century, many stone direction posts were erected across Cornwall during the 18th and 19th centuries. They are singular and remarkable in their variety and are noted in the appropriate chapters of this book.

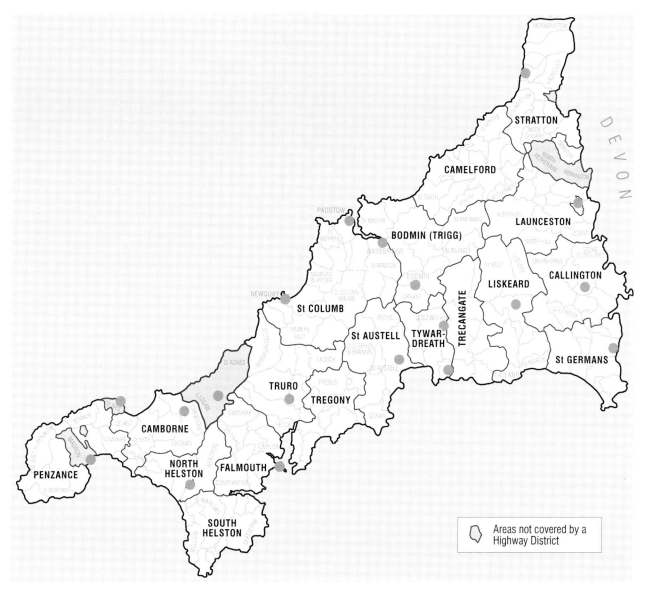

Highway District outlines

PARISHES AND DISTRICT HIGHWAY BOARDS

Maintenance of all roads which were not taken up as turnpike roads remained the responsibility of the parishes through which they ran. The 1835 Highways Act removed the obligation of Statute Labour, but replaced it with a highway rate to pay for maintenance within the parish. This maintenance could be of a lower level than that required on the turnpikes, because usually the traffic density was much less.

Some parishes erected milestones on their roads. These milestones were contemporary with the turnpikes and reflected the design and style of the time. No written records have been found so far, to date any parish milestones in Cornwall.

While the 1835 Act allowed parishes to group together to form Highway Districts, this did not happen in Cornwall until a further Act was passed in 1862 (25 & 26 Vic. C.61). With a number of exceptions, Cornish parishes were grouped together by the Justices into seventeen Highway Districts with highways administered by a District Highway Board. Each parish retained one or more waywardens to supervise the practical work of road repair. Some Highway Districts erected milestones.

11

CORNWALL COUNTY COUNCIL

Turnpike Trusts were set up for a period of 21 years to improve the roads under their care and to pay off the loans raised for the work by charging tolls. Invariably at the end of this period the work was not completed and much of the debt was still outstanding, so a Renewal Act was sought to continue the Trust's work. This pattern of renewal continued into the 19th century, but increased competition from the growing number of railways in Cornwall reduced the revenue from freight. When the railway bridge across the Tamar was opened at Saltash in 1859, the rail network could take passengers to anywhere in England. The days of long distance horse-drawn road travel were coming to an end. Roads were still needed and the turnpike roads remained the arteries of the road system, but they were finding it harder to pay their way and travellers were ever more vociferous about the rising tolls charged.

One by one the turnpike trusts began to be wound up. The 1878 Highways and Locomotives Act created 'Main Roads' with some central funding for maintenance. Main Roads were roads that had been turnpikes and roads declared 'Main' at Quarter Sessions. They were administered by the county highways board.

In 1889 Cornwall County Council came into being and one of its top priorities was to set up a Highways Committee to take over the running of the Main Roads. The Highways Committee received a huge number of requests from the District Highway Boards to add their busiest parish roads to the list of Main Roads so that some of the burden of maintenance could be taken by the County.

One of the conditions laid down by the County Council for adopting a road as Main seems to have been the erection of milestones prior to adoption. Other County Councils had a policy of upgrading or replacing milestones on old turnpike roads they took over, but only Cornwall insisted that ALL roads which were to be made Main, and so receive increased maintenance funding from the county rate, should have milestones.

This was very important for the study of

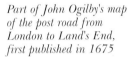

Part of John Ogilby's map of the post road from London to Land's End, first published in 1675

milestones, because Cornwall County Council was able to stipulate that any road to be adopted as a Main Road must first have milestones of an approved type erected along it. Since the county was divided into an eastern and a western highway division, each with its own County Surveyor, there can be seen to be two distinct styles of 'handover' milestones, one in each half of the county. Not only was Cornwall special in erecting new milestones on roads at this late date, but they erected granite stones where other counties used cast iron mile posts.

Cornwall County Council has passed into history, replaced by the Unitary Authority called Cornwall Council. The County Council preserved the milestone legacy it inherited and added a new layer of roadside history in the form of its own special milestones.

MAPS

The history of roads is found on maps as much as it is in books. Early maps showed the relative position of towns with perhaps a straight line to indicate how they were linked. As maps improved through the 18th and 19th centuries they gave more and more detail of roads and roadside features. The first really useful map for Cornwall's roads was John Ogilby's *Brittania* published in 1675. This showed the main post roads on a series of strips with accompanying notes and carefully measured distances and directions. Cornwall is fortunate to have been the first county to be mapped at one inch to one mile by Joel Gascoyne in 1699, giving invaluable information about the road network at the time. Thomas Martyn published his one inch county map in 1748, which gives a wonderful view of the roads shortly before Cornwall's first turnpike trust for roads leading to Truro. Christopher and John Greenwood published maps of all but five of the English counties between 1817 and 1834. Their map of Cornwall has proved the most reliable source for information on turnpike roads. Note that the numbers showing distances at one mile intervals on their map refer to calculated distances and do not record the location of milestones. The Ordnance Survey one inch maps show road improvements during the 19th century. Commercially available copies of these maps need to be studied with care. Different sheets of the Ordnance Survey map were updated in different ways throughout the 19th century. Railway information was usually added but road improvements were sometimes overlooked. The large scale six inch and twenty five inch Ordnance Survey maps mark the accurate location of milestones and show information about distances, but do not copy the inscriptions on individual milestones. Comparison of the first edition Ordnance Survey maps of 1880 and the second edition of 1907 shows how milestones were set up on roads taken over by the new Cornwall County Council, matching the listings published in the county newspaper at the time.

SW355248 B3315 Sennen, the first milestone in England. 1407760

CHAPTER ONE
WEST PENWITH

The far western tip of the Cornish peninsula from Penzance to Land's End, contains some of the most elaborate and beautiful milestones in the county, and some of the most primitive. It is unique in having three sets of enigmatic milestones with numbers only, each set having a different destination. The large number of so-called finger stones - stones with carved pointing hands - is a special feature of this area.

THE FIRST MILESTONE

The most westerly milestone on the British mainland must be at or near Land's End. This might be expected to be some large monument giving distances to the major cities, or perhaps to the other corners of our island. There is a modern signpost that does this within the Lands End Experience complex of buildings, but the first and last milestone is a very low key affair.

In the past, Land's End was not easy to find without a local guide. Budding author Wilkie Collins visited Cornwall in the summer of 1850. His book *Rambles Beyond Railways* published the following year was a great success. He describes an old milestone marked simply with the number 1:

> I have already said, that the stranger must ask his way before he can find out the particular mass of rocks, geographically entitled to the appellation of the 'Land's End'. He may, however, easily discover when he has reached the district of the Land's End, by two remarkable indications that he will meet with on his road. He will observe, at some distance from the coast, an old milestone marked 1, and will be informed that this is the real original first mile in England; as if all measurement of distances began strictly from the West! A little further on he will come to a house, on one wall of which he will see written in large letters 'This is the first Inn in England', and on the other: 'This is the last Inn in England'; as if the recognised beginning and end too, of the Island of England were here, and here only! [1]

Today, the real original first milestone in England is not easy to find. It is no longer on the main road. Comparing Ordnance Survey maps published in 1925 and in 1934 reveals that the

line of the road to Land's End changed. A short cut appears to have been made between these two dates, by-passing the hamlet of Trevescan and reducing the distance to Land's End by about ¼ mile. To find the milestone, leave the modern A30 and take the old loop into Trevescan. Turn right where B3315 joins, and immediately on the right, set between massive granite boulders in the boundary wall around the outbuildings of Trevescan Farm is a straight sided monolith with a pyramid top – the first milestone (SW355248). Sadly the rectangular recess with the large carved number 1 which Wilkie Collins saw has fallen away due to a fault line in the granite. A hole drilled horizontally through the milestone shows where an attempt has been made in the past to hold the two parts of the stone together. Without reference to other similar stones it would be hard to identify this as any more than a block of granite surrounded by hundreds of other granite blocks on this rocky extremity.

However, its neighbour the second milestone is in better condition. This milestone stands near the turning to Sennen Cove, opposite Sennen School. The school building is dated 1880, but the milestone is older than this. The milestone is built into an old stone wall, a Cornish hedge, between the road and a recently created footpath. The milestone must have been there before the stone wall was built (SW362260). The milestone design is most unusual and distinctive. It is, as Collins describes, marked simply with a number, in this case **2**, which stands proud of a rectangular field cut away from the dressed face of a rectangular granite stone with a pyramid top.

The run of milestones is complete. Milestones 1, 2, 3, 4, 5, 6, 7 and 8 all survive. At 9, on the outskirts of Penzance, there is a replacement in a different style (SW455295). This triangular section milestone with a pyramid top once had cast iron plates, but now has an inscription in the stone surface, reading **PENZANCE 1; LANDS END 9**. It probably dates from about 1890.

Almost one hundred years before Wilkie Collins, William Wynne and his family visited

SW362260
Sennen School. 69855

SW372271 A30
Trevedra Farm. 1406869

SW387273 A30
St Buryan. 69611

SW402275 A30
St Buryan. 69610

Land's End.
CYRUS REDDING 1842

dismantling lengths of stone wall. Nevertheless, Mr Wynne noted milestones recently erected, not on the enclosed coach way, but on the more direct horse way which crossed unfenced land.

> A Short Relation of a Journey into Cornwall in the year 1755 and what occur'd to me worthy of Remembrance.
>
> I set out from Little Chelsea with wife and daughter in the coach and 4 horses. Son and servant on horseback . . .

Some days later he writes:

> Next day we set out from pensance for the Lands End. 'Tis 10 miles the horse way and miles stones Lately set up, but the Coachway is at least 12 miles to Senan.
>
> In our way, there is a Quaker Burying Ground enclosed with a wall of stones.
>
> About 3 miles from hence is Senan Churchtown... The coach would go no further and 'tis two good miles to walk to the point of land called Land's End, a great part of it is narrow stony way so that a Coach could not pass without pulling down their stony Hedges, which has and may be done if desired.
>
> Some of the way the Coach came, we were forced to get out and to be Lifted over stones, some of which Lay across the road and bigger than any at Stonehenge . . . impossible to be removed but by Gunpowder. [2]

It seems likely that these 'miles stones lately set up' in 1755 were the same series that Wilkie Collins noted in 1850. The first turnpike trust in Cornwall was established for roads around Truro in 1754. The milestones on the horse way, which is now the A30, are therefore at least as old, if not older than the oldest turnpike milestones in Cornwall.

PENZANCE AND ST JUST TURNPIKE TRUST

In 1863, very late in the turnpike era, an application was made by a new trust to levy tolls

Land's End. While Wilkie Collins was on foot, the Wynnes travelled by coach. This meant they could not take the shortest route to Land's End, the 'horse way' or 'rode', but had to follow the easier 'coach way' or 'carriageway', which was more than four miles longer. Even this better route was obstructed by huge rocks requiring manhandling of the coach. To reach Land's End itself with the coach would have involved

SW417280 A30
St Buryan. 1407091

SW431280 A30
Sancreed. 1406886

SW443288 A30
Paul. 69564

SW455295 A30
Penzance.

SW426315 A3071
Madron. 1405971

SW397326 B3318
Sancreed. 69815

SW386334 B3318
St Just. 1406916

SW389340 B3318
St Just. 1405968

on a turnpike road from St Just in Penwith to Penzance. The application to the Secretary of State was for a new main road and three branches:

> The main road from Saint Just to the boundary of Penzance, in length about 6 miles 3 furlongs and 130 yards
> A branch road, from the main road, to Nancherrow, 3 furlongs 150 yards in length
> A branch road, from the main road, to Pendeen, 2 miles 1 furlong and 30 yards in length
> A branch road from the last-named branch road to Trewellard, 1 mile 1 furlong in length

The destinations show that this was a road for commercial traffic, serving the tin mines at Pendeen, Trewellard and St Just and the foundry at Nancherrow. The Nancherrow road is still called Turnpike Road or New Road. Milestones survive on the two northern branches, to Pendeen and Trewellard, both roads now classified as B3318. On each branch is a milestone with the single number **6** and south of their junction is a milestone with the single number **5**. On the main road, now the A3071, east of Newbridge (built 1843) is a milestone with the single number **3**.

At first glance these milestones look identical to the old milestones on the Land's End road described above. They have the same single number standing proud of a rectangular field cut away from the dressed face of a rectangular granite stone with, this time, a truncated pyramid top. More careful comparison will show how much crisper the edges are on these newer stones. Looking at the two turnpike trust 6-mile stones (SW386334 and SW389340) and the old Land's End 6-mile stone just east of the Tregonebris turn on the A30 (SW416280), the numbers are very different. While the turnpike trust numbers are sharp edged and almost an 8

with a gap, the old number is worn and looks like a large inverted comma. Crucially, and confusingly, the numbering on the turnpike milestones starts at the Penzance end with numbers increasing as the journey goes west, while the old milestones count down the miles to zero at Land's End.

MILESTONES AND A NEW BRIDGE BEFORE THE TURNPIKE

On the line of the main turnpike road, at the correct distance in relation to the other surviving milestones along the A3076, is a tall, thin milestone with a rounded top, rectangular in cross section with an incised inscription, reading **FROM PENZ 5** (SW395311). The carving looks old, but on the back is an even older inscription. While the front carving is all in capitals, on the back are three lines of carving in upper and lower case separated by three incised lines. **From Penz 5** is in a very old style.

We know that milestones existed on this road before the 1863 turnpike. One is mentioned in a newspaper. The *West Briton* of 26 May 1843 reported a 'New Bridge to be built at Newbridge, Sancreed by Mr Edward Harvey of Penzance at 3rd milestone on St Just road'. This reference to milestones on this road pre-dates the turnpike road by 20 years. Today, the 3rd milestone is a crisply carved stone with a raised number **3**, erected by the turnpike trust (SW426315).

One mile west of the five mile stone is a second survivor of the pre-turnpike series (SW379309). It tends to be rather buried in the undergrowth and is 60 yards west of a farm gateway. It is inscribed **FROM PENZ 6** in an identical style to the five mile stone. It leans against the Cornish hedge and its back is not accessible to see if it, too, has been reversed and re-carved.

The roads of West Penwith were busy with

SW395311 A3071
St Just (front). 1405977

SW395311 A3071
St Just (back). 1405977

SW379309 A3071
St Just. 69225

heavy commercial traffic in the early 19th century. Mines along the north coast were flourishing, but there were no natural harbours to carry away the tin and copper ore by sea or to bring in the coal needed to power the steam pumping engines which kept the mines dry even when they ran out under the sea. Everything had to enter or leave West Penwith by road.

In 1834 Nicholas Holman moved his foundry from Copperhouse, Hayle to Tregeseal, St Just to supply boilers, stamps and other heavy equipment to the local mines. Holman was involved in the new bridge at Newbridge as described by Clive Carter:

> The foundry was always supplied by road from Penzance, finished products being similarly transported in the opposite direction, as well as the products of the St Just mines. This section of

The wealth of West Penwith was in its mines. Botallack Mine, St Just. CYRUS REDDING 1842

the North Cornwall coastline was too rocky and exposed to allow the construction of a safe harbour. Until the advent of the motor vehicle, first the mule trains and then the wagon convoys were the sole means of transport between St Just and Penzance. The convoys of four-horse wagons ran daily, driven by rough and reckless individuals, distinguished by their dress of 'Sandford frocks and Billy Cock hats'. In summer the convoys were shrouded by billowing dust and in winter often grounded in the ford at Hallen Tachen. This was such a wagon trap that Nicholas Holman, worried by the interruption of supplies for his business, joined the mining fraternity in helping to pay for a handsome new granite bridge, which then saw the village change its name from Hallen Tachen to Newbridge.[3]

MADRON MILESTONES

There is one further group of milestones with a single number standing proud of a rectangular field. Remember this design occurs nowhere else in Cornwall. It can be found only in West Penwith.

Jane Powning of Cornwall Council's Historic Environment Service searched the 1st Series Ordnance Survey 6 inch maps and found a set of four milestones between Morvah churchtown and Madron. Two of the milestones have been located on the ground. The one immediately south of Morvah on what is now B3306, is built into a granite wall and is therefore older than the wall (SW403353). The milestone is heavily weathered, it has a horizontal crack below the carved number, the top is rounded, not pyramid

Map (left)

WEST PENWITH MILESTONES WITH MILAGE ONLY

Land's End c.1750 ○
Pre-turnpike ●
Madron Parish □
Penzance Turnpike 1863 ■
Turnpike route ▪▪▪▪▪▪

A rare parish milestone at Morvah, 4 miles from Madron.
SW403353 B3306
Morvah. 1406889

SW416345
Madron. 1406892

shaped. The number **4** stands proud of a cut away rectangular field. The stone is 4 miles from Madron.

One mile towards Madron, in the location shown on the 1880 map is a weathered and lichen encrusted stone (SW416345). It has what could be a truncated pyramid top, and clearly a recessed dressed rectangular panel on the front face, but there is no raised number 3.

THE FINGERSTONES OF WEST PENWITH
Stones with pointing hands exist elsewhere in Cornwall. There are three in the far east of the county and two on the Lizard. Nowhere are they in such profusion and variety as here in West Penwith. They are a real feature of the area and are justly celebrated. In their survey presented to the St Just and Pendeen Old Cornwall Society in 1994, Peter and Ruth Stenner christened these stones 'finger stones'.

A number of the stones are dated, though the dates seem to have changed over the recent decades, depending who last painted that particular stone! The dates given here are those which best fit the incised numbers in the rough granite. The stones are listed in the order given by Mr and Mrs Stenner:

1. On the Sennen turn B3306/A3071 to the west of St Just is a quadrant shaped stone with a rounded top and inscriptions on the two flat faces. The stone is at a T-junction, but details of only two directions are shown. A black painted hand with a large black cuff points south **TO ST BURYAN 5 MILES TO LANDS END 6 MILES.** A second black painted hand with a similar cuff points east - **TO PENZANCE 6¼ MILES AD 1836**. This is the commonest date on the dated fingerstones and matches a high point in tin production in the region. In 1780 Cornwall produced 19,022 blocks of tin. This had risen to 29,321 blocks in 1838.

The finished tin, in blocks each weighing from 3.34 to 3.35 cwts (about 170 kg) had to be

SW374309 A3071
St Just. 69222
Old and new waymarks.
The first of the West Penwith fingerstones.

taken overland to a stannary town to pay duty. Penzance and Hayle were stannary towns serving Penwith.

If a mule or packhorse carried two blocks of tin, this gives an idea of the traffic on the roads at this time. This was not a quiet backwater, visited only by tourists, but a busy industrial area.

Figures for the individual stannary towns show how great the tin production was in the west compared with the east of the county in 1838:

Truro	10,297 blocks
Penzance	12,423 blocks
Hayle	5,452 blocks
Calstock	393 blocks
Morwelham	756 blocks [4]

2. Near what is now Land's End Airport, at a junction of B3306, there is a very similar quadrant shaped stone with a rounded top and inscriptions on the two flat faces. On the right hand face a hand with a cuff points south **TO LANDS END 4 MILES**, below which a second cuffed hand points north **TO ST JUST 2 MILES**. On the left hand face a cuffed hand points south-east **TO ST BURYAN 3 MILES AD 1836**. On this stone, the edges of the oval recesses for each cuffed hand have been picked out in black paint. These two fingerstones are so similar they must have been made at the same time. The road through St Buryan was the main southern route to Penzance at this time (as shown on the county map in *Cornwall Illustrated* published in 1831).

3. At Crows-an-Wra is the most elaborately decorated milestone in Cornwall. It stands on a wide grass verge in front of the Wesleyan chapel beside a wheel-headed granite cross at the St Just turn from the A30. The stone is a narrow quadrant in cross section with an elaborate, overhanging top.

On the right face a hand without a cuff points north-west **TO SAINT JUST 3½ MILES**, though the **½** has not always been painted. The carving of the number **3** and in particular of the word **MILES** is very ornate. There is a flower head shape in the top right hand corner. A small square recess near the base shows where there was once a benchmark. The removal of the benchmark suggests that the stone has been

1 *SW374309 A3071 St Just. 69222*

2 *SW379286 B3306 St Just Airfield. 69220*

3 *SW395276 A30 Crows an Wra, St Buryan. 69652*

4 *SW376273 A30 St Just. 69227*

5 *364261 A30 Sennen. 69854*

6 *SW381309 A3071 St Just. 69224*

7 *SW407318 (right face) A3071 Sancreed. 69812*

7 *SW407318 (left face) A3071 Sancreed. 69812*

moved in the 20th century, probably during road improvements.

There are no pointing hands on the left hand face, but the inscription **TO PENZANCE 5¹/₂ MILES. TO LAND'S END 4¹/₂ MILES**.

The front edge of the stone is decorated with a barley twist pattern picked out in black paint and a black painted isosceles triangle.

On all three of these fingerstones the place name curves in an arc around the top of the number giving the distance.

4. Going south, by the junction of B3306 with A30 is the Quaker burial ground mentioned by William Wynn in his journal of 1755. Standing on the grass verge is the next fingerstone. This is triangular with a flat top and two dressed faces. The place names are carved in an arc as on the other stones, but the distance and **MILES** are on the same level and the pointing hands are not in recessed ovals.

On the left face, a black hand with a cuff points north **TO SAINT JUST 3 MILES**. (Note that Saint is written in full, not abbreviated to St.) On the right face a black hand with a cuff points east **TO PENZANCE 7 MILES**, below which a similar hand points west **TO LANDS END MILES**. In the photographs taken by Mr Stenner in 1992, the recessed blank space before **MILES** had the distance **2³/₄** painted in.

This stone stands 300 metres further from Land's End than the 3-mile stone in the old series mentioned earlier. The distance to Land's End was reduced when the loop of road through Trevescan, past the one mile stone, was by-passed by the A30 in the late 1920s. Presumably the fingerstone originally gave a bigger distance, which had to be cut out, hence the square recess.

5. On the A30 at the next junction north-east of the turn to Sennen Cove is a dated fingerstone giving directions but no distance – a guidestone rather than a milestone. This is a large flat-topped quadrant. The left hand face is inscribed **TO PENZANCE** with the town name in an arc above a black, cuffed hand pointing northeast along the main road and the date 1834. The right hand face has a black cuffed hand pointing southeast **TO BURYAN and PAUL**. On this face the script is italic with **and** in an elegant lower case. This suggests that the two faces were not carved at the same time, or perhaps were carved by two different people.

6. At the Sancreed turn on A3071 east of St Just is a flat-topped quadrant guidestone with a unique inscription in intersecting curves set in large recessed panels on each flat face. The right

The third fingerstone at SW395276 A30 Crows an Wra. 19th century guide stone and medieval cross, both marking the way

hand face has a black, cuffed hand pointing southeast **TO SANCREED CHURCH TOWN AND PAUL**. The left hand face has a black, cuffed hand pointing east to **PENZANCE DIRECT ROAD A.D. 1835**. The direct road was the one which was made a very late turnpike in 1863.

7. Further east on A3071, about 150 metres east of the B3318 junction, a fingerstone points up a farm track. This track, which climbs to a splendid viewpoint at the top of the hill, is the old road to Pendeen before the 1863 turnpike was set out on the easier gradient of the modern B3318. The fingerstone is a narrow quadrant with a semicircular top, beautifully carved and carefully painted. The right hand face has **SAINT** in an arc above a lace-cuffed outlined hand pointing northwest up the farm track, then **JUST NORTH ROAD and MORVAH**. Pendeen used to be referred to as Saint Just North. The left hand

21

8 *SW406317 A3071*
Sancreed. 69811

9 *SW393333 B3318*
St Just. 69228

face also has **SAINT** in an arc above a similar lace-cuffed outlined hand pointing west then **JUST CHURCH TOWN 1819**. This is the earliest dated milestone in West Penwith.

8. At the junction between A3071 and B3318 is a flat-topped, triangular fingerstone with an uncarved back. This must date from 1863 when the new turnpike to Pendeen was made. The right hand face has a black hand pointing northeast to **PENDEEN**. The left hand face has a black pointing hand pointing west to **ST. JUST**.

9. Where B3318 forks and to the north of where the older road over the hill rejoins the 1863 turnpike is a fingerstone with pointing hands in oval recesses. In 1992 the hands were white in a black oval. More recently the hands have been painted black with the curled fingers delineated and the oval outlined. The stone is a flat-topped quadrant. On the left hand face the hand points northwest to **TREWELLARD 1 MILE ST JUST 3 MILES**. Only **TREWELL** could be fitted in to an arc across the stone, and **ARD** has been added above at the end in slightly smaller script. On the right hand face the hand points north to **PENDEEN COVE 2 MILES MORVAH 2 MILES**.

10. The fingerstone at Portherras Cross,

where the northern arm of B3318 joins B3306, has a record four pointing hands. The stone is rectangular in cross section with a flat top. The hands and the style of inscription are the same as those on the previous stone at the fork in B3318, except there are no problems here with long names. At the top of the left hand face a hand in an oval recess points southwest to **PENZANCE 6 MILES**. Below this a hand in an oval recess points northeast to **PENDEEN 1 MILE**. A square recess near the base may once have contained a benchmark. At the top of the right hand face a hand in an oval recess points southeast to **ST JUST 3 MILES**. Below this a hand in an oval recess points northwest to **MORVAH ZENNOR 1836**. The similarities between this and the previous fingerstone would suggest that they were both of the same date, 1836.

11. The old road to the east of Morvah took a long loop inland before rejoining the modern path of the north coast road B3306 at Trevean. The fingerstone at the most inland point of this loop, where the road to Madron and Penzance branches off has pointing hands in two directions only. This is the road which carries the two worn survivors of the four Madron milestones shown

10 *SW388344 B3306*
St Just. 1405974

11 *SW414348*
Morvah (left face)
1410391

11 *SW414348*
Morvah (right face)
1410391

12 *SW370318 B3306*
St Just. 1405980

13 *SW438373 B3306*
Zennor. 70570

14 *SW451380 B3306*
Zennor. 426214

15 *SW376237 B3315*
Polgigga St Leven.
69748

16 *SW401248 B3283*
Sennen turn. 69609

17 *SW400246 B3283*
St Buryan. 69608

18 *SW398241 B3315*
St Buryan. 69607

on the 1880 Ordnance Survey map, yet the fingerstone does not mention Madron. The pointing hands are elegantly carved with a narrow cuff, but simply painted black all over. On the left face of the narrow quadrant stone with a rounded top, the hand points northeast to **MORVAH AND St JUST**. On the right face the hand points north to **ZENNOR AND St IVES**. No distances are given.

12. In Nancherrow just north of St Just Churchtown is a triangular fingerstone with pointing hands in oval recesses similar to 9 and 10 above, suggesting that it too dates from 1836. On the left face the hand points west to **BOTALLACK 1 MILE**. The **ACK** of Botallack runs off the face and is carved on the chamfered front edge of the stone. On the right face the hand points north to **MORVAH 4 MILES** up the steep climb of No Go By Hill which bypasses the loop of B3306 through Botallack.

13. At the junction east of Treen on B3306 is the worst spelt fingerstone in Cornwall. On the left face, not only is St Ives reduced to **STIVS**, but the S's are both reversed. The distance is given as **6 M** and there is a benchmark near the base. On the right face, a cuffed hand points south, splitting Penzance into **PENZ** above the hand and **ANCE** below with the distance as **6 M** again.

14. West of Zennor where a road leaves B3306 to climb the steep side of Trewey Hill there is a quadrant fingerstone with the names on both faces split by the pointing hands. On the left face reads **PENZA**, hand pointing southeast, **NCE 6 M**. The right face reads **MOR**, hand pointing southwest, **VAH 4 M**.

15. The last of the true pointing hand fingerstones is on the B3315 at Polgigga near Porthcurno. This gives directions and distance to two tourist attractions. The stone is a narrow quadrant with a semicircular top. On the left face the hand in a recessed oval points north to **LAND'S END 2½ MILES**. On the right face a similar hand points east to **LOGAN ROCK 1¾ MILES**.

There are three further pointing stones in West Penwith, but these use arrows rather than pointing hands.

16. To the west of St Buryan on B3283 a flat topped square stone bears an arrow pointing south to **St LEVAN** on the left face and an inscription but no arrow on the right face along the side turning **TO SENNEN**.

17. A few yards further south, a battered

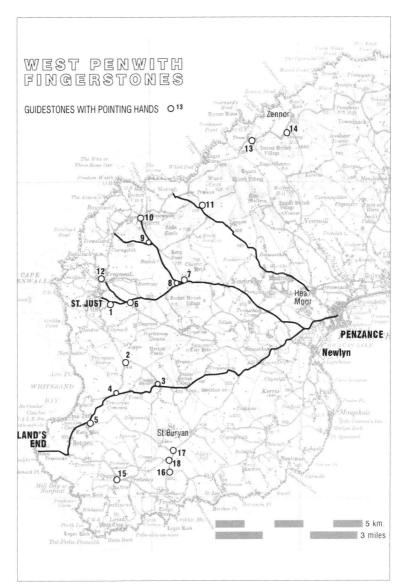

narrow quadrant of stone would lead you off B3283 on a short cut west to **St LEVAN** or allow you to continue south to the **LOGAN ROCK**.

18. The last stone is at the junction of B3315 and B3283 at Sparnon. The triangular stone has large arrows, but the writing is only painted, not incised. As the paint wears and is renewed the writing moves up and down the stone and occasionally names change places. When last visited it read **St BURYAN PENZANCE** with an arrow pointing northeast on the left face, and **LAMORNA NEWLYN MOUSEHOLE** with an arrow pointing east on the right face.

Published by W. Penaluna May. 1817.

PENZANCE

To the Inhabitants of Penzance this Plate is Inscribed By their obedient Servant W. Penaluna

Penzance, published by W Penaluna 1817. CORNISH STUDIES LIBRARY

CHAPTER TWO
PENZANCE, REDRUTH AND HAYLE

The road from Hayle to Penzance was transformed in 1825 by the construction of a long causeway and bridge across the River Hayle. This turnpike was extended with a more direct road to Penzance in 1837. The road east from Hayle to Redruth, marked by magnificent but largely neglected pre-turnpike milestones had to wait until 1839 before an improved route finally took shape. While a number of secondary routes retain good sets of milestones, the Redruth to Penryn Turnpike has few surviving stones and even these are under daily threat from modern heavy traffic.

THE POST ROAD
John Ogilby's strip map of 1675[1] shows the main post road to the west from Redruth running north of Crowan Church and just south of St Hilary Church. This would make it climb from Redruth to Four Lanes, then through Praze an Beeble and over Relubbus Bridge to Marazion. The post road then ran along the sands to reach Penzance. The bridge at Relubbus is mentioned in 1300[2] and there is a Roman milestone preserved in the church at St Hilary, suggesting that this is a very old route indeed. However, this did not become the main turnpike road.

HAYLE TO PENZANCE
If you had wanted to travel to Penzance before 1825, you would have been well advised not to go via Hayle. To travel west from Hayle it was necessary to ford the River Hayle. This could be accomplished at low tide in favourable conditions, with the help of a guide. At high tide the river was half a mile wide and the sandy river bed was continually shifting.

Stockdale noted:

> At low water, a certain part of the river may be crossed in a chaise, but when the tide is coming in, it is very dangerous, owing to the quicksands.[3]

In 1698 Celia Fiennes, on her return journey from Penzance, chose the safer alternative further south across the bridge at St Erth, rather than risk fording the river at Hayle on horseback:

> I continued my returne from Pensands to Hailing (Hayle), and now the tide was down, and so much

St Erth Bridge

land appeared which lay under water before, and I might have forded quite a crosse, many that know the country do but I tooke the safer way round by the bridge.[4]

The bridge at St Erth is very old. Charles Henderson quotes John Leland's *Itinerary* of 1538 which said that the bridge was 'made a 200

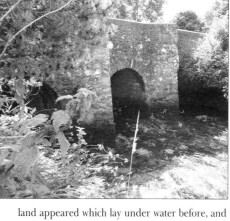

Trewinnard Coach
ROYAL INSTITUTION OF
CORNWALL

yeres syns and hath a three arches. Afor ther was a ferry.' Charles Henderson notes that:

> In 1816, Davies Gilbert, Esq., of Tredrea, procured a grant of £50 and spent as much out of his own pocket in getting the bridge widened. At this time it was still carrying the main road from London to Penzance, but in 1825, the Hayle Causey was opened a mile lower down the river and this became the highway.[5]

A VERY EARLY COACH

In the Royal Cornwall Museum, Truro, pride of place in the main exhibition area on the ground floor is given to the *Trewinnard Coach*. The Museum describes the coach as 'one of the earliest in existence in Britain, comparable in date to the Baskerville landau (1698) at Nottingham Industrial Museum and the 1696 carriage of the Speaker of the House of Commons in London. It is not dissimilar in style to some of the early coaches in the national Coach Museum in Lisbon, and its original owner was reputed to have been a Spanish ambassador.' By 1757 the coach was the property of Chistopher Hawkins Esquire of Trewinnard near St Erth. He and his wife Mary used the coach twice every Sunday to travel to church in St Erth. Accompanied by servants to assist if the coach should become stuck, the procession was quite a spectacle at a time when farmers brought in the harvest on pack horses. The journey was a little over a kilometre, using a bridge close to the manor house and the gentle gradient of the riverside Green Lane to reach the parish church.

The coach has a massive timber frame and a relatively small enclosed passenger compartment

suspended on long leather straps from the four corners of the frame. Secondary straps serve to steady the passenger compartment, but the potential swaying and rolling movement on a journey must have defined the term 'travel sickness'.

The undercarriage was used for the last time to carry Mary Hawkins' coffin to St Erth church in 1780. There is a vault for the Hawkins family in the churchyard. In 1909 the carriage was acquired by the Royal Institution of Cornwall and restored by J. Fuller and Co of Bristol for display in the Royal Cornwall Museum.

HAYLE – BOUNDARY STONES AND BUSINESS RIVALRY

Hayle is an 18th century new town. There is no such place marked on Joel Gascoyne's county map of 1699. The development of Hayle began with the establishment of the Angarrack Smelting House in 1704 and the beginnings of a port. The Cornish Copper Company came to Copperhouse in 1756, and John Harvey opened his iron foundry in 1779. Harvey and the Cornish Copper Company became fierce rivals in the supply of materials to the mining industry. Keeping the port free of sand and silt was a major preoccupation and a major cause of dispute, but trade was brisk, serving the new industries locally and the mines inland.

When Henry Harvey succeeded his father, the dispute between the two companies became even fiercer, drawing in local gentry despite their unwillingness to take sides. The purchase of a small parcel of land and the construction of a new and larger hotel to serve the town was part of a dispute over industrial waste pollution and disease.

Hawkins Family tomb, St Erth

Boundary stone number 3, Hayle SW558370

Boundary stone number 1, Hayle SW558370

In the centre of Hayle, immediately south of Foundry Square, a triangle of land is fronted by the old and new White Hart Hotels which face north towards Foundry Square. The land is completely built up, with Philps' Pasty Shop at its southern apex.

In the narrow one-way road on the south-east side of the triangle, near the corner of the back wall of the pasty shop yard, is a rectangular stone 18 inches tall (SW558370). One side of the stone is against the wall and cannot be read. The other three sides each bear a large Roman capital letter – **P**, **P** and **T** respectively.

Walk round the corner to the pasty shop entrance to find another similar stone at the southern apex of the triangle of land, on the pavement away from the wall (SW558370). All four sides are visible and carry similar large Roman capital letters to the first stone, reading – **T** (facing west), **P**, **P** and **P**. There should be a third stone at the north end of the triangle, but this has not been found.

Edmund Vale[6] mentions Penpol Pond as the land bought and drained by Henry Harvey to build the New White Hart alongside the Old White Hart. The New White Hart opened in the summer of 1838. In August 1830, cholera came to Hayle. Suspicion was directed to the 'nuisance adjoining the White Hart' – the stagnant water of Penpol Pond. A series of maps in the book show how Penpol Pond was a triangle of land in Phillack parish jutting into the surrounding St Erth parish. Studying the maps, it can be seen how the triangle of land now surrounded by roads was once the triangular Penpol Pond.

The most useful map is the earliest 'Copied from one surveyed and drawn by David Palmer, 1810', because this marks four 'Stones showing the ancient course of the River.' The stones numbered 1, 2 and 3 on this map delineate the triangle of Penpol Pond and the boundary between Phillack and St Erth parishes. The fourth stone is beside 'A walled bridge built by Harvey', and again lies on the boundary between the two parishes.

The letters **P** and **T** on the two stones which have been found match the estates in the two parishes. These are indicated on the same map – Trelissick owned by Col. Rodd in St Erth parish, and Penpol owned by Mr. Millett in Phillack parish.

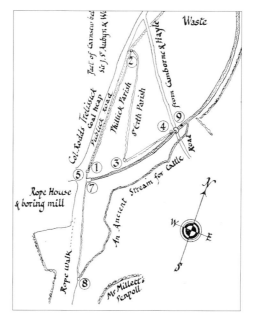

Extract from David Palmer's map dated 1810 showing boundary stones numbered 1, 2, 3 and 4

SW551366 Hayle Bridge Causeway date stone 1825

Grigg's Quay the road went to Rose an Grouse and joined the road from St Erth Bridge near Cockwells. From Ludgvan lower town it followed Long Lane to Gulval before dropping steeply down to the coast and into Penzance.

In 1836 plans were drawn up to improve the road west of Ludgvan with a new line of road to meet the road from Helston near Long Rock.[8] An Act of Parliament in 1837 confirmed the extension of the Trust's control along what is the current line of the A30 trunk road (7 WIV c ii). The milestones between Penzance and Hayle date from this period.

The milestones are of an elaborate design, with a triangular pyramid top and a triangular main section, joined to a square section base by triangular stops. A large amount of information was squeezed onto each of the two main faces in rather small letters. The inscription is carved in Roman capitals with a deep incision for the heavy strokes and a very narrow shallow incision for the light strokes. This style of inscription does not weather well, even on granite, and has usually been repainted in a much simpler style. Many of the milestones have suffered considerable damage on what has always been the main motor road through Cornwall. All in all, these are not pretty milestones, but their survival on such a busy road makes it worth the effort to seek them out. All eight milestones are still in place, from the one mile stone outside the coach depot (SW485311) to the milestone in front of the Cornish Arms in the centre of Hayle (SW564378).

The old pre-causeway route over St Erth Bridge is marked by just one surviving guide stone at a T-junction west of the bridge (SW536344). Black painted hands point towards St Hilary in one direction and St Erth in another. There is no indication of the third direction, to Penzance and Marazion.

HAYLE BRIDGE AND CAUSEWAY

Despite the shifting sands in the Hayle River, the town of Hayle prospered because of its link to the sea. The dangerous tidal ford was superseded by the Hayle Bridge Causeway Turnpike Trust, under 'An Act for building a Bridge and making a Causeway and Turnpike Road from or near Grigg's Quay, in the Parish of Uny, Lelant, over Hayle River and Sands, in the Parish of St Erth, to Carnsew Quay, through Hayle Foundery, in the said Parish of St Erth, and Pen Poll, in the Parish of Phillack' (6 GIV c. iv). The cost of construction was to be recovered by tolls of ½d for each foot passenger, 1d for each horse, 2d for a cart, and 6d for a coach or chaise.[7] There is a date stone, 1825, on the north side of the road at the east end of the causeway, where the road to St Erth turns off (SW551366). The date is carved into a horizontal inset disc on the parapet.

Beyond the new causeway, the road to Penzance remained tortuous. From the toll bar at

HAYLE TO ST IVES

C & J Greenwood's *County Map of Cornwall* published in 1827 shows a toll booth (T.B.) at Grigg's Quay at the western end of the newly built Hayle Causeway. The road from here to St Ives is marked on the map with a heavy line, indicating that it was a turnpike road. Distances of 11, 12 and 13 miles, measured from Redruth are marked along the road on the map. The Greenwood map of Cornwall has proved very reliable in all other areas, and it is odd that there is no other evidence for this road having been a turnpike at any time.

SW485311 A30
Penzance. 1405965

SW501314 old A30
Ludgvan. 70385

SW511325 A30
Ludgvan. 70367

SW521338 A30
Ludgvan. 70368

SW531350 A30
Ludgvan. 70379

SW543360 A30
Ludgvan. 426203

SW553371 B3301
Hayle. 70151

SW564378 B3301
Hayle. 70185

There are only two milestones on the A3074 between Grigg's Quay and St Ives.

In the 19th century, the road was maintained by the St Ives Urban Sanitary Authority (USA) as far as the ecclesiastical parish boundary between St Ives and Lelant. Beyond this parish boundary the road was maintained by the Camborne District Highway Board (HB).

On 6 November 1890 the *Royal Cornwall Gazette* published a list of 'Roads recommended by the Road Committee of Cornwall County Council to be made main and adopted by the County'.

Two entries in the Gazette list are relevant here:

St Ives USA: St Ives through Trelyon to Lelant
Camborne HB: St Ives to Hayle Causeway

The Camborne Highway Board erected the milestone in Lelant (SW543373) three miles from St Ives and an identical stone two miles from St Ives (SW530382) in Carbis Bay, but no milestone one mile from St Ives has been found. Such a milestone would have been erected by the St Ives Urban Sanitary Authority.

The design of these two Camborne Highway Board milestones is of a style copied from the nearby Redruth to Penzance turnpike – a triangular main section with square base and

SW536344
Guide stone at Tredrea
Lane, Ludgvan. 70414

SW543373 A3074
St Ives

SW530382 A3074
St Ives

SW474317 B3311
Gulval

triangular pyramid top - but with the inscription on cast iron plates, rather than carved into the stone surface.

Sadly the Carbis Bay milestone has lost its plates. Funding is being sought to have replacement plates cast.

PENZANCE GUIDESTONES

In 1970, a number of triangular guidestones stood at junctions on secondary roads leading out of Penzance. One with pointing hands stood at Heamoor, half a mile south of Madron. Another with cuffed, pointing hands was on the St Ives to Penzance road half a mile north of Chyandour at the Heamoor turn. Both these have been lost where junctions have been opened up to improve sight lines. One survives near Gulval (SW474317) where the road to Zennor branches off the Madron road at the top of Green Lane Hill, but sadly the painted inscription is no longer legible.

One outlier stone is to be found on what is now the B3311 St Ives to Penzance road on a sharp bend and road junction below Castle an Dinas (SW494347). The stone is battered and quite hard to spot beneath modern road furniture. Rectangular in cross section with a flat top, it is inscribed **PENZANCE ROAD** with the date **1812**. A shallow carved square between the main inscription and the date suggests that a bench mark may have been removed from the stone. The design, inscription and date of this stone are all unique.

BOUNDARY STONES WITH RAISED CARVING

There are two surviving boundary stones of an original four that were erected in 1687 to mark where the unusually circular boundary of the Borough of Penzance was crossed by the main roads into the Borough. One stands at the back of the footpath, against the wall of No.8 Chyandour Cliff (SW478309) on the main road to central Penzance from the east. The other is to the north of Penzance at Nancealverne, on the east side of St Clare Street. It stands at the back of the footpath, against the wall of the cricket ground, opposite the fire station (SW466308).

Both boundary stones have the same inscription **P 16 87** – wrapped around three faces of the stone, and raised above a recessed field in a similar style to the single number West Penwith milestones described in the previous chapter.

A commemorative plaque was erected in 1867 to mark the removal of one of the other boundary stones when Alverton Road was widened. The plaque reads **B S 13FT 6IN S 1865**, which tells us that the boundary stone stood 13ft 6in south of the plaque, i.e. in the middle of what is now the main road, but was removed in 1865.

The fourth stone stood at Wherrytown and is presumed to have been lost when the Esplanade was developed. (See the famous painting *The Rain It Raineth Every Day* by Norman Garstin in 1889, which shows the Esplanade but no trace of the boundary stone. Penlee House Gallery, Penzance)

The definitive book of Penzance is *The History of the Town and Borough of Penzance* by P. A. S. Pool, published by the Corporation of Penzance in 1974. In his book, Mr Pool describes the Charter of Penzance, granted by King James I in 1614, as follows:

> The Charter defines the bounds of the Borough, not as usual by reference to convenient topographical features such as streams and roads but as an artificial line formed by a circle of half-mile radius from the middle of the town – the Market Cross in Green Market.

SW4941 3471 B3311
Ludgvan. 70366

SW478309
Penzance Boundary stone 1687
Chyandour Cliff. 1408085

SW466308
Penzance 1687 boundary
stone. 1408102

SW464301 Lost boundary
stone, Alverton Road, Penzance

SW478309 Chyandour Cliff, Penzance Borough Boundary Stone 1687

Later, on page 43, he describes how in 1687:

> ...the Corporation spent £1-19s-6d on four bound-stones and another £1-10s-0d on setting them up at Chyandour, Chapel St Clare, Alverton and Wherrytown, where roads crossed the borough boundaries. The first and second are still to be seen (inscribed 1687), the third has been removed and superseded by a later stone, and the fourth seems to have vanished without trace.[9]

Cyrill Noall, who wrote the book of *Cornish Mail and Stage Coaches*, also wrote a book about Penzance, in which he describes the ceremony of Beating the Bounds of Penzance:

> At somewhat rare intervals the Councillors (of Penzance) themselves indulged in the good old custom of 'beating the Borough bounds'. In 1854, the Mayor, Richard Pearce, and Corporation assembled at the Green Market Cross, whence they proceeded to the western boundstone at Alverton, passing round the Borough limits to inspect other boundstones at Chapel St Clare and Chyandour. Taking to the water at Albert Pier, the 'beaters' followed a seaward course marked by buoys to visit the last boundstone at Wherrytown. Various ancient practices were observed on the way, the Corporation also receiving the hospitality of several gentlemen over whose lands they passed, the pleasures of the day concluding with a five o'clock dinner at the Union Hotel.[10]

A more recent boundary stone stands on B311 above Gulval and well outside the half mile radius of the old boundary. Tucked into the bottom of the hedge, this stone is inscribed **BOROUGH OF PENZANCE 1934** marking the expanded boundary before the Second World

War (SW481320). There may be other similar boundary stones still to be rediscovered around Penzance.

HAYLE TO REDRUTH – MILESTONES BUT NO TURNPIKE

Most of the heavy goods to and from the industrial sites of Hayle must have gone by sea. The old road from Hayle to Redruth was suitable for pack horse trains, but not for heavy wheeled traffic. It climbed from what is now Foundry Square in the centre of Hayle to High Lanes, crossed a steep valley at Guildford and a very steep valley at Angarrack, ascending 'Steamers Hill' to Connor Downs and then a further long descent and long, steep climb on either side of Roseworthy. This route is shown as the main road from the end of 'Hayle Bridge and Causeway' on C & J Greenwood's county map of Cornwall in 1827.

The same route is shown on the Ordnance Survey 1-inch map Sheet 33, Penzance which shows a dog-leg diversion at Guildford to go under the railway viaduct. The current one was built in 1886, replacing an earlier timber structure of 1852. The map was re-engraved in 1839, bringing the map up to date with such improvements as the Hayle to Penzance turnpike road, mentioned above.

The old road crossed into Camborne parish as it climbed from Roseworthy. This section of road survives as a stony track between SW617397 and SW624402. From Treswithian the road

SW481320 B3311 Penzance Boundary stone 1934

SW481320 B3311 Penzance Boundary stone 1934 showing location

SW559370
Hayle. 70246

SW573376
Hayle. 1408993

SW587384
Steamers Hill, Hayle.
70164

SW601391
Angarrack lane,
Gwinnear. 70107

veered north away from Camborne churchtown along Gilly Road, now called Weeth Road, to Parcanbowan and then along Eastern Lane and North Roskear Road to Tuckingmill. Another very steep descent and climb was encountered at Tuckingmill, with a final very steep descent and climb beyond Pool at Blowinghouse to arrive at last in Redruth.

The original milestones survive all along this pre-turnpike route! It is quite extraordinary that when the turnpike road from Hayle to Redruth was finally opened in 1840, the milestones on the old road were not removed. The old milestones have a similar design to those mentioned near Land's End, and to the Penzance boundary stones of 1687. They are square in cross section with a square pyramid top. The carving on two adjacent faces reveals a raised number and letter on a recessed rectangular field in the same style as the Land's End milestones.

One face bears a large **P** and a number giving the mileage to Penzance. The other face bears a large **L** and a number giving the mileage to Land's End, ten miles further than Penzance. The similarity in design between the two sets of milestones and the agreement in distance to Land's End suggests that both sets were erected in the same period between 1740 and 1750.

The first of these old milestones is just off Foundry Square in Hayle. It has been cemented into the garden wall of No.3 Penpol Road so that only the **18 L** face is visible. (SW559370). Climb the hill past Hayle School to High Lanes. At the start of the descent to Guildford is a block of granite set on the bank. The legend is rarely noticed by the casual observer. This is **9P, 19L** (SW573376).

The old road was cut in two by the Hayle by-pass in 1986. Once over the new bridge, the old road can be rejoined and the steep drop and climb through Angarrack experienced. Where Steamers Hill becomes Angarrack Lane, a lichen encrusted granite milestone is carved **10P, 20L** (SW587384).

Among the shrubs along the garden walls of the modern bungalows of Connor Downs, outside No.3, is **11P, 21L** (SW601391).

Beyond this point the old road is buried beneath the 1840 turnpike. A short section of the original route can be seen north of the turnpike where the descent to Roseworthy has been eased between SW606394 and SW611394.

The trail goes cold in the back streets of Camborne. The milestone which once stood here **14P, 24L** survives in a new housing development in the grounds of what was known as Lower Rosewarne Farm and Gladys Holman House (SW649403). The milestone was moved here long before the modern houses were built. Its removal from its original location may be linked to an earlier housing development in the grounds of the old house.

The milestone in Pool, **16P, 26L** has been re-sited on the south side of the road in front of the chapel (SW671415). A commemorative plaque was put up near the milestone which describes it as a 'Turnpike Milestone', which it is not. All these milestones are older than the first turnpike in Cornwall. They are all 'Pre-Turnpike Milestones'.

The milestone at SW688417, **17P, 27L** was lost when the roundabout for the Redruth by-pass was constructed in 1965.

The last milestone in this series, **18P, 28L** is at East End, Redruth, in an angle of house walls on the pavement in front of No.32 (SW702422).

A further group of similar milestones continues as far as Mitchell, and will be referred to in a later chapter.

SW649403 in 2007.
New houses have been built but
the milestone has been
protected. Camborne. 66638

SW671415 A30
Carn Brea 508046. A plaque on
the wall calls this a Turnpike
Milestone, which it is not.

SW702422
East End, Redruth. 66816

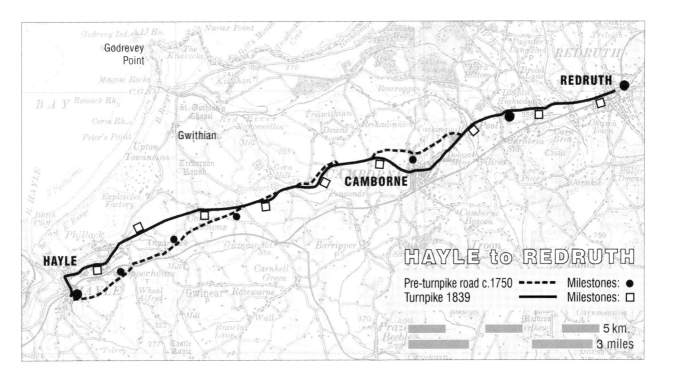

HAYLE TO REDRUTH TURNPIKE

Go back to the milestone outside the Cornish Arms on Commercial Road in the centre of Hayle. This triangular milestone on a square base was the last milestone on the turnpike from Penzance to Hayle using the Hayle Causeway and it was the starting point for the next phase of road improvement, proposed in an Act of Parliament in 1839 (2 & 3 V c194), a new line of road between Hayle and Redruth.

The Hayle end of the new road is described in a 'road book'* published in Exeter shortly afterwards:[11]

> Our road leads through Copperhouse, and shortly after passing the old smelting house, we cross an arm of the Hayle creek, and a tramway of the Redruth railway, which at this spot runs level with the road. On the left, close to the sand hills are some newly erected arsenic works. The turnpike road, within the last ten years, has undergone great improvements; and we here make a gradual ascent to higher ground, keeping

within a short distance of the railway. As the tourist approaches Camborne he will perceive on every hand indubitable marks of the great mining districts he is entering,- the country is desolate looking;- instead of tall forests clad in lively green, he perceives tall chimneys vomiting volumes of black smoke,- and mounds of earth and rubbish, too barren to produce the scantiest vegetation.

This was the route of the A30 trunk road until the Hayle by-pass was constructed in 1985. The 1985 by-pass goes north of Connor Downs before sweeping south of Hayle towards the western end of the Hayle Causeway, crossing the River Hayle on a modern bridge. A pre-by-pass guidebook published in 1965 remarks:

> The traveller usually gets his first view of Hayle from the top of Connor Downs on the main A30 road – the Land's End road.[12]

The guidebook goes on:

> The section of road north of Hayle was originally built and maintained by the enterprise of the local gentry who subscribed to its cost. It was opened in 1840 and from then until 1891 all users had to pay a toll. The Turnpike Inn at Connor Downs and the old toll houses on the road are reminders of these early days when the many hundreds of mules and packhorses which were then based on Hayle,

---

* Road books were once popular travelling companions. They contained tables or strip maps with descriptions of the road in varying amounts of detail. The most popular road book was produced by Daniel Paterson and ran to 18 editions between 1771 and 1829.

carried inland the seaborne traffic through the town's busy port.

Visitors who care to take the old road via the now quiet backwater of Angharrack village will realise the difficulties which faced the traveller before the construction of the turnpike.

Turnpike trusts were not profit making organisations. They were set up by subscription from local gentry as described in the guide book. Money made from tolls was spent on road improvement. The increased movement of goods and people did benefit the local gentry because they were all involved in local business.

The new turnpike ran alongside a new railway line at Hayle. In the rivalry between the two transport systems it was the railway that emerged victorious in the 19th century. An Act of Parliament of 27 June 1834 incorporated the Hayle Railway Company. 'At that time packhorses carrying ore converged on the port in large numbers and the necessity for a railway became more and more evident, especially in view of the success of the Redruth and Chacewater' - horse drawn railway opened in January 1826 to the south coast of Cornwall.[13]

The line was opened from Hayle Foundry to Pool in December 1837. The first passenger train ran between Hayle and Redruth on 22 May 1843. Two hundred people in two passenger carriages and three wagons travelled free on this first day. The regular passenger service used 'mixed trains' with coaches being attached to the rear of the goods wagons.[14]

Cyril Noall describes how the coach companies responded. The *Four Burrow Hunt* coach was:

> ...put on the road in 1849 for the express purpose of competing with the Hayle Railway a few years after that line commenced its passenger service. The railway directors, realising that a considerable passenger-carrying potential existed between Penzance and Truro, made arrangements for horse-omnibuses to link Penzance with Hayle at one end of the line and Truro with Redruth at the other. "Through" passengers changed at Hayle and Redruth – a somewhat inconvenient arrangement – but the fares were quite low – 3s 3d first, 2s 3d second and 2s third class respectively. Time was lost in changing from 'bus to train and from train to 'bus when performing this journey, whilst the horse buses themselves were rather slow vehicles, which resulted in a poor operating schedule.
>
> Perceiving this, a group of local coach proprietors,

Crotch, Ward & Co., decided to put on a fast day coach, which they named the *Four Burrow Hunt*, to run direct between Penzance and Truro without any change. Its route lay via Chacewater, Redruth, Camborne and Hayle, and it commenced running on October 16th 1848. The coach was scheduled to leave Pearce's Hotel, Truro every morning at a quarter past seven, and to arrive at Ball's Union Hotel, Penzance at 10.40, returning the same evening at five o'clock, reaching Truro at 8.30pm.[15]

The service was faster than the train and did not involve changes but the fares were higher – 3s outside and 5s inside.

The railway was here to stay, however, and in 1852 the West Cornwall Railway was completed between Truro and Penzance. The *Four Burrow Hunt* faded from the scene, but the *Fairy* coach began operations in 1856, running from Penzance through Hayle, Camborne, Redruth, Truro and across the River Tamar to Plymouth to link with the train to London. Brunel's Royal Albert Bridge at Saltash linked the Cornish railways with the rest of Britain in 1859 and the coaches could no longer compete.

SW577386
Carwin Rise, Hayle.
70152
The milestone survived these roadworks in 1999.

The milestones of the 1840 turnpike survive. The first milestone is on the eastern side of the roundabout at the eastern end of the Hayle by-pass. Leave the roundabout on what now appears to be a minor turn eastwards towards Connor Downs. Almost buried in the grass verge, opposite the filling station, in front of a motel, a battered triangular stone with a pyramid top bears the inscription **HAYLE 1 MILE, PENZANCE 9, LANDS END 19** on the left hand face and **CAMBORNE 5 MILES, REDRUTH 8, TRURO 17** on the right hand face (SW577386). The milestone has settled into the ground over the years and the square base is no longer visible.

In Connor Downs the main road is called Turnpike Road. The second milestone is not far from the Turnpike Inn on the opposite side of the road (SW592392). The triangular section shaft is joined to the square base by the familiar triangular stops found on milestones throughout the west of Cornwall at this date. At one stage the small, faint inscription had been over-painted incorrectly with the wrong distances to Camborne and Redruth. The same problem occurred on the next three milestones. All show traffic damage and considerable difficulty in picking out the small lettering neatly in black paint. The last of these is in College Street, Camborne, to the east of the roundabout where the old pre-turnpike main road runs further north along Weeth Road (SW637404).

The level of the new turnpike road was raised to cross the deep valley at Tuckingmill on the line of the pre-turnpike road, and again to cross the deep valley at Blowinghouse between

SW592392
Connor Downs. The new Turnpike Road became the A30 until the dual carriageway bypass of 1984

SW592392
Connor Downs. St Austell brewery sign showing the origins of the inn.

SW592392 Connor Downs, Gwinnear 1409024

SW608394 Horsepool Road, Gwinnear 1410449

SW622399 Camborne 1410393

SW637404 College Street, Camborne 66650

SW663412 Old A30 Carn Brea. 66732

SW679415 Agar Road, Carn Brea. 490344

SW695419 West End, Redruth. 1409467

Pool and Redruth. The milestone in Pool stands on the pavement in front of a large modern store (B&Q). It is a similar design to the previous stones found on this road, but there is much less writing and the larger, neatly inscribed lettering is carried on a slightly recessed rectangular field – **CAMBORNE 1, PENZANCE 15** on the left hand face and **REDRUTH 2, TRURO 11** on the right hand face (SW663412).

The milestone built into the garden wall of No. 49 Agar Road in Pool is in very good condition. It carries the full inscription and has no recessed rectangular field – **CAMBORNE 2 MILES, HAYLE 6, PENZANCE 16, LANDS END 26** and **REDRUTH 1 MILE, TRURO 10** (SW679415).

The last milestone in the series is in a recess of the garden wall of No.32 West End, Redruth. It has the clearer, simpler inscription on a recessed rectangular field – **CAMBORNE 3, PENZANCE 17** on the left hand face and simply **TRURO 9** on the right hand face (SW695419).

The two milestones with shorter, clearer inscriptions may be replacement stones, or they may have had the older shallow inscription removed, hence the shallow rectangular recess, before being re-carved. There is no firm evidence at present to confirm either of these two possible explanations for their different wording.

MILESTONES TO PORTREATH

The harbour at Portreath was an easy downhill run from the mining district surrounding Redruth. Heavy industrial traffic supported the

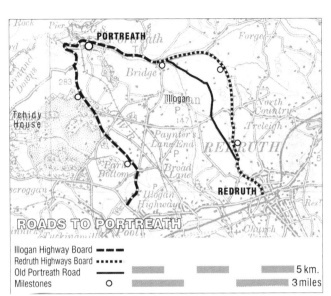

ROADS TO PORTREATH

Illogan Highway Board	▬ ▬ ▬
Redruth Highways Board	• • • • • •
Old Portreath Road	▬▬▬
Milestones	○

5 km.
3 miles

building of the first mineral tramway from Scorrier down the valley to Portreath in 1812. A branch of the Hayle to Redruth railway was opened in December 1837 to run from Carn Brea to Portreath. However the roads were also busy with traffic.

The road from Pool to Portreath was maintained by the Illogan Highway Board. It used to run right up to the church in Pool, but the last southern section was cut off by the A30 by-pass in the 1980s. In 1890 the Illogan Board applied to Cornwall County Council for the road to be made Main.[16] This required the erection of milestones at Park Bottom (SW665429) and at Penpraze (SW656442). At the same time the Illogan Board applied for the road from Portreath to Bridge, the modern B3300, to be made Main. The milestone in Portreath (SW659452) is on this road. The Portreath milestone has a rectangular recess and simplified inscription, suggesting that it has been recarved.

SW665429 Cot Road, Illogan 66756

SW656442 Cot Road, Illogan 66752

SW659452 B3300 Portreath 66791

SW675448 B3300
Redruth. 1409062

SW688446 B3300
Redruth. 66836

SW690430 B3300
Redruth, 66841

From Bridge to Redruth there are two roads. The Old Portreath Road climbs past Laity Farm along a high ridge. The New Portreath Road follows the gently gradient of the valley bottom through Gilbert's Coombe. The new road was built and milestones erected by the Redruth Highway Board in 1890. The full stop after the number on these milestones is unique. The milestone at the head of Gilbert's Coombe (SW690430) is inscribed **REDRUTH T.C. 1. MILE**. T.C. stands for town centre.

REDRUTH TO PENRYN TURNPIKE ROAD
A Trust was set up by Act of Parliament in 1762 (3 GIII c.lii) to turnpike the road from the mining district around Redruth to the quays on the River Fal. The preamble of the Act records the route as:

> From New Street and Pig Street in Penryn respectively to Higher Water gate and thence to Redruth through Ponsanooth and Gwennap Moors and the parishes of Gluvias, Perran Arworthal, Stithians, Gwennap and Redruth.

Two trusts were already in existence, controlling roads to Penryn. The Truro Trust (1754) had a route which entered the town from the north. The Helston Trust (1761) entered Penryn from the west. The Redruth road entered Penryn from the north-west, climbing Browns Hill where there was a toll gate to reach the main street of the town (called Pig Street).

By this date, Falmouth was the more important harbour and all three trusts sent their traffic over the old St Thomas Bridge, which existed as early as 1275 on their way to Falmouth.[17] The old bridge was approached down the steep, narrow, twisting St Thomas Street from Penryn town. The traveller from Truro would first have to climb the steep, narrow Truro Lane to reach Penryn then risk the

SW785344 Truro Lane, Penryn, the turnpike road from Truro

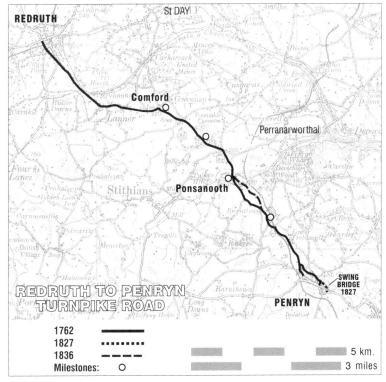

(above) Site of Penryn old bridge.

(right) Penryn new bridge (site of 1827 swing bridge)

descent of St Thomas Street, while the traveller from Redruth had a choice of climbing Browns Hill or New Street hill and then descending St Thomas Street.

The solution was to build a new bridge. The Act of 1827 (7&8 GIV c.18) allowed the Redruth Trust to build a new road from the bottom of New Street to Sowell's Quay and to build a bridge across the Penryn River. To allow traffic to reach the docks along the river, the bridge was a swing bridge made in cast iron by Harvey of Hayle. The approach road is now called Commercial Road. The swing bridge was not replaced by a fixed bridge until 1936.[18]

Some improvements were made to the road over the years, but the basic route changed little from that in the original Act, being much the same as the modern road. The main exception was between Ponsanooth and Burnthouse where in 1832 a new route was proposed to ease the gradients. In 1836 the old road at Ponsanooth was to be 'forthwith abandoned by the Trust'.[19]

We know that the Trust put up milestones, probably from its beginning. In 1840 the trustees at their meeting in Comford instructed that 'the road be re-measured and the milestones be accurately placed commencing from Penryn Bridge.'[20] In 1896 new milestones were proposed to replace the old stones.[21] Only four milestones remain today.

The milestone south of Comford (SW736397) is knocked sideways, broken and illegible. A triangular milestone with a triangular pyramid top is half-buried at the road edge near Pengreep (SW749388). No inscription is visible. In Ponsanooth at the start of the long climb of the improved turnpike route, a triangular milestone joined to a rectangular base by triangular stops is inscribed **REDRUTH 5 MILES, CAMBORNE 8 MILES** on the left face and **PENRYN 3 MILES, FALMOUTH 5 MILES** on the right face (SW758377). A similar milestone survives just north of the very busy junction with the A39 from Truro despite being knocked over in 2006 (SW769365), inscribed **PENRYN 2 MILES, FALMOUTH 4 MILES** on the left face and **REDRUTH 6 MILES, CAMBORNE 9 MILES** on the right face. There is a photograph in the Courtney Library, Truro[22] of this milestone on its side in 1970 after an earlier, similar traffic incident. Note that these last two milestones are on opposite sides of the road.

SW736397 A393 Comford

SW749388 A393 Gwennap

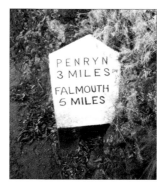

SW758377 A393 St Gluvias 66532

SW769365 A393 St Gluvias 66513

HELSTON AND
THE LIZARD

Helston is at the centre of a web of roads lined with milestones, yet only the main east-west route was ever a turnpike. While the origin of most of the milestones has been established, some early ones are still shrouded in mystery.

This area boasts the most southerly milestone in Britain, just half a mile from Lizard Point. The Royal Navy Air Station at Culdrose was built over a complex of roads, and milestones were moved about to make room for aircraft and helicopters. The tragic death of a Highway Surveyor in 1797 is recorded in a churchyard on the Lizard.

OBJECTION TO A NEW TURNPIKE ROAD BEING BROUGHT NEARER TO PENZANCE THAN MARAZION

Not everyone saw the advantages of the turnpike road system. Some saw only an increase in the cost of travel:

TOWN OF PENZANCE
At the Guildhall of the said Town the Second day of December in the year of our Lord One Thousand Seven Hundred and Sixty (1760) Whereas a Petition has been presented to the Honourable House of Commons for carrying a Turnpike road from Penryn in the County of Cornwall to and thro' the Borough of Helstone and to and thro' the several towns of Marazion and Penzance to the Land's End in the said County We whose names are hereunto subscribed being the Mayor & Majority of the Aldermen & Commonalty of the said Town assembled on this occasion Having Duly weighed and considered the many disadvantages that necessarily must arise from setting up Turnpikes further to the Westward of Penryn than the said Town of Marazion Have Resolved in Conjunction with the Neighbouring Parishes to oppose the said Petition from being carried into a Law and do Hereby agree consent and impower The worshipful the Mayor to employ one or more solicitor or solicitors and to pay him or them out of the Corporation Stock or fund and to take such steps as shall be thought proper for the more effectual preventing Turnpikes from being set up nearer to the said Town of Penzance than the said Town of Marazion, As witness our hands the day and year above said

Jn Tonkin Mayor

Alex. Reid
Thos. Vigurs
Thos. John
Andrew Vigurs
Alex. Read Junior
Sam. Grenfell
John Ballen
Thos. Sidwell Junior
John Mitchell
Uriah Tonkin
G. Borlase
W. Visick
J. Tonkin
Hr. Borlase

This is transcribed from a photocopy of a manuscript in CRO/WT in *The Book of Penzance* [1]

HELSTON TURNPIKE TRUST

The petition from the Mayor of Penzance stopped the new turnpike at the western end of Marazion, so that travellers to Penzance must complete their journey, albeit free of toll, along the foreshore.

'An Act for amending & widening the Road leading from the Town of Falmouth, in the

SW513311
Longbridge Marazion

SW513310
Marazion new bridge
1837

of his carving that was at fault, or did he carve the wrong inscription? The corrective work proved satisfactory, however, because in 1766 an entry reads: 'The Guinea for each milestone to be paid to Dennis Read & William Williams for cutting the same.' Most of Dennis Read's re-carved milestones were replaced when new sections of road were built under the renewal Act of 1833 (3 & 4 WIV c.14). There is one possible survivor and perhaps two others showing his original work.

Serious road works were undertaken in the early days of the Helston Trust to make the through route fit for the traffic of the time. A summary in 1765 in the Minute Book states: 'Roads from Falmouth thro' Penryn Helston & Marazion to West of Bridge have been created and compensation will be paid for land taken.' Roads were not merely widened and the potholes filled in, but private land was acquired and new roads were created.

An example of this is the road west from Helston. After crossing the medieval bridge by the site of the priory of St John, the traveller was faced with the steep climb to Sithney Common up Sithney Old Hill. A wider sweep of road was constructed avoiding the first and steepest part of the climb. This is shown on Greenwood's 1827 map and must pre-date the more radical changes to the turnpike road made in the 1830s.

The Bridge at Marazion at the western end of the turnpike road is called 'Longbridg' (without an 'e') on Gascoyne's map of 1699,[3] but the road on his map ends at the river's edge south of the bridge. Longbridge was a County Bridge in 1898 when Cornwall County Council took over responsibility for the county's roads. Writing in the 1920s, Charles Henderson notes that 'there is a new bridge near the shore on the road from Marazion to Penzance, but the old bridge with two pointed arches of the 18th century survives further up the stream.' [4] This would suggest that the Helston Turnpike Trust repaired the ancient 'Longbridg' as part of their initial road building programme, the new bridge mentioned by Henderson now carries the modern traffic and is dated 1837. The fact that the Act specifies 'Two Hundred Feet to the Westward' of the bridge shows that the road over the bridge and the approaches were to be maintained by the Turnpike Trust.

County of Cornwall, through the towns of Penryn, Helston & Marazion, and from thence to and over Marazion River and Bridge, and Two Hundred Feet to the Westwards of the said River and Bridge' was passed by the House of Lords in 1760 (1 GIII c.xxxii).[2]

As the previous chapters have shown, a turnpike road did reach Penzance from Hayle seventy-seven years later in 1837, and, eventually, a turnpike road was established from Penzance westwards to St Just in 1863, but there was never a turnpike to Land's End. Did the Mayor of Penzance save his townsfolk from unnecessary charges for travel, or did he delay the development of Penzance by preventing easy access to heavy traffic from further east?

While the first Turnpike Minute Book for the Helston Trust was lost in a fire in the early years of the Trust's existence, all three subsequent books survive, covering a period from 1763 to 1880. Two early entries refer to the milestones which the Act required the Trustees to set up. In 1765 it was recorded that

> ... whereas the letters & numbers on the milestones are not made to the good liking of the trustees by Dennis Read ... it is ordered that the said Dennis Read... shall take out the letters & numbers ... & insert such as five or more of the Trustees shall approve.

Quite what was wrong with Dennis Read's original inscription is not clear. Was it the quality

DENNIS READ'S MILESTONES
The connection to Falmouth was important because Falmouth was the port for international

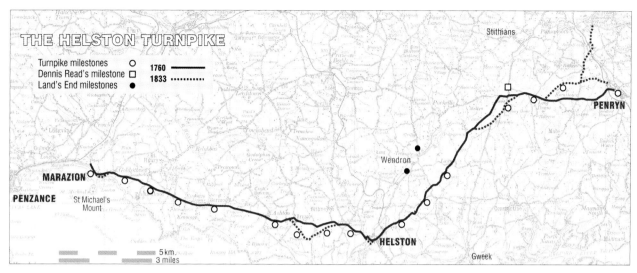

mail, but the main route east from Helston led through Truro. In 1761, the Truro Turnpike was already established with a route through Stithians to Tretheage Bridge (SW729361). A spur from the new Helston turnpike at Rame Cross was built to link with this road and it is on this spur that a possible survivor of Dennis Read's original milestones still stands.

Opposite the turn to Little Trewince is a rectangular milestone with a battered pyramid top. The back face, now turned away from the road, has a recessed panel with a deeply incised inscription, **H 7** (SW728346). The adjacent face to the right has a recessed panel with no inscription. The size and style of this milestone matches those on the road from Hayle to Redruth mentioned in the previous chapter. These have remarkable raised lettering on a recessed field. Perhaps Dennis Read used raised lettering which was not to the satisfaction of some of the Trustees – an old-fashioned and laborious style – and he was required to remove the raised lettering, a relatively simple task and recarve the milestone with more modern, clearer and more long lasting incised lettering.

The recessed field and the incised **H 7** now face away from the road. On what is now the front face of the milestone there are two lines of inscription, worn and battered but picked out in black paint. This reads **H 7, T 10** - Helston 7 miles, Truro 10 miles – the correct distances along the respective turnpike roads.

LAND'S END MILESTONES

Between Helston and the turn to Carn Menellis, on what is now the B3297, are two milestones, one mile apart, of a design similar to the 1740s milestones on the Hayle to Redruth road (SW674304 and SW681317). Both milestones are approximately 12 inch square in cross section with a pyramid top. The inscription is carried by large raised carving on a recessed rectangular field on two adjacent faces. Like the Hayle to Redruth milestones, these give the distance to **L** for Lands End, but here the second face gives the distance, 2 and 3 miles, to **H** for Helston.

These may be two of the original milestones carved by Dennis Read that failed to meet the approval of the trustees.

In 1833, major new road works were undertaken, and the rest of Dennis Read's milestones were replaced with a new design of triangular milestone on a rectangular base. On B3297 both old and new milestones survive. The new design milestones stand a few yards from the old Land's End milestones.

SW728346
Wendron (front) 66328

SW728346
Wendron (back) 66328

SW674304 B3297
Wendron 66325

SW681317 B3297
Wendron 66323

NEW ROUTES

New lines of road were set up both east and west of Helston. The renewal Act of 1833 (3&4 WIV c.14) details a whole series of new pieces of road:

1. from the current road near The Star Inn in the village of Trewannack in the parish of Wendron, and passing through the parish of Wendron, to rejoin the same road about Two hundred and forty Yards to the eastwards of the Blacksmith's Shop at Trewennack aforesaid.

This is a minor diversion to avoid a narrow corner in Trewannack.

2. from the said Road from Helston to Penryn, about Four Miles and One thousand four hundred Yards from Helston, and passing through the Parishes of Wendron and Stithians, to rejoin the same Road about Six Miles and One thousand five hundred and eighty Yards from Helston.

This transferred the turnpike to the higher, more southerly, of two parallel roads already in existence. Map evidence suggests that both roads were used before the Act. Greenwood's 1827 map shows the more southerly route as the turnpike, while the 2 miles to 1 inch county map published by G & J Cary in 1832 shows both parallel routes of equal importance, i.e. both turnpikes. The higher route gives fewer hills on the Falmouth route, but adds a steep climb to the road from Truro. However, as we shall see from proposal number four, the route to Truro was about to undergo a radical change.

3. another new Piece of Road diverging from the said Road from Helston to Penryn at or near the Western End of the Long Downs in the Parish of Mabe, about Seven Miles and Seven hundred and thirty yards from Helston aforesaid and passing through the Parishes of Mabe and Gluvias and the Borough of Penryn, to join the Redruth Turnpike Road at or near the Western End of a certain Street called Pig Street, in the Borough of Penryn aforesaid.

This was a very significant route change. The old turnpike ran from Long Downs (SW176340) through Mabe Burnthouse and into Penryn along Helston Road (SW770345). The new road avoided the steep inclines at Mabe Burnthouse with a broad sweep to the north via Treliever Cross then down the valley to Treliever Road at the north end of Penryn town. Pig Street is now called West Street.[5] Most importantly, the new route ran along part of the Redruth Turnpike Trust's road and over the new swing bridge.

4. from the said last-mentioned new Line of Road, commencing at or near Treliever in the Parish of Mabe. And passing through the parishes of Mabe and Gluvias, to join the Truro Turnpike Road about Six Miles and Two hundred Yards from Truro.

From Treliever Cross, partly on existing roads and partly along a new line entirely, a road was built to link with the Truro Trust's road to Falmouth, making the old Truro to Helston road through Stithians a backwater. All three turnpike trusts co-operated in planning the new road system around Penryn.

5. at the Western End of a certain Street called Coinage Hall Street. In the Borough of Helston, and passing through a part of Bullock lane and the Lower Green to rejoin the present Road at the Foot of the Alms House Hill.

This new road was to ease the steep gradient and tight bends at the western exit from Helston before crossing the bridge at St John's.

SW524307 Marazion Toll House and gate post. (right) The gatepost beside Marazion's toll house gives an idea of the size of the toll gate

SW797376
*Old Road, Falmouth.
OOPS (out of position
stone)*

SW784344
*Lower Street Penryn
365854*

SW754346 A394
*Mabe left face (in
2008) showing
wartime defacement*

SW754346 A394
*Mabe right face,
recently repainted in
1997*

SW740343 A394
Stithians right face

6. another new Piece of Road commencing at the junction of the old with the present turnpike Road at Antron in the Parish of Sithney, and passing through the Parishes of Sithney and Breage, to rejoin the present Road at the Western End of the Village of Breage.

This was to avoid the steep gradients crossing the deep valley to the east of Breage.

7. and another New Piece of Road, of the length of Two hundred and forty Yards or thereabouts, diverging from the said present Road at a Place called the Bold Turn, in the Town of Marazion, and to rejoin the said present Road at a Place called the Old Turnpike House, in the said Town of Marazion.

There is a Toll House at the eastern end of Marazion, but the building is not older than the 1833 road improvements. It is remarkable that one of the massive toll gate posts survives beside the toll house.

Triangular milestones, with triangular pyramid tops, joined to rectangular bases by triangular stops, line the whole length of this new route from the centre of Penryn all the way to Marazion.

The most easterly milestone was 1 mile from Falmouth and 1 mile from Penryn. It stood on a garage forecourt but disappeared in 1968-9. It was rediscovered in a garden a few yards away in 2013.[6]

The next milestone, Falmouth 2 (SW784344) is a well-preserved example in the centre of Penryn, beside a pedestrian crossing.

Falmouth 3 is missing.

Falmouth 4 (SW754346) has had the inscription chiselled off, but has been repainted on the damaged surface. Many milestones were defaced in 1940, when the threat of invasion was imminent.

Falmouth 5 (SW740343) has been more neatly defaced, but now bears no legend.

In 1837 the Helston Turnpike Minute Book records 'Stone direction posts to be erected at Rame Cross and Long Downs' to direct travellers along the new sections of road. A tall, rectangular pillar with a pyramid top had an inscription on one face, but this has been chiselled off. The direction post at Rame Cross survives in good condition. It is in the triangular style of a milestone but rather slender in cross section (SW727339).

At Longdowns, next to a millennium boundary stone erected by Mabe Parish, is a tall rectangular granite pillar with several lines of writing on one face which have been chiselled off (SW746340).

Falmouth 6 is in place (SW726338), but Falmouth 7 and Falmouth 8 are missing.

Falmouth 9 (SW693305), 10 (SW683293) and 11 (SW672283) complete the eastern set of milestones, surviving a new road layout on the outskirts of Helston completed in 2007.

SW746340 A394
*Defaced guide stone and millenium parish
boundary stone, Mabe*

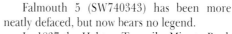

SW727339 A394
*Wendron 66391 left
face*

SW727339 A394
*Wendron 66391 right
face*

SW726338 A394
Wendron 66390

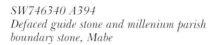

SW693305 A394
Wendron 66376

SW683293 A394
Wendron 511889

SW672283 A394
Wendron 511887

SW686299 A394
Wendron 66311 left face

SW686299 A394
Wendron 66311 right face

At the crossroads between the 9 and 10 mile stones is a direction post in the same triangular style. The inscription on the direction post bears no relation to the inscription recorded by English Heritage when the direction post was listed in 1988 (SW686299).

On the western road, from Helston to Marazion, all ten milestones survive, though most are rather battered by the heavy passing traffic.

TRELOWARREN MILESTONES
The road to Gweek, branching at Butteriss Gate from the main Helston to Falmouth road A394, carries a complete set of five milestones giving the distance, not to Gweek, but to Trelowarren. The ancient manor of Trelowarren is mentioned in the Domesday Book, held with the neighbouring properties of Halliggye and Treal by Thurstan. The present owners, the Vyvyan family, acquired the property by marriage in 1427 in the reign of Henry VI.

Gweek, at the head of the tidal Helford River, is a port with a long history. In the 14th Century it was the main port of Helston, whose burgesses controlled the trade.[7] Exports from the mines of Wendron parish were shipped from here, while coal and timber were imported. The Truro river barges called here regularly until just after the Second World War.[8]

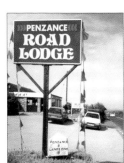

SW648279 A394
Helston 385568

SW632280 A394
Sithney 65932

SW621279 A394
Breage 65704

SW607284 A394
Breage 65703

SW592288 A394
Breage 65702

SW576291 A394
Breage 65701

SW560294 A394
Breage 65700

SW545300 A394
Perranuthnoe 70009

SW530305 A394
Turnpike Road,
Marazion 69994

SW516306
A394Marazion 69908

SW718328
Wendron 66329

SW714314
Constantine 66029

SW710298
Constantine 66028

SW706281
Gweek 66106

SW706266 B3291
Gweek 66130

The milestones are tall and thin with primitive carving, breaking up the inscription to fit the narrow stone. The most northerly is inscribed:

**FROM
TRELO
И
WARRE
VII**

That is seven miles from Trelowarren House. While most of the milestones have the **N** added above the **E**, only this milestone has the **И** carved backwards (SW718328).

The most southerly of this set of milestones is **From Trelowarren III** and stands at the west end of the bridge in Gweek (SW706266). Charles Henderson tells a story about the third milestone:

The quaint 18th century milestones giving the mileage to Trelowarren will be noticed on this road, proof that when the road was first made fit for carriages, only those going to the great houses had occasion to go on wheels. One of these milestones (the third) lay for many years in the river at Gweek, but was found and restored by the care of Mr T. Bowden.[9]

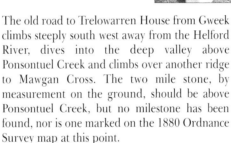

The old road to Trelowarren House from Gweek climbs steeply south west away from the Helford River, dives into the deep valley above Ponsontuel Creek and climbs over another ridge to Mawgan Cross. The two mile stone, by measurement on the ground, should be above Ponsontuel Creek, but no milestone has been found, nor is one marked on the 1880 Ordnance Survey map at this point.

In 1832, Sir Richard Vyvyan built a new road from Gweek to his home at Trelowarren. This followed the Helford River south east from Gweek and then climbed the gentle gradient of the valley from Ponsontuel Creek south west to the crossroads at Rosevear. The new road, called Gweek Drive, turned eastwards just north of Garras to enter the grounds of Trelowarren through a splendid gateway. As the Drive climbs through parkland a milestone, said to have been made by Thomas Eva of Gweek for Sir Richard, is inscribed;

**FROM
TRELO
WARREN
I
MILE**

The crisp stonework and neat carving show that this milestone (SW706242) is very different to the much older milestones north of Gweek.

SW706266 B3291
Gweek 66130
This milestone beside the bridge at Gweek was rescued from the river.

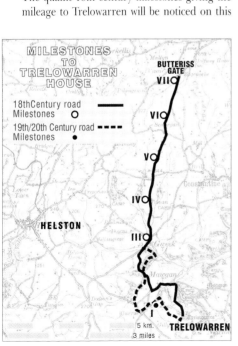

SW706242
Trelowarren, Mawgan in Meneage 65342

SW645265 B3304
Helston 385560

SW642280
Sithney 511886

SW639283 A394
Sithney 65926

There was a two mile stone on Gweek Drive, but it can no longer be found.[10] The old and new sets of Trelowarren milestones do not match distances. Travelling from Trelowarren to Gweek along Gweek drive, the distance is more than three miles.

PENROSE HOUSE GUIDE STONES
There is a group of three guide stones on the route from Penrose House, south west of Helston, to Sithney churchtown. All three stones are of the same unusual design with elaborately cuffed pointing hands and neatly carved lettering on a tall granite post. There is a guidestone at the southern end of Squires Lane, one at the junction with Gipsy Lane, and one where the route crosses the Helston turnpike, the modern A394. 'Squire's Lane' can be seen to link 'Squire' Rogers' house at Penrose with the church at Sithney.

Penrose House is a large property with grounds overlooking Loe Pool, a fresh water lagoon separated from the sea by Loe Bar, a bank of sand and shingle. 'The property belonged for ages to a family named Penrose, the name of the estate, which becoming extinct, it was sold to Mr. Hugh Rogers, whose son is the present owner.'[11] *Cornwall Illustrated*[12] gives a fuller account:

> About two miles south-westward from Helston, is PENROSE, which is reputed to have been the seat of a family so named, from a period antecedent to the Conquest until the year 1744, when the elder branch becoming extinct by the death of John Penrose, Esq., the manor descended, under his will, to his niece, Mrs. Cuming; who, in 1770, sold the whole to Hugh Rogers, Esq., father of John Rogers, Esq., the present owner. This gentleman has made considerable additions to the old manor house, which is embosomed in woods, and delightfully situated near the sloping margin of a little creek on the western side of the LOOE POOL.

It seems most probable that the three guidestones giving directions to Penrose were set up by the owner of Penrose. The most northerly of the three stones (SW639283) is at the crossing point of the new line of the Helston to Penzance turnpike announced in the *West Briton* on June 28 1833. The guide stone at this point gives directions to Helston and Penzance, as well as to Penrose and Sithney. This suggests that the guidestones were erected shortly after the new turnpike road was completed.

Milestones and guidestones to private houses

are unusual. Cornwall has other examples at Tregothnan, Heligan and Mount Edgcumbe.

CARN MENELLIS MILESTONES
To the north of Wendron, branching off the B3297, a route can be traced along country lanes through Lezerea, Porkellis, Penmarth, across the corner of Stithians Reservoir, past Penhalurick to rejoin the B3297 on Buller Downs south of Redruth. The route is lined with rectangular, pent-topped milestones. All the milestones give distances to Helston, Redruth and a place not marked on the maps called Carn Menellis. Penmarth is not mentioned on any of the milestones. At the crossroads in the centre of the Penmarth is a house once known as Carn Menellis Post Office and Stores. It closed at the start of this century. Some years before this the inhabitants of Carn Menellis decided that they preferred the name, Penmarth, and the old name disappeared.

On the high central spine of Cornwall, this area has a long mining history. The roads would have carried industrial traffic to both the north and south coasts. The milestones are marked on the 1880 Ordnance Survey map, where none are shown on the parallel B3297. Was this the main route until the B3297 through Four lanes and Burras was made a Main Road in 1889?

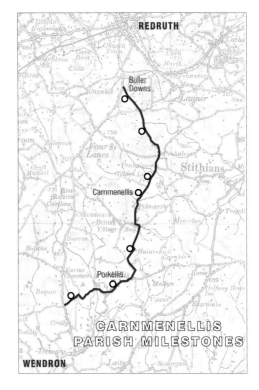

SW681331
Wendron 66324

SW694334 Wendron
1410384

SW701347
Wendron 66327

SW704364
Wendron 427864

SW708371
Wendron 1400355

SW706384
Stithians 66229

SW698398
Redruth 66800

The milestones are in two groups. The southern four stones give distances to Carn Menellis with an odd half mile. Those further north give the distance to Carn Menellis as 1, 2 and 3 miles respectively. The southern group give a total distance between Helston and Redruth as 10 miles, e.g. **Helston 4, Redruth 6**, while the northern group place Helston and Redruth 10¾ miles apart. Both these are underestimates. The more direct route along B3297 is

10 miles, while the Carn Menellis route is 11 miles. The discrepancy in distance suggests that the two groups of Carn Menellis milestones were put up by two different bodies. It seems most likely that this was the Parish in each case, since minor roads were the responsibility of the parishes. However, while the southern group all lie within the parish of Wendron, only two of the northern group of three are in the parish of Redruth, the most southerly being a few yards over the border into Wendron parish.

Parish milestones are rare, even in Cornwall. This complete set of milestones is the best example in the county.

LIZARD GUIDE STONES

In 1697 Justices in Highway Sessions were authorised to set up "direction stones or posts" at "cross highways" (8&9 WIII c.16). While milestones at regular intervals along a road are very useful, a direction stone set up at a junction is invaluable to a stranger travelling without a local guide or a map.

SW775224
St Keverne guide stone
64690

SW775224
St Keverne 64690

SW744218
St Keverne 64686

SW773198 B3293
Coverack turn, St Keverne

Three guide stones survive on the Lizard peninsula. All are in the parish of St Keverne and two bear the date 1838. They are flat-topped, pillars of course grained granite. Weathering has made the inscriptions hard to read unless picked out in black paint. Crude pointing hands show the direction. Perhaps these were more delicately carved when new. The stone west of Tregowris (SW775224) has inscriptions on two faces. On the stone north of Traboe (SW744218) only the inscription on the north face survives. The other dressed face can no longer be deciphered. Below the surviving directions are the inscribed letters **I.B**, **I.P** and **I.T**. No explanation of these has been found.

The third guide stone is at the junction of B3293 and B3294 (SW773198) and carries just one surviving inscription and pointing hand to Coverack.

KILLED BY A BIDDAX

Since 1555 when they were first required to take responsibility for their roads, parishes had appointed a highway surveyor to supervise maintenance and repair work. This was not a popular job, more of a duty. It was unpaid and only householders with a certain minimum income could be elected to the post. To ensure that the surveyor was not distracted by other duties, the Highways Act of 1835 exempted the following from duty as Highway Surveyor –

> ...peers and Members of Parliament; justices of the peace; clergymen and dissenting ministers; practising barristers; solicitors; members of the college of physicians; members of the college of surgeons; dentists; apothecaries; officers of the superior courts; officers of the army and navy; non-commissioned officers, drummers and privates in the militia; officers of the customs and inland revenue, and of the post-office; registrars of births, deaths and marriages; and masters of workhouses and relieving officers.[13]

While an irksome duty, the surveyor's task was not normally considered dangerous. With little traffic and no heavy machinery for road repairs, how could a surveyor die in the line of duty? Yet this is the unfortunate fate of Richard Roskruge in 1797.

A memorial stone set into the bank near the porch of the church of St Anthony in Meneage (SW782255), in the north-east corner of the Lizard, tells the story and adds a poem of forgiveness to the man who caused the surveyor's accidental death:

St Anthony in Meneage memorial to a Surveyor Killed by a Biddax

THIS STONE
Is dedicated to the Memory
OF
Richard Roskruge
WHO WAS
Killed in the Execution
Of his Office as Surveyor of the
Highways by a Blow on his Head
With a Biddax 14th August
1797 aged 66
Years
Doom'd by a Neighbour's erring hand to die
For him my Spirit breaths from Heaven a sigh
O while Repentant Prayers the Deed atone
Be mine to waft them to the Eternal Throne
ALSO OF JOAN HIS WIFE
Who died 17th August 1824

A biddax or 'beat axe' is a West Country tool still in use today. It is similar to a pickaxe. The careless back swing of such a tool could easily catch a bystander a nasty or even a fatal blow.

MAIN ROADS

When the Turnpike Trusts began to be wound up, after 1870, their roads were declared Main Roads. The county authorities paid one half of the expenses of maintaining a main road to the local highway board, provided the work was approved by the county's surveyor.[14] Other highways could be declared a main road, if it could be shown that they were sufficiently important. For example, if a road joined two important towns or if it served a busy railway station, an application could be made for main road status. It was in the interests of local highway boards to upgrade their roads to main roads, because of the extra money they could obtain towards the cost of maintenance. Before adoption, all such applicant roads were inspected by the county's surveyor, who in Cornwall required milestones to be erected.

All the roads declared 'main' in the public notices placed in the *Royal Cornwall Gazette* in the 1890s have milestones from this date. This can be checked by comparing the First Edition Ordnance Survey map of 1880 with the Second Edition Ordnance Survey map of 1907. Milestones are shown on newly adopted roads on the Second Edition, but are absent on the First Edition which pre-dates their adoption.

NORTH HELSTON MAIN ROADS
On 6 November 1890 the *Royal Cornwall Gazette* published a list of 'Roads recommended by the Roads Committee of Cornwall County Council to be made main and adopted by the County'. The new County Council had appointed two Divisional Surveyors. The list covered roads in both the Eastern and Western Divisions of the county.

North Helston Highway Board, consisted of the parishes of Breage, Wendron, Sithney and Germoe, meeting in the Vestry Rooms, Sithney. It applied for three roads to be made main:

Helston to Porthleven (now numbered B3304)

Helston to Sithney Cross to Nancegollan (now the B3303 to Camborne)

Helston via Croswolla to Pencoys (now the B3297 to Redruth)

To link with these, in the same public notice, Camborne Highway Board asked for roads to be made main from:

Botito to Nancegollan (Botito is now called Botetoe Bridge on B3303)

Botito Bridge to Camborne (B3303)

Hayle by St Erth Praze to Trenwheal (now B3302 Hayle to Helston road)

Redruth Local Board, in the same public notice, applied for the road to be made main from:

Redruth Station by Clinton Road and Wheal Buller towards Helston excluding streets (now the B3297 over Buller Downs to Pencoys)

Clinton Road was built by the Redruth Local Board in 1879.

It can be seen that Helston missed an

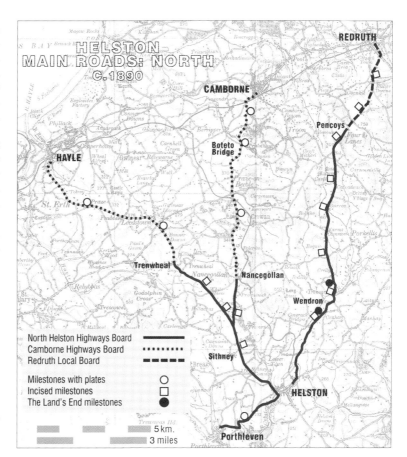

SW640376 Botetoe Bridge B3303 two miles from Camborne

application for its end of the B3302 and perhaps failed to bring its end of B3303 up to standard. This was rectified in 1892 when a second schedule of roads to be made main was published

SW638347 B3303 and SW604343 B3302 from the Philbrick archive. The original caption reads - PHOTOGRAPHS 1969-70 - MANY PLATES TORN OFF JULY 1972

All the milestones are of the same basic design, probably specified by the Surveyor for the Western Division, T. J. Hickes. This was based on the milestones used by the Helston Turnpike Trust – triangular with a triangular pyramid top and rectangular base joined by triangular pyramid stops. Camborne Highway Board attached cast iron plates carrying the inscriptions on its milestones, while Redruth carved the inscription into the stone faces. North Helston used plates on its Porthleven road, but carved inscriptions elsewhere. Unfortunately almost all the cast iron plates disappeared in the 1970s. Photographs in the Philbrick archive in the Royal Cornwall Museum show cast iron plates in place in 1969. It is hoped to use these photographs as a guide to produce replacement metal plates.

On B3302, milestones with missing plates survive at St Erth Praze (SW575351), Leedstown (SW604343) and near Pengwedna (SW622319), while the two North Helston Board incised milestones remain intact in Sithney parish (SW632307 & SW639292). There was a milestone at Tolroy, midway between St Erth Praze and Hayle. It had lost its plates, but someone had painted a 'plate' with **HELSTON 9** on one face. Sadly, this milestone disappeared without trace in 2009.

in the *Royal Cornwall Gazette* on 4 February, including:

2 miles 3 furlongs 27 poles from Sithney Common to Nancegollan

2 miles 2 furlongs 36 poles from Balaam's Corner to Binnerton Bridge (Trenwheal)

All these roads gained milestones between 1880 and 1907, the dates of the two Ordnance Survey maps. It seems logical to conclude that they gained their milestones in order to be made main, either before 1890 or before 1892.

SW575351 B3302
St Erth

SW604343 B3302
Milestone Cottage, Crowan

SW622319 B3302
Breage

SW632307 B3302
Sithney 1142171

SW639292 B3302
Sithney 65933

Disappeared in 2009
SW562359 B3302
Tolroy, St Erth 70288

SW643390 B3303
Camborne

SW640376 B3303
Crowan

SW638347 B3303
Crowan

SW636307 B3303
Sithney 65979 and 65934

SW674304 B3297
Wendron 66326

SW681317 B3297
Wendron 66322

SW678332 B3297
Wendron 66321

SW678348 B3297
Burras bridge,
Wendron 66362

SW682364 B3297
Wendron 66320

SW684379 B3297
Carn Brea 66698

SW694391 B3297
Carn Brea 66696 (Note
subtle change of inscription
from Helston Highway Board
to Redruth Highway Board)

SW678348 Burras bridge and milestone on
B3297

Enigmatic bridge stone at Burras bridge

SW699405 B3297
Redruth 66799 (Opposite
Redruth Town sign)

On B3303, the one mile stone from Camborne has one plate still attached (SW643390). Stones with missing plates survive at Botetoe Bridge (SW640376) and near Clowance House (SW638347). The North Helston incised milestone is in good condition, opposite the Crown Inn at Crowntown (SW636307).

On B3297, the first milestone from Helston is missing, but 2, 3, 4, 5, 6 and 7 remain in place. The only distinction between these North Helston Board stones and the last two milestones to Redruth (SW694391 and SW699405), erected by the Redruth Local Board, is the location of **MILES**. The Redruth stones have miles on the same line as the distance, for example **8 MILES**, while the North Helston stones have **MILES** on a separate line below the distance. The survival rate in the county is very good for the incised stones, but the stones with metal plates, once they have lost their plates, have become very vulnerable to loss. It is hoped that replacement plates will help to ensure the milestones' future.

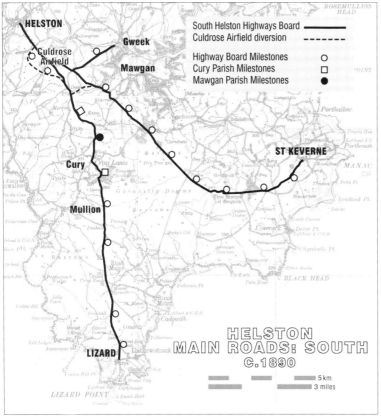

HELSTON
MAIN ROADS: SOUTH
c. 1890

South Helston Highways Board ——————
Culdrose Airfield diversion - - - - - - -

Highway Board Milestones   ○
Cury Parish Milestones   □
Mawgan Parish Milestones   ●

*SW664262 A3083
Helston, incised on one
face only*

*SW671251 A3083
Mawgan in Meneage.
Moved from Gweek road when
Culdrose air base was built*

SOUTH HELSTON MAIN ROADS

South Helston Highway Board, covering the Lizard peninsula, combined the following parishes: St Keverne, Mawgan in Meneage, Cury, Mullion, St Martin, Manaecan, Gunwalloe, St Anthony, Grade, Landewednack, Ruan Major, Ruan Minor.[15] Meetings were held at 'The Inn in the parish of Mawgan in Meneage'.[16] Was there really only one inn in the entire parish?

A public notice in 1890 declared that 'South Helston Main Roads have been repaired and should be taken over from 1 October 1890.'[17] This referred to three roads:

Helston to Lizard Point (now the A3083)

Helston to Gweek (now B3291)

Helston to St Keverne (now B3292)

The construction of the military airfield at RNAS Culdrose in the Second World War caused considerable disruption to the road network immediately south of Helston. While most of the milestones have survived, some have been displaced from their original locations.

The original road to Lizard Point was a continuation of Meneage Street from the centre of Helston. This ran across what is now the main runway, where there was a turn for St Keverne. The Gweek road turned off the St Keverne road near the public car park at the south east corner of the airfield.

Studying the 1880 Ordnance Survey map, there are milestones marked at 1, 2, 3, 4 and 5 miles south of Helston on the Lizard road. These must be milestones that pre-date the 1890 handover to Cornwall County Council announced in the *Royal Cornwall Gazette*. In addition, there are two milestones on the side road through Merries and Gilly to White Cross, but these have not been found on the ground. The map records a distance to Helston only for all of these milestones. There are no milestones further south and no milestones on either the Gweek or St Keverne roads.

The 1907 Ordnance Survey map shows milestones all the way to the Lizard and milestones to Gweek and to St Keverne. These extra milestones correspond with the road improvements referred to in the public notice of 1890.

A further public notice in 1892 refers to roads to be made main in the Helston Urban Sanitary Authority.[18] These include 1 mile 6 furlongs on the Lizard road.

The first milestone, now at SW664262 on the diverted A3083 road, in front of the boundary fence of RNAS Culdrose, originally stood at SW668261, the continuation of Meneage Street which is now within the airfield boundary. This milestone is of the late 19th century pattern – triangular with a pyramid top, rectangular base and triangular pyramid stops. **HELSTON 1 MILE** is incised and painted on the right hand face. **GWEEK 2 ¾ MILES** is painted but not incised on the left hand face. This milestone would have been erected to comply with the public notice of 1892. It is the only milestone erected by the Helston Urban Sanitary Authority.

The second milestone, fatter and squatter than the first milestone, but to the same design, is incised **GWEEK 1 ¾** on the left face and **HELSTON 2** on the right face. This now stands at SW671251 on the line of the diverted A3083, just south of the main entrance to HMS Seahawk. It was originally at SW674250 where there are now military buildings south east of the main runway.

The next milestone in this series is **GWEEK ¾, HELSTON 3** on B3291 near Trevilgan Farm (SW695260). This is in its original position, matching the 1890 public notice about South Helston Highway Board main roads.

Returning to the main Lizard road, A3083,

SW695260 B3291
Gweek road Mawgan in Meneage

SW685234 A3083
Cury parish

SW694224 A3083
Mawgan in Meneage parish

SW694209 A3083
Cury parish

SW697195 A3083
Mullion

there are three quite remarkable milestones. The three mile stone is south of Little Polwin Cottage, by a farm gateway (SW685234). It is a rectangular milestone with a flat top, inscribed on the side facing the road, **FROM HELSTON III MILES**. This is not an 1890 main road milestone, but a Cury parish milestone, pre-dating the 1880 Ordnance Survey map. It differs in design from the next milestone south (SW694224), which is rectangular with a rounded top and different style of inscription, **4 MILES FROM HELSTON**, and is in Mawgan in Meneage parish. However, a further mile south the road is back in Cury parish, and the fifth milestone matches the third milestone – rectangular with a flat top, inscribed **FROM HELSTON V MILES** (SW694209). It seems reasonable to conclude that these are milestones erected by the individual Parish Highway Boards, before they were combined to form the South Helston District Board in 1863.

Continuing south the A3083 enters Mullion parish where the six mile (SW697195) and seven mile (SW697179) stones are the triangular 1890 type. A3083 Mullion The eighth milestone is

SW697179 A3083
Mullion

SW700148 A3083
Landewednack.

SW703132 A3083 Lizard Head, Landewednack. *The most southerly milestone in Britain*

SW695246 B3293
Mawgan in Meneage

SW706236 B3293
Mawgan in Meneage

SW718225 B3293
Mawgan in Meneage

SW729213 B3293
Mawgan in Meneage

SW740202 B3293
St Keverne

SW755198 B3293
Trelanvean, St Keverne

SW771198 B3293
St Keverne Beacon

SW784206 B3293
St Keverne

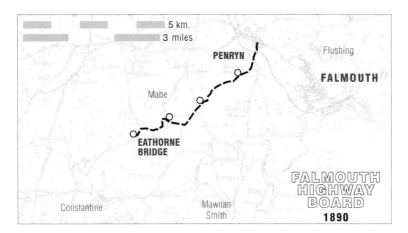

5 km.
3 miles

PENRYN

Flushing

FALMOUTH

Mabe

EATHORNE
BRIDGE

Constantine

Mawnan
Smith

FALMOUTH
HIGHWAY
BOARD
1890

ten miles from Helston and half a mile from St Keverne is anomalous (SW784206). To avoid obstructing the entrance to Treskewes Farm, this milestone is on the opposite side of the road to all the rest, so its inscriptions are reversed. **HELSTON 10 MILES** is on the left face and **ST KEVERNE ½ MILE** is on the right face.

FALMOUTH MAIN ROADS

In order to mention all the surviving milestones in the Helston area, it is necessary to consider the Falmouth Highway District. From 1863, this local board covered the parishes of Constantine, Gwennap, Budock, Stithians, Gluvias, Mawnan, Mylor, Mabe, Perranarworthal and Falmouth.

In 1890 the Falmouth Highway Board applied for one road to be made main from:

Penryn to Eathorne – 4 miles [19]

This is along the road from Penryn to Gweek (B3291), linking the Lizard peninsula to Penryn and all places east without needing to go through Helston town. Eathorne Bridge is the boundary between the parishes of Constantine and Mabe, four miles from Penryn. No application to make the remainder of the road from Penryn to Gweek a main road has been found, and there are no milestones between Eathorne Bridge and Gweek.

Work to bring the road up to standard was slow. At last, in June 1892 it was announced that

missing. The ninth (SW700148) and tenth milestones, the most southerly on the British mainland (SW703132) (There are milestones on the Channel Islands) are in Landewednack parish and are the triangular 1890 South Helston District Board designs. Note that none of these 1890 milestones carry the word **MILES** or **MILE**.

The road to St Keverne, B3293, turns off the A3083 Lizard road south of RNAS Culdrose. The two mile stone from the 1890 set is missing, the only loss caused by the construction of the airfield. All eight of the remainder survive in their original locations. The very last milestone

SW742311 B3291
Eathorne Bridge,
Constantine.
Note the Mabe parish boundary
stone beyond the bridge.

SW754316 B3291
Budock 66427

SW766322 B3291
Budock 66431

SW779330 B3291
Budock 66432

among the new roads repaired and taken over as main roads by Cornwall County Council was the road from:

> Penryn Drawbridge to Eathorne – 4 miles 1 furlong [20]

The 'Penryn Drawbridge' would be the swing bridge built in 1828 and taken over from Falmouth District by Cornwall County Council as a county bridge in 1889.[21] All four milestones, of the triangular design with carved letters, survive on this stretch of road.

CRILL CORNER

One final item of roadside furniture remains to be mentioned within this area. A guide stone once stood in the middle of a three way junction, but has been moved to the road edge to improve the flow of modern traffic. Tucked into the shrubbery at the road junction known as Crill Corner, south of Budock Water (SW783310) is a granite pillar over six feet tall. The lower part of the stone is rectangular in cross section. One half of the stone has been cut away across a diagonal to form a triangular section upper part. This gives directions to **PENRYN**, **MAWNAN** and **FALMOUTH** respectively on its three faces, with the date 1828 on the wider diagonal face beneath **MAWNAN**. No other stone of this design has been found in Cornwall.

SW783310
Crill Corner guide stone
Budock 66422

A Truro Trust milestone on the Falmouth Road A39 near Killiganoon, Feock 63294 SW805408

CHAPTER FOUR

TRURO

Truro is not the oldest town in Cornwall, but it has fought long and hard to become the most important.

The Domesday Book makes no mention of Truro,[1] but the borough was given a charter in the 12th century by Reginald, Earl of Cornwall in the reign of Henry II.[2] A spit of land between the rivers Allen and Kenwyn, where they join to form the tidal River Truro, was a natural site for a trading settlement. Sea going ships could reach Truro from the magnificent haven of Carrick Roads. A land route north lay between the two rivers, while fords and bridges led to routes east and west. East Bridge over the River Allen, in Old Bridge Street is named in the 13th century, while West Bridge over the River Kenwyn is first mentioned in 1434.[3] With the advantage of its location, linking land routes and sea routes, it was logical that Truro should be made a coinage town in 1327, assaying tin from the surrounding mining area. Truro prospered and was proud of its prosperity.

However, Truro has always been a long way from London and at times the town struggled because it was so far to the west. In the 15th century, the eastern half of Cornwall was more successful than the western half. In 1540 Truro was among the decayed towns of Cornwall listed in an Act of Parliament as being in need of repair.

Truro was a centre of communications. John Ogilby published his *Britannia* in 1675 to show the post roads of Britain – the roads that carried the Royal Mail. Two of Ogilby's three post roads through Cornwall terminate at Truro. The northern post road through Launceston, Camelford and St Columb Major reached East Bridge down Mitchell Hill. The central post road from Liskeard, Lostwithiel and Grampound came past Pencallenick and over St Clements Hill to East Bridge. Only the south coast route from Plymouth through Looe and Fowey bypassed Truro, crossing further south by the King Harry Ferry on its way to Lands End.[4]

When Celia Fiennes visited in 1698, she found Truro was at a low point in its history. She said Truro was:

> ...formerly a great tradeing town and flourish'd in all things but now as there is in all places

Truro from the river,
CYRUS REDDING 1842

their rise and period, soe this which is become a ruinated disregarded place.[5]

The first use of coal for smelting tin in 1702, at Calenick, just south of Truro, and the development of copper mining in the 1720s brought new wealth to Truro. However, the growing port of Falmouth took away much of the sea trade. In 1722 Daniel Defoe noted 'trade is now in a manner wholly gone to Falmouth, the trade at Truro being now chiefly for the shipping off of block tin and copper ore, the latter being lately found in some mountains between Truro and St Michael's'[6]

ROADS INTO TRURO – THE FIRST TURNPIKE TRUST IN CORNWALL

At a time when all heavy goods in the county was still transported by pack animals, it showed imagination on the part of local entrepreneurs to propose the improvement of 'several Roads leading from the Borough of Truro' in the first Turnpike Act in Cornwall in 1754. (27 GII c. xxi)

The plan was to improve all the heavily trafficked roads radiating from Truro:

The northern post road from Launceston was to be a turnpike as far as Mitchell.

The central post road was to be a turnpike as far as Grampound.

The Falmouth road, via Calenick

The original turnpike road to Grampound through the grounds of Trewithen House

WEST THROUGH CHACEWATER TO REDRUTH:

SW811446 A390
Truro 377396

SW796450 A390
Truro 509210

SW780450 Threemilestone, Kenwyn 63286. The
only village in England named after a milestone

SW764450
Green Bottom, Kenwyn
63284

SW749443
Chacewater 63161

SW734444
Chacewater 63104

SW719439 A3047
St Day 66896

SW708428
Mount Ambrose,
Redruth 66835
This **FROM TRURO 8
MILES** milestone has
been recarved

Smelting House and Higher Carnon was to be a turnpike as far as Penryn.

The south west road through 'Penwethass and Bisso Bridge to Tretheage Bridge' would link with the south coast post road to Land's End.

The road through Chacewater to Redruth would carry industrial traffic from the mines in the west.

The road to Short Lane's End would gather in the industrial traffic from the north coast mines around St Agnes.

Improvements took time. In the summer of 1755 William Wynne travelled by coach from Redruth:

> ...after dinner by Lord Falmouth's mines and tin works to Truro. Two miles of which are new turnpike road and about one mile on the other side of Truro, in consequence of a late Act of Parliament. [7]

It was soon realised that two of the routes listed above were not well chosen and their line was improved by an Act of 1756 (29 GII c.lxxii) 'for changing and altering two roads of Truro Turnpike Trust'.

The Falmouth road was altered to avoid the Higher Carnon River crossing (SW783408) because 'from Callenick Smelting House over Lower Carnon (SW786400), Perranwell and thence to Cassaws Water is shorter by a Mile.' (29 GII c.lxxii)

The link to the south coast post road ran parallel to the Falmouth road for much of the way, so it made sense to run it along the Falmouth road as far as Perranwell and then to branch off 'over Perran Downs to Pellene Cross to and over Tretheage Bridge' towards Helston. The original route can be followed from Truro city centre up Chapel Hill, across the ring road by the football ground then down to the valley bottom at Treyew Mills. Climbing the hill past Penweathers and crossing two more steep valleys before dropping to the Carnon River crossing on Bissoe Bridge, the traveller could begin to wonder at the choice of route, and there are still more hills to come. This original route shows no sign of turnpike improvement and has no milestones.

NORTH: The A39 road north from Truro was improved in 1997. All but one of the old milestones survived this

SW846540 Plaque on A39 overbridge near Trispen commemorating opening of bypass in 1997

SW833462 Bodmin Road, Truro 508975

SW833477 A39 St Clement 508978

SW840490 on cycleway St Erme 63930

SW842505 Trispen, St Erme 63931

SW846520 west of overbridge St Erme 63932

GONE SW846536 St Erme 63933 Lost to road works 1997

SW857544 Opposite Mitchell Farm, St Newlyn East 63962

The 1754 Act required 'milestones to be erected and distances measured from Truro Bridges', i.e. East Bridge and West Bridge. From the start, the Truro Trust had a standard design of milestone. This was rectangular in plan with a semi-circular rounded top, carrying the inscription **FROM TRURO** so many **MILES**. With the exception of the London Road built by McAdam, this design of milestone was used on all the Truro Trust roads throughout the long and successful life of the Trust. This standard design can make it difficult to date Truro Trust milestones. Crisp corners and neatly incised inscriptions suggest a mid 19th century date, while strangely shaped numbers and in particular an **s** on the end of 'miles' which is falling over, suggest an original mid 18th century milestone. Most Truro milestones have worn, rounded edges and many have a recessed area on the front face where they may have been re-cut. These may be original milestones which have been refurbished by the Trust rather than being replaced..

All the Truro Trust roads from the 1756 Act onwards still carry an almost full set of milestones, which is a wonderful achievement. Subsequent Acts added new roads and by-passed old ones, but the milestones were left in place. This makes the Truro Trust unusual. Other Trusts removed the milestones from their old

EAST:

SW888477 Probus 508950

SW904478 Probus 508361

SW916486 A390 Probus 508362

SW931484 A390 Grampound 508363

SW843437
Malpas Road, Truro
377499

SW836437
Malpas, St Clement
351276

roads when they were superseded by new routes. For example, the Helston Trust left no milestones through Mabe Burnthouse when it built a new road into Penryn in 1833.

Truro's bold lead in 1754 was justified when in 1760 a whole spate of Turnpike Acts was applied for by the other towns in Cornwall. Truro expanded its road network in 1773 (13 GIII c. cxii) by applying to Parliament for permission to turnpike three more roads:

> From Coinage Hall Street across a new bridge to be built at the Steppings and via Sunny Corner to Mopas (Malpas). (This would give access from the river at low tide. Malpas is still used today as the low tide terminus by the ferry from Falmouth to Truro.)

> From Short Lane's End to Four Burrows. (This links to the 'spine road' of the county, later to be designated the A30.)

> From the third milestone on the Redruth road to Three Burrows. (This is another link to the spine road A30.)

A settlement grew around the 'third milestone' to become the only place in Britain named after a milestone – Threemilestone.

In 1782 Truro applied to add three more roads (22 GIII c.89):

> Short Lane's End to Callestock Burrow, on the Cross Road leading from Marazanvose to Zelah. (The 'Cross Road' is the A30 spine road again. Describing it as a Cross Road not a Highway suggests that it is of secondary importance. The roads were terminating on Cornwall's watershed, but were being fed by the mining districts to the north, not traffic moving along the ridge.)

> Two Burrows (Allet SW795485) to Perran Almshouse (SW789494). (This is another link terminating on the spine road. There is no milestone on this road, because it is less than one mile long.)

> Three Burrows (SW745469) to St Agnes Almshouse. (The Almshouse was on the outskirts of St Agnes (SW720494). The last Truro milestone on this road is **FROM TRURO 7 MILES** at SW727484.)

The Trust maintained its roads to a high standard, though, in the late 18th century, goods in Cornwall still travelled on the backs of animals rather than in wagons.

SW816459 B3284
Truro city boundary,
Kenwyn 508974

SW809472 B3284
Shortlanesend,
Kenwyn 63276

SW798483 B3284
Kenwyn 63275

SW783487 B3284
Kenwyn 63274

SW765488 B3284
Perranzabuloe 63681

SW765457 A390
Kenwyn 63273

SW754466 A390
Chacewater 63272

SW809487
St Allen 63920

SW808502
St Allen 63919

SW738473 B3277
St Agnes 63751

SW727484 B3277
St Agnes 63750

James Forbes visited Cornwall in the last decade of the century. He was born in London in 1749. At the age of sixteen he went to Bombay to work for the East India Company. In 1780 he became Collector and Resident at Dubhoy. His *Oriental Memoirs* were published between 1813 and 1815. He travelled in Europe and published *Letters from France* in 1806, which was an account of his captivity during the Napoleonic wars.

He travelled to Cornwall in 1794, leaving his house at Stanmore on 18 September with his wife, Rose, and his daughter, Eliza, in his own coach driven by his own coachman. During the trip, James wrote letters to his wife's sister, Anne, describing and commenting on what he saw on his way to Land's End. He says:

> I have seldom seen a neater town than Truro; the best streets wide and airy, with good houses and well furnished shops, all paved in the modern style, their names at the corners, and the lamps at convenient distances.

On his way back from Land's End, on October 24, he:

> ...dined at Redruth, and fully intended to go the direct road from thence to St Michael (Mitchell), a stage of over 13 miles over the downs; but it is not a turnpike road, and having lost our way in the morning, and setting in for a cloudy and wet afternoon, I preferred going to St Michael by the way of Truro, which only increased the journey by two or three miles.
> The road in this stage was excellent, and the country softened and improved on approaching Truro, where we arrived as the day began to close.

The direct road from Redruth to Mitchell, mentioned by Forbes, is now the A30 trunk road, the main road through Cornwall. The Forbes family left Truro for Mitchell the following day

on another well maintained Truro Turnpike road:

> After breakfast I set off for St Michael's, a short stage of seven miles, and a fine day and a good road through an enclosed and cultivated country, moderately hilly, soon brought us thither.

He comments on the traffic:

> ...and all we met with on the roads in this country are the farmers' wives and daughters carrying their commodities on horseback to the market-towns; or carriers with a long string of pack-horses, loaded with tin ore for the smelting-houses, or bringing sea sand from the coast to the inland parts for manure, or dressing as it is called in Cornwall, which is said to render the land very fertile. (Lime rich sea sand was used to improve acid moorland soil.) [8]

Walsingham Place, Truro

SOUTH:

SW819435 A39
Truro 508973

SW813421 A39
Kea 63398

SW813420
Old Falmouth Road,
Playing Place, Kea
508971

SW805408 A39
Feock 63294

SW794396 A39
Feock 63295

SW782388 A39
Mylor 63584

SW771379 A39
St Gluvias 443405

SW770363 A39
St Gluvias 66514

SW777365
Old Falmouth Road St
Gluvias 428071

SW781350
Old Falmouth Road,
Truro Hill, Penryn
365685

SW766386
Old Tretheague Bridge
road, Perranarworthal
63583

SW751384
Old Tretheague Bridge
road, Stithians 509239

SW741374
Old Tretheague Bridge
road, Stithians 427860

SW731363
Old Tretheague Bridge
road, Stithians 509235

SW741372
Stithians 66227

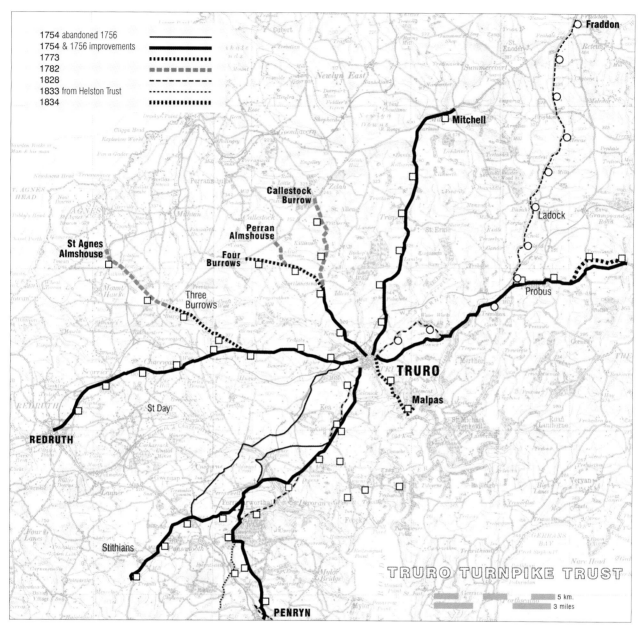

Legend:
1754 abandoned 1756
1754 & 1756 improvements
1773
1782
1828
1833 from Helston Trust
1834

Fraddon

Mitchell

Callestock
Burrow

Perran
Almshouse

St Agnes
Almshouse

Four
Burrows

Ladock

Three
Burrows

Probus

St Day

TRURO

REDRUTH

Malpas

Stithians

TRURO TURNPIKE TRUST

5 km.
3 miles

PENRYN

THE NINETEENTH CENTURY

The powers of the Trust were renewed in 1802 (42 GIII c.iv) and an Act of 1817 (57 GIII c.xliv) allowed for an increase in tolls, but with reductions in toll according to the width and construction of the wheels of the waggon. It was thought that wider wheels would cause less damage to the road surface.

Real improvements to roads were made by the better drainage of a slightly cambered road profile, by surveying new routes which avoided steep hills and by the simpler method of road repair requiring a single layer of well graded stones.

These were the techniques developed by John Loudon McAdam, which allowed a rapid growth in the use of wheeled traffic, even in Cornwall.

THE McADAM PERIOD

The renewal Act of 1828 (9 GIV c.iii) introduced new lines to make great improvements to the gradients on the main post road from Falmouth, through Truro towards Bodmin and Launceston. A series of new sections of road were built, parallel to the existing road between Truro and Penryn. A new route was found to the east, avoiding the steep climb of St Clements Hill and

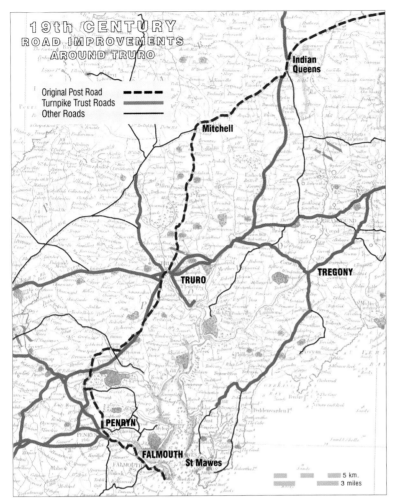

opening a route up a river valley through Ladock to join the Bodmin Trust's and the Haleworthy Trust's turnpikes near Indian Queens.

Paraphrasing the lengthy legal wording of the Act, the trust sought permission to:

Demolish all or part of a house occupied by Thomas May on the south side at the east end of Bodmin Street and add the land to the turnpike to Grampound.

Build a New Road from the east end of St Austell Street to rejoin the present road near Kiggon Bridge (SW856455) and to disturnpike the old road over St Clements Hill past Pencallenick. (There are no milestones on the disturnpiked road today.)

The road from Truro to Mitchell was described as 'narrow, steep and incommodious' – the standard phrase used in applications for major road improvements. This was the road Forbes

described as 'a good road through an enclosed and cultivated country, moderately hilly' in 1794. A New Road was proposed, diverging from the Grampound road at the foot of Truck Hill (SW884475) and passing by the Northern Valley through the several parishes of Probus, Ladock and St Enoder to join the road from Truro to Bodmin at Penhale near Indian Queens.

New Pieces of Road between Truro and Penryn: Diverging near Plynt's Barn and rejoining near Killiganoon 2 miles 1430 yards from Truro. This is the A39. The 'Old Falmouth Road' leaves the roundabout on the Truro ring road and runs through Calenick to Playing Place. The first milestone was moved onto the new road (SW819435), but the second milestone is still on the old road in Playing Place (SW813420).

Diverging at Killiganoon, 3 miles 550 yards from Truro, across the Carnon River and the Redruth and Chasewater Railway to Devoran, along the north side of Perran Creek to rejoin the present road near Rapson's Mill on Perran Wharf. The old road crossing the river at Lower Carnon and on to Perranwell has no milestones and so must have been successfully disturnpiked.

Diverging at Belle Vue through fields west of the present road, crossing the present road 230 yards below Penryn Town Turnpike Gate, through fields east of the present road and over the Head of the Creek to join the Redruth turnpike near the bottom of New Street. This is a link on the outskirts of Penryn to avoid the steep descent of Truro Hill. Its description matches the road called Durgan Lane in modern Penryn.

A New Road was needed from Perran Wharf to join the present turnpike from Truro to Tretheage Bridge at Pellean Bar or Gate. This was a very short link so that traffic to Helston could make use of the improved crossing of the Carnon River.

Replace Chapel Hill with a new road to Penryn 60 yards from the Barrack Ground to join the present Redruth road at Chapel Hill Gate.

Demolish houses in Kenwyn Street and build a New Road towards Redruth from the entrance to Bosvigo Lane westwards to rejoin the present road near Bosvigo Barn.

The existing road from near Mitchell Hill Gate to Moresk Mill (St Clement parish) was to be made Turnpike. This is Moresk Road in Truro.

This is a very long list, including some major new road building. A Half Inch map published by G&J Cary in 1832 shows all these road improvements as well as the old turnpike road.[9] This map also shows the Helston Turnpike Trust's new road from Treliever Cross to Cuckolds Corner mentioned in Chapter 3. This road was proposed by the Helston Turnpike Act of 1833 (3&4 WIV c.xiv) and marked out in 1834.[10] The Cary map of 1832 shows the road complete. It seems that Messrs Cary based their map on green paper proposals to Parliament rather than on an actual survey. This is supported by their marking of Bodmin Trust roads, which were proposed but never built, on the same map (See later). Despite being a little premature, the Cary map gives accurate information about the roads in this chapter. The Treliever Cross to Cuckolds Corner road, although built at the expense of Helston Turnpike Trust was administered by the Truro Trust and carries **From Truro** style milestones.

The trustees needed someone to supervise this grand scheme of improvements and they did not want second best. They wrote to John Loudon McAdam in 1825 to seek help and advice in operating their roads more efficiently. Not only was J. L. McAdam at the height of his fame as a road engineer and surveyor at this time, but he was also the head of a dynasty of surveyors. His three sons, William, James and John Loudon, were all surveyors, as were his four grandsons. McAdam senior passed the letter from Truro to his eldest son, William, who was the family expert in the West Country.[11] William McAdam believed that the new construction and maintenance techniques developed by his father, and his cost cutting management style would produce better roads at a lower price. He took on the role of Surveyor for the Truro Trust from 1825 to 1833. He handed over to his son, Christopher, in 1833.

A UNIQUE MILESTONE DESIGN

The new road from Truro to the east which by-passed St Clements Hill and Pencallenick before taking a sinuous line up the valley from Tresillian to Ladock and on to Penhale was clearly intended for long distance traffic. It had a new design of triangular milestones with inset cast iron plates on two sides, facing up and down the road. While one plate on each milestone gave distances to Truro and Falmouth, the other plate gave distances, grandly, to London, as well as to Bodmin.

It is very rare to have the details of milestones in written contemporary accounts, but in 1830 the Truro Turnpike Order Book[12] records:

Monday 10 May: 'Benjamin Bowden having undertaken to provide 12 triangular new mile Stones according to the plan now produced for the sum of 13s per stone – Resolved – That the Clerk be requested to enter into an agreement with him accordingly.'

Wednesday 26 May: 'That in case Benjamin Bowden the Contractor for the new mile Stones shall perform his contract to the satisfaction of the Trustees or whom so ever they shall appoint [William McAdam?], the Trustees present at this meeting recommend his being allowed 2s per mile Stone in addition to the sum agreed to be paid to him for such mile Stones at the meeting held on the 10th instant.'

Monday 19 July: 'Resolved - that the distance from London be mentioned on the plates to be laid on the new mile Stones.'

Monday 1 November: 'Resolved – That the Clerk do pay Benjamin Bowden the sum of £12-6s-11d the amount of his bill for new mile stones.

'Resolved – That the Clerk do pay Perran Foundry Company the sum of £11-2s-0d the amount of their Bill for Castings for New Mile Stones.'

From these entries it is clear that the milestones were designed to have metal plates and that the legend on the original metal plates was to include the distance from London.

The two plates on each side of all the milestones in the series are the same size, but the inscriptions are recorded in a different style and size of lettering. These differences are consistent throughout the series. The 1880 OS map gives only two distances, for example: Truro 12 and Bodmin 11 is marked on the map for the milestone at SW911580. It is standard practise on these maps to give no more than two destinations, no matter how many are shown on the actual milestone. It is not the omission of the Falmouth and London distances, but the discrepancy in the Bodmin distance which is noteworthy. The 1907 OS 2nd Series 6 inch map shows the distances at the same location as Truro 12 and Bodmin 12¼, which agrees with the Bodmin distance on the milestone. Bodmin appears to have moved 1¼ miles between 1880

SW838457 A390 Truro 508951

SW851460 A390 St Clement 508982

SW876469 B3275 Probus 508983

SW886479 B3275 Probus 508984

SW890493 B3275 Probus 508985

SW892508 B3275 Ladock 508986

SW899522 B3275 Ladock 508987

SW906535 B3275 St Enoder 507772

SW902551 B3275 Ladock 507782

SW904567 B3275 St Enoder 71307

SW911580 Blue Anchor, St Enoder 507740

and 1907! Putting together the differences in style of the two metal plates on each milestone and the difference in distance to Bodmin on the two editions of the OS map suggests that the Bodmin mileplates on the milestones in this series were replaced between 1880 and 1907. This was probably at the instigation of the new Cornwall County Council which took over the maintenance of this road in 1889.

There is a question here about why the original plate gave what now appears to be an incorrect distance to Bodmin. This may be explained by the flurry of road building activity in Cornwall around 1830. Not only the Truro Trust, but also the Bodmin Trust was active with new road schemes. In 1829 (10 GIV c.xix), 1833 (3 & 4 WIV c.lxxxix) and again in 1835 (5 & 6 WIV c.cv) the Bodmin Trust put forward proposals for new sections of road, some of which were never built. It has been mentioned that John Cary's half inch county map dated 1 July 1832 shows a maze of turnpike roads around Bodmin, including those which were never built.

The Truro Trust had the Perran Foundry Company cast its plates with the distance to Bodmin, and then the Bodmin Trust's plans changed, making the distance on the Truro plates inaccurate. The next milestone north, after the Bodmin 12¼ quoted above, is a Bodmin turnpike milestone erected after the 1835 Act. It is a stone milestone, carved **B 12** for Bodmin 12 (SW913584). It is a ¼ mile from the Truro Trust's McAdam milestone. It seems surprising that Truro did not correct their mileplates, but the evidence from the Ordnance Survey maps of 1880 and 1907 suggests that the correction was not made until after the Trust had been wound up in 1874.

No other Cornish Trusts chose to use cast iron plates. The Helston Trust proposed 'new milestones with Cast Iron Plates as on Truro turnpike to be erected' on a new branch from Treliever to Perranvale,[13] but put up carved stone milestones instead. The Truro Trust did not adopt McAdam's plated milestone design elsewhere on their network, persisting with the standard **FROM TRURO** so many **MILES** design in stone until the end.

Although the milestone in Tresillian village has been lost, 11 of McAdam's original 12 milestones still survive in their original location. They record the high water mark of turnpike road construction in Cornwall. The road's gentle gradient and sweeping bends provided ideal conditions for rapid coach travel. This road was the A39 main road to Truro until the mid 1990s. There was no room in the narrow valley to straighten McAdam's sweeping curves or to widen the road to a dual carriageway to accommodate the needs of our modern traffic, so a new route into Truro was constructed by upgrading the A3076 Mitchell to Truro road and reclassifying this as the A39. This Mitchell to Truro road, the new A39, with its hills and valleys, was the original Truro Turnpike road used by James Forbes. It had been replaced by McAdam's Ladock valley road in 1830. McAdam's 'London Road' has been downgraded to become the B3275. Road building has come full circle!

THOMAS HICKES, SURVEYOR

When William McAdam agreed to take on the role of surveyor for Truro, he wrote that he would appoint a sub-surveyor. Since he was also surveyor for Launceston Trust and for trusts in Devon, the appointment of a local sub-surveyor to supervise the work on the new roads was essential.

Thomas Hickes was born in Gloucestershire in 1805. Between 1823 and 1836 he lived at Elm Cottage in Moresk Manor, Truro. It seems likely that Hickes was the young sub-surveyor appointed and trained by William.

In 1836, both William McAdam and John Loudon McAdam senior died. In the same year Christopher McAdam handed over the Surveyorship of Truro's turnpike roads to Thomas Hickes. In 1849, the Truro and Redruth Turnpike Trusts merged (12 & 13 V c.xliv). Effectively, Truro took over the running of the Redruth Trust's roads from 1849. Hickes remained the Truro Trust's surveyor until the Trust was wound up in 1874, when he was aged 69. He was paid three year's salary for loss of office and promptly found employment with one of the Highway Districts that took over the disturnpiked roads. His son, Thomas James Hickes, was appointed Surveyor to the new Cornwall County Council, when it was set up in 1889.

Thomas Hickes, senior, invented a 'Mile Meter' in 1843. This was a three wheeled hand cart with one very large wheel, carefully made to have a circumference of exactly one pole (5.5

yards). The large wheel was connected by gears to a dial to record the distance in miles, furlongs and poles. When Thomas James Hickes left Truro to live in Oxford in 1906, the Mile Meter came into the possession of the Royal Cornwall Museum in Truro. Until recently, it stood in the central display area in the museum, beside the Trewinnard Coach, a Victorian carriage and an early bicycle. According to the remarks on the accession documents of the museum 'The machine was sold at auction at Elm Cottage, the residence of T. J. Hickes, County Surveyor and son of the Inventor, when the former was leaving Truro for Oxford.' The purchase price was 15 shillings. The accession notes give the date of invention as 1843. A letter to Major Parkin at the Museum from T. J. Hickes in May 1906 describes the machine as follows:

> The Road measuring machine was invented by my Father, and made by Carvasso, who was a carriage builder on Lemon Quay where the coach factory is now. At that date there was a constant request for the length of Roads, and to save the wearying task of measuring with Gunter's Chains; to do it quicker, and to avoid

Members of Fraddon & Penhale Improvement Committee celebrate the replacement cast iron plate on the 1830 Truro Turnpike milestone in Blue Anchor in April 2009 (SW911580).
PHOTO:
MARILYN THOMPSON

The Measuring Wheel of Thomas Hickes.
COURTESY ROYAL INSTITUTION OF CORNWALL

the risk of losing a length, or even more, my father invented the Mile Meter, (underlined in the letter) and it proved a pleasant success. It cost him £34.

Thomas Hickes was not the first person to invent a measuring wheel. Smaller, single wheeled machines were standard surveying equipment in the late 17th century. A cartouche in John Ogilby's *Britannia* of 1675, shows such a wheel, together with a surveyor's chain. The compass rose on Joel Gascoyne's *Map of the County of Cornwall Newly Surveyed* in 1699, shows a change in fashion of clothes worn by the surveyors, but an almost identical measuring wheel to the one depicted in Ogilby's book. Both wheels are a similar size, coming to mid-thigh of the surveyor pushing them as one might a lawn mower. Both have a dial of some sort below the pushing handles. Neither surveyor is watching his wheel, suggesting that it

recorded the distance automatically – he did not count the number of turns.

The National Trust has a measuring wheel which was on display at Saltram House, near Plymouth. It is mahogany with a brass dial behind a large glass cover. The dial has two hands like a clock and was calibrated in yards, poles, furlongs and miles. The diameter of the wheel was 31.5 inches which gave a circumference of 99 inches, or half a pole. Measuring wheels of this design continued to be made through the 19th century, now called 'waywisers' in the antiques world. There is a good example of a Waywiser in the Oxford History of Science Museum. This is very similar to the National Trust example and was made by Thomas Wright and William Wyeth in London in 1740 or 1741. Mr Hickes built only one of his machines.

Not only did Mr Hickes make his own measuring machine, he also made his own road roller. This is still in occasional use on an estate near Truro. It is now modified to be towed by a tractor, rather than by a team of horses, but can be identified by the legend cast into the rim of each massive half of the roller - TRURO TRUST THOMAS HICKES SURVEYOR 1838.

PRE-TURNPIKE MILESTONES
The milestones between Hayle and Redruth mentioned in Chapter 2 continue along the road from Redruth as far as Mitchell, on the road that James Forbes declined to use in 1794. We know there were milestones on this road, because they are mentioned in the Cornwall section of Lysons' *Magna Britannia* in 1814:

The old road from the north of Cornwall to the

Road roller inscribed TRURO TRUST, THOMAS HICKES SURVEYOR *1838* PHOTO: ROGER FOGG

Land's End branched off at Michell; this road which has long been disused for carriages, **though its mile-stones remain**, and it still keeps its place in the road-books, passed through Zealla, Redruth and Crowless to Penzance.[14]

The success of the Truro Trust's roads diverted traffic going to and from the west of the county through Truro, rather than using the more direct ridge route from Mitchell to Redruth, along the county's spine. The road between Mitchell and Redruth was never made a turnpike, despite its modern importance as the county's main artery.

The milestones along the ridge route, which was to become the A30 trunk road, are similar in design to the Hayle to Redruth pre-turnpike milestones, with recesses on two faces containing a raised letter and number. The letter **P** for Penzance is replaced by an **R** for Redruth, while **L** for Land's End continues to be used.

At Carland Cross at the top of the hill to the west of Mitchell, the Truro turnpike turns off the ridge road. At the time of writing, there is a large roundabout here, next to a wind turbine farm. Here is the first milestone, 12 miles from Redruth. Two of its faces have been re-carved, probably in 1890 when this road was taken over as a Main road by the new Cornwall County Council. Incised on opposite faces are **BODMIN 17 M** and **PENZANCE 30M**. **R 12** survives, in raised letters in a recessed rectangle, but **L 40** has been lost under the new inscriptions (SW845539).

The old milestones continue, at one mile intervals, with the extra inscription obscuring one or other of the original raised letters for the next six miles – Redruth 11, 10, 9, 8, 7, 6. To find the **9 R** milestone, leave the modern A30 and trace the original road through Zelah (which Lysons spelt 'Zealla'). The milestone is to the west of the village, against the wall of a converted chapel at the foot of a steep climb (SW808512). Sadly, the sequence has been broken by the disappearance of the **7R** milestone, found to be missing in 2009.

The next three milestones in the series have been defaced a second time, when their County Council inscriptions were erased during the Second World War. It seems likely that they were moved from the roadside during the War, since the **5R** milestone is now where the **4R** milestone

SW845539 A30
St Erme 508473

SW831532 A30
St Erme 508472

SW816525 A30
St Allen 63916

SW797502 A30
Perranzabuloe 63714

GONE in 2009
SW785492 A30
Perranzabuloe 63271

SW771486 A30
Kenwyn 63270

SW757479 A30
Perranzabuloe 63680

SW745468
Chacewater 63105

SW733458
Blackwater, St Agnes
1406160

Tresillian Toll House A390 SW869465; Toll House at Brighton Cross on the London Road, now B3275 SW904543

Toll House at Brighton Cross on the London Road, now B3275 SW904543

should stand, to the west of the roundabout complex at Chiverton Cross (SW745468). Five miles (SW757479) and three miles (SW733458) from Redruth are marked by milestones with completely blank faces, but clearly the same shape as the others in the series.

Unfortunately the **2R** and **1R** milestones were lost to road improvements, when the Redruth by-pass was built in the later 20th century.

TOLL HOUSES

Toll gates were erected on all the Truro Trust's roads radiating from the town, with a toll gate keeper at each to collect revenue from the passing traffic. Each gate would have a toll board displaying the charges for the various types of vehicle.

The Trust built a number of houses for its toll gate keepers over the years. Ten are known to survive.[15] Most of these are instantly recognisable as toll houses, because they have windows set an angle to look up and down the road, and often what appears to be a blanked out window, where the toll board would be mounted. There would need to be a gate or a chain to control access from side roads along the turnpike road. Sometimes these too had a toll house. On the road from Truro to Penryn there were six toll houses in total, belonging to the Truro Trust, though not all functioned for the whole of its history.

At the end of the turnpike era, the toll houses and other toll collecting equipment were sold off. An advertisement in the *West Briton* of 17 December 1874 announced:

> For Sale, Toll Houses, Toll Bars, and other Effects belonging to the Truro Turnpike Trust, viz:
>
> PENRYN ROAD
>
> Plynt's Barn - Toll-house, stable, tool-house, granite and wooden posts, gate and toll-boards
>
> Callenick - Toll-house, granite post and toll-board
>
> Playing Place – wood post and toll-board
>
> Carnon Downs – Toll-house with wood shed, granite and wood posts, and gate
>
> Carnon Hill – Wood post and chain, toll board and stand
>
> Carnon Bridge – Toll-house, granite posts, toll board and stand
>
> Sticker Bridge – Granite and wooden posts, toll board and gate
>
> Penryn Gate – Toll-house, granite and wood posts, toll board, gate, windlass and chain
>
> Michell Down – Toll-house, granite and wood posts, toll board and gate

All this was on just one of the Trust's roads. There were similar lists for the other roads.

BOUGHT FOR A FIVE POUND NOTE

An interesting comment appeared in the same newspaper a few weeks later, on 28 January 1875:

> Many of the old turnpike gates and houses

belonging to the Truro turnpike trust have been dismantled and taken down, but others are still remaining. Most of them were sold for a mere song, some of the houses having been bought for a five pound note. In some cases those who purchased the houses would like them to remain; but if the boards reconsider their previous determination as to their removal, the properties would have to be put up again by public auction, as for occupation purposes, instead of removal, the properties would in some cases have been sold for twenty times the amount.

It is fortunate that so many of the toll houses survive, though few are lived in now. Having a front door intentionally at the very edge of a busy road, and usually a single storey with perhaps three rooms, means toll houses are both noisy and rather cramped.

KING HARRY FERRY AND THE FLUSHING ROAD

The road to the King Harry Ferry on the River Fal is an old route. It was on the southern post road described by Ogilby in 1675.[16] Today it branches off the main Truro to Falmouth road at Playing Place. There are three **From Truro** milestones between Playing Place and King Harry Ferry (SW815409, SW823397 & SW838396), and an extra **From Truro** milestone on the turn to Feock near Goon Piper (SW818393), yet King Harry Ferry does not appear as a destination in any of the Turnpike Acts. Apart from the milestones, there is no evidence that this road was part of the Truro Trust's network.

On the road from St Gluvias, Penryn, to Flushing, the waterside community opposite Falmouth harbour, there are two unusual milestones. They give the distance to Penryn as one and two miles respectively (SW796350 &

SW808344). Their shape is reminiscent of the standard **FROM TRURO** so many **MILES** design, but the inscription is in lower case lettering and the distance is in Roman numerals, e.g. **II From Penryn**.

POST-TURNPIKE ROADS
ST AGNES
The original Act of 1754, setting up the Truro Turnpike Trust, makes no mention of a road to St Agnes. The Act of 1782 (22 GIII c.lxxxix) added a road from 'Three Burrows in Kenwyn to St Agnes Almshouses'. This explains why the distinctive Truro Trust milestones stop at the 7 mile stone on the B3277 (SW727484). The next milestone, one mile further on, is triangular with a sloping top and a square base. It has two cast iron plates on two faces (SW719497). These are replacement plates made by the St Agnes Improvement Committee, a local charity, in 2011. Another milestone of the same design

King Harry Ferry with Cornwall Vintage Motorcycle Club members boarding.
PHOTO:
MARILYN THOMPSON

SW796350
Mylor 63579

SW815409 B3289
Feock 63399

SW823397 B3289
Feock 63297

SW838396 B3289
Feock 63328

SW818393
Feock 63296

SW807343
Mylor 63472

SW719497 B3277
New plates made in 2011
by St Agnes Improvement
Committee

SW719503 B3277
St Agnes 508475

SW728452
Blackwater, St Agnes

stands at the road junction a few hundred yards nearer St Agnes village with its original cast iron plates intact (SW719503). There is a third milestone of this design to the west of Blackwater (SW728452). This lost its plates in 2009. These milestones were erected by the St Agnes Highway Board in 1890 when the roads were handed over to Cornwall County Council.

The *Royal Cornwall Gazette* of 6 November 1890 published a list of 'Roads recommended by the Road Committee of Cornwall County Council to be made main and adopted by County'. The entry for 'St Agnes HB' reads:

Pressingoll to Vicarage at St Agnes
Chiverton Arms to Four Hundreds   1m 6f

Four Hundreds was once an important location though the name has now disappeared. In the 19th century it defined the village of Blackwater.

Blackwater is a village three miles south-east of St Agnes, in the ecclesiastical parish of Mithian on the road between Redruth and St Columb. Here the four hundreds of Powder, Pyder, Penwith and Kirrier meet.[17]

The exact meeting point is SW722443, near the Crossroads Motel and the site of Scorrier railway station.

In 1890 James Hickes, the County Surveyor held a meeting at Pressingoll (SW721492) with the representatives and surveyors of the Highway Board to inspect the two roads to be made Main. He gave detailed instructions, including a description of the milestones he required:

Recommendation – Chiverton Arms (SW744469) to Four Hundreds – sides to be cut and levelled and hedges trimmed.

Mileposts to be set up – granite with diagonal faces and cast iron tablets on a square base.

Direction posts at Four Turnings and Red Lion Inn.

Widening at Blackwater near Wheal Busy Corner at 3 mile post

From Pressingoll to Penwinnick Corner he asked for similar work, including mile posts of the same style.[18]

A unique milestone stands at the entrance to what is now a car parking area near the sea at Blue Hills, St Agnes. This beautiful spot was once a heavily industrial mining landscape. The stone is inscribed **1 FROM MILESTONE** and is one mile from the St Agnes Highway Board milestone at the road junction in the village (SW727517).

PERRANPORTH

Truro Turnpike Trust maintained the road only part of the way to Perranporth. In the 1754 Act (27 GII c.xli) the road came as far as Shortlanesend. In 1773 (13 GIII c.cxii) a section from 'Shortlanesend to Four Burrows' was added. These sections of road bear the milestone design typical of the Truro Trust – tombstone shaped, with the inscription **FROM TRURO** so many **MILES**.

The next four milestones to Perranporth are a completely different, triangular design with a massive rectangular base. The inscription is not cut in to the stone surface, as would be standard practice in Cornwall, but carried on metal plates attached to the two dressed surfaces.

In the *Royal Cornwall Gazette* of 6 November 1890, the list of 'Roads recommended by Road Committee of Cornwall County Council to be made main and adopted by County' gives the entry for 'West Powder HB' as 'Shortlanesend to Perranporth'. One of the requirements for adoption as a Main Road, with the subsequent

SW727518
Blue Hills, St Agnes
1 FROM MILESTONE

SW755496 B3284
Perranzabuloe

SW754511 B3284
Perranzabuloe

SW755527 B3284
Perranzabuloe

SW757540 B3284
Perranzabuloe

county funding for repairs, was that milestones were set up before handover. No milestones are shown here on the 1st Series Ordnance Survey 6 inch map of 1880. Four milestones are shown on the 2nd Series map of 1907. Milestones were set up in 1890, with metal plates giving distances to Truro and Perranporth, prior to the road being adopted as a Main Road by Cornwall County Council.

SCORRIER STATION

Scorrier station opened in 1852 but does not exist any more having closed in 1964. But along the B3298 Scorrier to Comford road the milestones give distances to Scorrier Station.

There are three milestones to Scorrier Station. They correspond to an entry in the Royal Cornwall Gazette of 4 February 1892 headed 'Cornwall County Council Schedule 2 of

Main Roads'. The relevant entry reads 'Falmouth Highway Board: Comford to Four Hundreds'. These milestones are similar in design to the Perranporth milestones – triangular on a massive square base – but have the inscription carved into the stone, not carried on cast iron plates. Time has shown this to be a more durable method of inscription.

MINERAL TRAMWAYS GUIDE POSTS

The tramways and mineral railways have been linked together since 2000 by the Mineral Tramways Heritage Project to form a network of traffic free cycling and walking routes exploring the industrial history of central Cornwall within the World Heritage Site. The routes are way-marked with sympathetically designed granite guide stones.

SW730411 B3298
St Day 66657

SW733426 B3298
St Day 66898

SW728438 B3298
St Day 66897

SW724441
Mineral Tramways Cycle route 2008 guidestone at Scorrier Station

SW816525 A30 St Allen 63916. Milestone reinstated May 2010

15th Century bridge at Wadebridge. The Wadebridge bypass bridge in the background opened in 1993.

CHAPTER FIVE
THE HALEWORTHY TRUST, COLAN, NEWQUAY AND ST COLUMB

The area to the north-west of Bodmin Moor has one turnpike trust with its mixed fortunes shown in its milestones. There are several other groups of local milestones and a considerable sprinkling of guidestones.

HALEWORTHY TURNPIKE TRUST

The Haleworthy Trust was set up by Act of Parliament in 1760 (33 GII c.xi) to turnpike the road 'From Haleworthy (SX180878) to the E end of Wadebridge' and 'from W end of Wadebridge into & thro' the borough of Mitchell (SW860545)'. The trustees thought that this new turnpike would link with the turnpike from Launceston, established in the same year, and the existing turnpikes radiating from Truro, to provide the main road through Cornwall for years to come.

Writing in 1838, Davies Gilbert records that 'The North road was for some years the great line of communication to the West of Cornwall.' And that Gilbert 'had heard from Rev. William Phillips (who died in 1784) that the making of the road was taken up rather as a matter of patriotism and to assist the undertaking he cut, with his own hands, the figures on the granite milestones which remain.'[1]

The Trustees came from the various towns along the route of the proposed turnpike – Camelford, Wadebridge and St Columb Major. It was already the main route into Cornwall from the east, skirting the northern and western edges of the forbidding waste and swirling fog of Bodmin Moor. Improving the road would increase traffic and bring more business to the towns, it was hoped.

In the early days of the Haleworthy Trust these hopes were realised, but in 1769 the Bodmin Turnpike Trust was established (9 GIII c. lxix) with a direct route across Bodmin Moor. 'This road so entirely superceded the former as to cause an entire loss of capital to those who contributed towards making it, and the road itself fell back to be inferior to that of most parish roads. It was however taken up as a new concern in 1835; a stage coach was established on it.'[2]

STAGE COACH RIVALS

In fact two stage coaches were established on the Haleworthy Turnpike, and the road itself was improved, with new sections and easier gradients, as described later. The rivalry between the two coach companies, Pearce Cockram & Co., proprietors of the Regulator coach, and A. Stephens & Co., who ran the Defiance coach, is colourfully described in Cyril Noall's *History of Cornish Mail and Stage Coaches*.[3] These two companies were already at odds on other routes in Cornwall. The worthies of Camelford, Wadebridge and St Columb applied to the proprietors of the Regulator for a coach service, but their request was turned down. The Defiance Company, when approached, agreed to give the route a service. However, shortly afterwards, the Regulator began running a competing service on the same route, despite its earlier refusal.

It might be thought that the locals would have been delighted to have not one, but two coaches. However this was not the case. There was bitter resentment at the earlier refusal of the Regulator to offer a service. The people of Camelford held a pro-Defiance meeting at the King's Arms Inn on 27 November 1835. They felt that the Regulator was in competition to drive the Defiance off the road, and that once this had been achieved, the Regulator's service would be withdrawn.

Mr Noall notes the last reference to the Defiance was in 1840, while the Regulator continued through Wadebridge until at least 1850.

HALEWORTHY TO CAMELFORD

Haleworthy or Hallworthy (SX180878) was a noted inn in the parish of Davidstow.

It is curious that the milestones on the road between Haleworthy and Camelford show the distance to Launceston, not Camelford. SX109839 A39 in Camelford Even odder is the design, because it is identical to the milestones further east on the Launceston Trust section of the road. There is no change in the milestones spacing or style on either side of Haleworthy. The last of these Launceston Trust style

SX175877 A395
Davidstow 67388

SX159874 A395
Davidstow 67387

SX144870 A395
Davidstow 505706

SX132862 A39
Forrabury & Minster 68667

SX109839 A39
Camelford 68544

*SX108839
Trefrew Road,
Camelford, Lanteglos*

milestones is **L 16** which is in Camelford itself, outside 33 Victoria Road (SX109839). On the Camelford side of this last milestone, at the corner of Trefrew Road, is a house now called Sunnyside, but labelled Turnpike on an early 19th century large scale map in Camelford Museum. The map shows named and numbered fields, like a tithe map. It shows a barrier across the main road and Trefrew road, suggesting toll gates. The map also shows a milestone labelled '16 miles to Launceston' where the **L 16** milestone stands. The map titled 'Camelford c.1816-20 printed by R.Cartwright, Warwick Place'. The Haleworthy Trust Renewal Act of 1825 still refers to 'the road leading from Haleworthy in the parish of Davidstow in the county of Cornwall to the East End of Wadebridge; and from the West End of Wadebridge into and through the Borough of Mitchell.' (6 GIV c.xl) In 1840 Richard Symons, clerk to the trust, reported that there were thirty-three and a half miles of road through ten parishes all repaired by the trustees. [4] To give this total, the distance must include the road north of Camelford as far as Haleworthy, still maintained by the Haleworthy Trust, despite the Launceston-style milestones.

A very old milestone was discovered in 2010, built into the end of the garden wall of a modern bungalow SX108839. The design of this milestone is reminiscent of the milestones near St Columb Major described below. The milestone discovery was not on the A39 through Camelford, but in Trefrew Road, a side road leading to Slaughterbridge.

The inscription, elegantly carved on the milestone, said that it was **I Mile To Camelford**, which the milestone in its current location was not. The really exciting thing about this milestone was the date carved on it, 1752, which

made it older than the Haleworthy Turnpike Trust of 1760. This makes it one of the oldest milestones in Cornwall, and its excellent condition makes it an exceptional find.

It seems clear that it had been moved, but from where and when? A milestone of this quality must surely have been made for the main road. One mile north of Camelford along the A39 brings you to what is now a lay-by, halfway between Redgates and Collan's Cross. Is this where the milestone once stood?

The map evidence provided by Camelford Museum shows that by 1820 the milestones north of the town gave distances not to Camelford, but to Launceston. The **L 16** milestone opposite the turn to Roughtor in Camelford is shown and described on the museum's map. So had the **I Mile To Camelford** milestone been removed by this date? The landowner who built the bungalow in the 1960s, where the milestone now stands, in Trefrew Road, had made his living as a monumental mason. Did he find the milestone, perhaps in the lay-by and decide to give it a new home? Careful inspection of the carved face of

Camelford and its neighbours hoped to prosper from the success of a turnpike road
CYRUS REDDING 1842

the milestone shows very neat repair work to two large holes, probably where the hinges for a farm gate had once been fitted. Detective work continues to try to find out more about this milestone.

CAMELFORD TO WADEBRIDGE

Camelford was a modest place, but had the advantages needed to grow, once the road was improved. Ogilby describes the pre-turnpike town as

> Cambleford, seated on the River Camel, a small town scarce numbering 50 houses, is in the parish of Lanicolas [Lanteglos] a mile distant, yet sends burgesses to Parliament, and is governed by a Mayor, Recorder and 8 Magistrates; has a small market on Fridays and 3 fairs yearly... having some inns affording good accommodation. [5]

Celia Fiennes reached Camelford from Wadebridge in 1698. The journey was wet and muddy which may have prejudiced her against the town:

> to Comblefford over steep hills 9 miles more, some of this way over Commons of black Moorish ground full of sloughs, the lanes are defended with bancks wherein are stones, some great rocks others slaty stones such as they use for tileing; Combleford was a little market town but it was very indifferent accomodations , but the raines that night and next morning made me take up there, till about 10 oclock in the morning it then made a shew of clearing up, made me willing to seek a better lodging. [6]

The road south of Camelford went through St Teath, Watergate and Trelill to St Kew Highway, then past Three Hole Cross to Wadebridge. This was the turnpike route until 1837, when a new

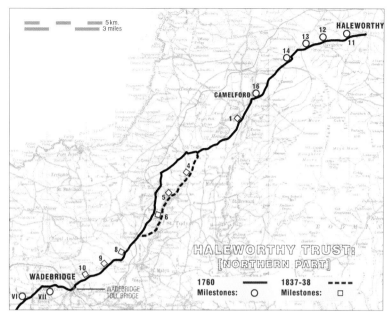

road was planned along the valley of the River Allen from Knightsmill to St Kew Highway.[7] Note that between 1834 and 1840 Christopher McAdam was Surveyor for the Haleworthy Trust, now renamed the Camelford, Wadebridge and St Columb Trust. No milestones survive on the pre-1837 route, but round topped tombstones give the distance to Camelford along the sinuous valley bottom road and all the way to Wadebridge.

1 CAM is at Valley Truckle beside the entrance drive to a house (SX097823). The **2 CAM** milestone at Helstone cannot be found. The **C 3** milestone at Knightsmill is not a milestone but a county bridge **C** stone, marking the boundary of road maintenance between the turnpike trust and Cornwall county, who were responsible for the bridge approaches, with the number 3 only painted on SX072806). **4 CAM**

SX097823 A39
Camelford 68527

County bridge stone
with painted number 3
SX072806 A39
Advent 68474

SX066792 A39
St Teath 505711

SX055780 A39
St Kew 351506

SX047766 A39
St Kew 351507

SX025747 A39
St Kew 505713

SX013738 A39
Wadebridge

SW999730
Egloshayle 505802

SW999730 Egloshayle
10 CAM in Castle
Canyke Depot 2011
awaiting repair and
re-erection

The bridge at Wadebridge divided the turnpike in two.
It had charged its own tolls from the 15th century. CYRUS REDDING 1842

(SX066792), **5 CAM** (SX055780) and **6 CAM** (SX047766) are set into the dry stone wall on the west side of the valley road, the opposite side to the River Allen. The **7 CAM** milestone just north of St Kew Highway was lost to road widening in the late 20th century. **8 CAM** (SX025747) has all but lost its number following repeated blows from the verge trimmer. **9 CAM** (SX013738) has been decapitated by the verge trimmer and now records just **CAM**.

10 CAM (SW999730), the last milestone north of the old bridge at Wadebridge was buried in a three metres high embankment near the roundabout of the Wadebridge by-pass when a new hardware store was built in 2007. The milestone was Grade II listed (Egloshayle 505802) and when plans were prepared to replace the hardware store with a supermarket in 2011, the milestone was recovered from beneath the embankment. It is hoped to re-erect the milestone beside the highway when the new supermarket is completed in 2013.

WADE-BRIDGE
The 15th century bridge across the River Camel at Wadebridge is the most spectacular ancient bridge in Cornwall. The original bridge had seventeen equally spaced arches and was over five hundred feet long. It was built by local subscription and maintained by the Wada-Bridge Trust set up by John Lovibond in 1476 and endowed with an area of land for raising funds. Tolls were charged for the use of the bridge and the trust survived until 1852 when the bridge was handed over to the County and a major widening scheme was undertaken. The bridge was widened again in 1963, before the bridge and town were relieved of their traffic by a new high level bridge and by-pass, begun in 1991. [8]

The Haleworthy Trust's road ended at the eastern end of the bridge and recommenced at the western end of the bridge. Distances were measured from Camelford on the north side of the bridge, and to St Columb on the south side. On both sides, the distance from the end of Wade-Bridge to the first milestone was less than one mile.

THE ST COLUMB MILESTONES
Between Wadebridge and Mitchell the Haleworthy Trust milestones give distances to St Columb Major. These milestones are massive rectangular blocks of granite, typically 18 inches by 15 inches in cross-section, with worn, rectangular pyramid tops. The inscription in

Toll House at Wadebridge, now bypassed and free from traffic. SX971725

letters up to 4 inches high is a mixture of upper and lower case, with the distance given in Roman numerals which is most unusual for Cornwall.

The first of these milestones, **VII MILE To Saint COLUMB**, stands on the grass verge in front of Tesco's supermarket, on the climb south out of Wadebridge town centre (SW975725), before reaching the modern (1991) by-pass. The elegant little octagonal toll house has been isolated in a cul de sac on the opposite side of the by-pass and is sadly neglected (SW971725).

The next milestone has crossed the road sometime in the 20th century, at a very narrow point, south of the Wadebridge showground (SW961718), but all the rest are on the west side of the road and all are in place as far as St Columb Major.

The original route in to St Columb from Wadebridge was through Gluvian. This involved a very steep descent with a gradient of about 1 in 6 to the stream crossing, then a steep climb up the other side of the valley into the town. In 1838 a loop to the west was introduced from the one mile stone, past Trevornick and the turn to Tregamere, entering St Columb at a higher level.

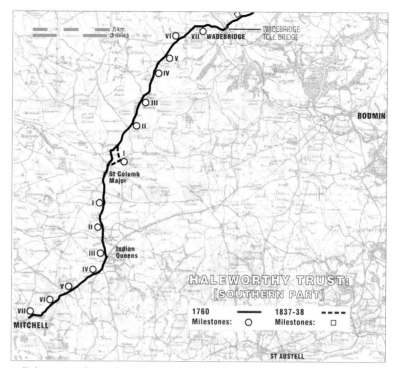

A link was made to the old road in the valley bottom where the toll house stood. A new toll house was built at SW915640 where the link road divides from the new road. [9]

The old tollhouse was falling into ruin, and in 1967 the Parish Council pressed for it to be demolished, while the St Columb Major Old Cornwall Society fought for it to be saved. It was restored by private enterprise and is now an attractive dwelling, still instantly recognisable as a toll house, with its prominent porch, jutting first floor window, and even a wooden settle outside for the tollgate keeper on fine days!

When the St Columb Major by-pass was built in the 1970s, the **I MILE To Saint COLUMB** stone was moved to the Tregamere turn (SW922644) so that it remained on the public highway.

South of St Columb Major, the same design

Toll House at St Columb saved from demolition in 1967 SW914639

SW975725 Wadebridge, St Breock 67677

SW961718 A39 St Breock 676798

SW951707 A39 St Issey 397160 St Breock 67679

SW943693 A39 St Issey 397162

SW 936680 A39 St Columb 71164

SW929665 A39 St Columb 71163

SW922643 Tregamere Lane, St Columb 71154

SW912618 A39
St Columb 71162

SW911602
Trevarren, St Columb
507527

SW912587
Fraddon, St Enoder
71310

SW905573
St Enoder 71308

SW891564
Summercourt, St Enoder
71305

SW878555 A30 resited
beside westbound
carriageway, St Enoder
71303

SW866548 A30 St
Enoder 71301

*Milestone discovered in
St Columb Road depot
December 2008; The
milestone from the depot, resited
beside A30 April 2009,
SW878555*

of milestone is continued. Despite a number of large scale road developments, all seven of these milestones remain in place, including two on the A30 dual carriageway. All these milestones are on the west or north side of the road, except for the **VI MILE To Saint COLUMB** stone (SW878555). St Enoder 71303This milestone, in effect, climbed over the wall, from the old A30 to the south side of the new dual carriageway A30, when the old section of road was sold to the local farmer. For some time the **VI** mile stone languished in the highways depot at St Columb Road after being recovered from the section of road that was sold. Eventually, arrangements were made with the Highways Agency contractors to have the milestone re-erected on the south side of the A30 dual carriageway, a few feet from its original location on the other side of a stone wall. No additional safety barriers were needed, because the A30 is below the old road at this point, leaving the milestone high up on the embankment.

TREBARWITH SANDS TURNPIKE TRUST
This trust was established in 1825 (6 GIV c.lxxxiv), to improve access for extracting sand from the seashore used for manure and to

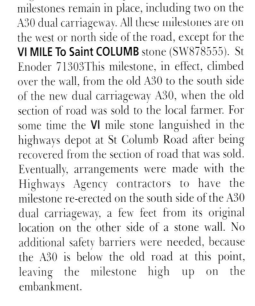

provide an export route for locally quarried slate. The turnpike ran from the coast towards the main road north of Camelford, but stopped at Condolden Bridge (SX092864).

At least one entrepreneur saw the opportunity for a much grander road, running across the moors to join the Bodmin to Launceston turnpike near Peverell's Cross (SX122721). As the following extract from the *Royal Cornwall Gazette* shows, he called a meeting in Camelford before the Act was passed. There is no newspaper report following the meeting, which suggests that it was not a success. Certainly, no road across the moor was built:

NEW ROAD FOR CARRIAGE OF MANURE
AND TRAVELLING,
BETWEEN CAMELFORD AND BODMIN
It Being in contemplation to apply to parliament for an Act for making a NEW ROAD for the better conveyance of Sand for Manure, from Trebarrow (Trebarwith) Strand in the parish of Tintagel, to the Road leading from Camelford to Tintagel, about the distance of three miles, the benefits of which will be much increased if this Road were extended into the interior of the neighbouring Parishes as far as to meet the Bodmin Turnpike Road to Launceston, about the Five Mile Stone, which might also be used as a better Road between Bodmin and Camelford…
…a Meeting at the King's Arms, Camelford on Wednesday 26th May at ten o'clock.
Dated May 6 1824 [10]

It seems that the turnpike was set up to improve the difficult section of an existing road. Greenwood's map of 1827 marks 'T.B.' at SX050864, just above the beach, where a stone cottage now stands called *Toll Bar*, and a

Toll Bar cottage. The Trebarwith Strand Trust of 1825 had two toll bars but no milestones.

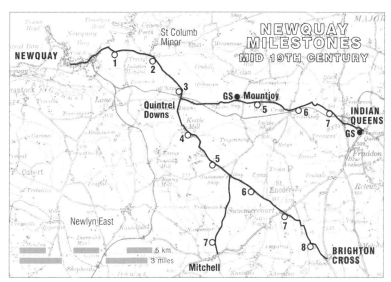

continuous turnpike route, denoted on the map by heavy edging to the road, past 'Conoldon Bridge' as far as Collan's Cross (SX121853) on the main A39 road.

In 1840 there were 2 miles 3 furlongs 17 poles of road through two parishes all repaired by the trustees, and 2 toll gates. [11]

A toll house has been identified near Condolden Bridge about two miles from the beach.[12] The first edition of the one-inch Ordnance Survey map marks a toll gate – 'T.G.' at this point (SX091863) and appears to show a building on the north side of the road. A toll charged at one gate would clear the traveller of a further charge at the other gate.

No milestones are recorded on this road and none have been found.

NON-TURNPIKE MILESTONES

NEWQUAY MILESTONES

In contrast to the massive milestones to Saint Columb Major, the Newquay milestones are slim and quite small, with a gable top. They run along the three roads which spread out from Newquay towards the A30 spine road: A392 to Indian Queens, A3058 to Summercourt and A3076 to Mitchell. The milestones on A3058 continue beyond the A30 at Summercourt to reach the Truro turnpike B3275 near the toll house at Brighton Cross.

The design of milestone is unique to Newquay. It exists nowhere else in the county. None of these roads were ever turnpikes. Who erected the milestones and when?

The local Highway Board seems the most likely candidate.

Newquay Highway Board was established under the Highways Act of 1835. All the Newquay style milestones are shown on the 1880 Ordnance Survey map. It seems likely that the Newquay milestones were set up between 1835 and 1880.

A milestone of a different design, on a minor road, feeding into the A392 at Mountjoy is dated

SW824620 A392 Henver Road, Newquay 508246

SW839617 A392 Newquay 71110

SW849604 A392 Newquay 508247

SW878601 A392 Newquay 508248

SW893598 A392 St Enoder 508250

SW907596 St Columb 507795

SW852590 A3058
Newlyn East 508256

SW861579 A3058
Dairyland, Newlyn
East 63995

SW874570 A3058
St Enoder 71302
*recovered from Staffordshire
and re-erected*

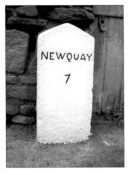

SW887560 A3058
Summercourt,
St Enoder 71304

SW897549 A3058
St Enoder 71306

BOTTOM OF PAGE:
(left) Newquay 6 found in Staffordshire by a member of the Milestone Society in 2005

(centre) The author and Andrew Hinsull with Newquay 6, recovered from Staffordshire and re-erected beside A3058 at SW874570 in 2006.
PHOTO:
MARILYN THOMPSON

(right) Celebrating the re-erection of Newquay 6 with the Mayor of St Enoder

1852. Logically, the Newquay milestones must predate this milestone. This narrows the date of erection to a period between 1835 and 1852, a period of prosperity and expansion in the area.

The passenger railway service to Newquay, which brought the town wealth as a holiday resort, did not commence until 20 June 1876. Until this date, visitors would have come to Newquay by road. The milestones were erected by the town's worthies on the Local Highway Board to guide paying visitors to the budding resort.

VULNERABLE MILESTONES

A vigilant member of the Milestone Society spotted a milestone in the front garden of a house in Staffordshire in 2005 which was inscribed **Newquay 6**. This had been beside the A3058 in 1995, but had been missing for a couple of years. Negotiations in Staffordshire and with Cornwall County Council resulted in the milestone being returned to Cornwall and re-erected with due ceremony in its original position in June 2006 (SW874570).

Sadly **Newquay 4** (SW863601) on A392

disappeared in 2007 near the entrance to a new depot for a construction company.

During the Second World War many milestones were buried beside the road and subsequently dug up and reinstated. Some were defaced by having the inscription chiselled off. A most unusual example is the **Newquay 7** milestone on A3076 (SW861551) which had the **NEWQUAY** inscription filled with cement. Examination suggests that an attempt had been

SW861550 A3076
showing WW2
cement obscuring
NEWQUAY

SW861550 A3076
re-painted
Newlyn East 508258

made to chisel off the inscription before the application of the cement. The cement proved almost as hard as the surrounding granite and could not be removed when the stone was repainted in 2009. **NEWQUAY** was painted over the smooth cement, but the anomalous **MILES** below the 7 was omitted so that this stone matched all the others on roads from the town.

St Columb Major to Newquay

There is an entry in the *Royal Cornwall Gazette* of 6 November 1890 showing the adoption as a Main Road by Cornwall County Council from St Columb Highway Board, the road from 'St Columb to Newquay'. This is now the A3059, which has triangular milestones with triangular pyramid tops at one mile intervals from the junction west of St Columb Major, through the village of St Columb Minor to the junction with A392, Henver Road on the outskirts of Newquay.

The first stone in the series is rather battered (SW896634). It had suffered repeated vehicle impacts, until a road straightening in 2007 moved the road away and improved the sight lines. It gives the distance to St Columb as 1¼ miles and to Newquay as 6 miles. It is curious that a St Columb Highway Board milestone does not measure in whole miles from St Columb, but from Newquay.

The next milestone is set away from the road, at the back of a wide area of grass on a bend (SW882634). This location is the result of 20th century road improvement. The milestone stands quite high, exposing the rectangular base and triangular stops that join it to the triangular upper section.

The last milestone is opposite the Wesleyan Methodist Chapel in St Columb Minor (SW838621). While all the other milestones are on the left hand, south, side travelling from St Columb Major, this one is on the opposite side. It

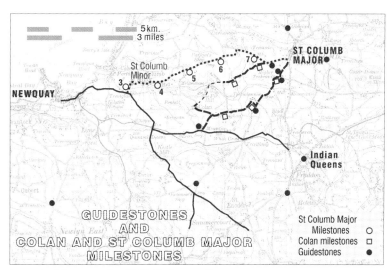

is marked here on the 1907 Ordnance Survey map. All the milestones were made together to a common design. Very faintly, through the layers of white paint, a second inscription can be made out on this milestone, identical to the inscribed and black painted inscription above it, but on the opposite faces. The milestone was manufactured to go on the left hand side of the road with the appropriate inscription, but this would have put it in front of the chapel, so it had to be re-carved to give the correct facings when on the other side of the road.

THE PADSTOW ROAD

The road between Halsars Grave and Padstow was recommended by the Road Committee of Cornwall County Council to be made Main and adopted by the County in 1890.[13] This is the road now designated A389. Halsars Grave is called Hals' Grave on the modern 1:25000 map at SW957715, where the A389 joins the A39 road to Wadebridge.

Except for some straightening just west of the milestone at Little Petherick, the road is

This milestone crossed the road in St Columb Minor. The original carving is just visible through the old paint. SW838622 Newquay 71119

SW896634 A3059 St Columb 71159

SW882634 A3059 St Columb 71158

SW867629 A3059 Colan 71015

SW852623 A3059 Colan 71013

SW838621 St Columb Minor, Newquay 71119

SW947717 A389
St Issey 397159

SW931718 A389
St Issey 397190

SW914721 A389
Broken in 2008.
St Issey 397158

SW908732 A389
Padstow 507529

SW909748 B3276
Padstow 396035

shown on C & J Greenwood's 1 inch county map of 1827, following its modern route. The sharp bend at this point on the old road, which still survives on the ground, is shown on the 1915 OS ½ inch map, Sheet 35, showing that the straightening took place in the 20th century, after the road had been adopted by the County.

All five of these squat triangular milestones, with their flat tops sloping towards the front corner, survive on this road, including the stone 1 mile from Padstow, now on the B3276, the original route of the Main road as adopted in late 1890 (SW909748). Their design is identical, suggesting they were all produced in one batch by the same mason. This is not the norm in Cornwall. There are no other milestones in Cornwall that match these in style.

ROADS TO COLAN

The survival of most of a group of milestones in the narrow lanes around the church of Colan, between Newquay and St Columb Major is remarkable. These milestones are the most lightweight, poorest carved and of the lowest quality stone of any in Cornwall.

The 1inch Ordnance Survey 1st Series map of 1870 shows two roads from St Columb Major to Colan, one on each side of the Porth River valley.

The more northern route stays on high ground to Nanswhyden before turning sharply south to cross the valley to Colan on a road which was never tarred and is now a green footpath across the fields. Three milestones are marked on this route on the OS 1:25000 First Series map sheet SW86, published in 1964, giving details of the inscription, including a milestone on the 'footpath' section (SW875622). The footpath section milestone has been missing for over twenty years.

The more southern route turns south, just past the first milestone, to cross the valley to Trebudannon and then on to Colan. Again, three milestones are marked on this route on the same OS sheet SW86, published in 1964. The last of this series, one mile from Colan Church, has disappeared since 2002.

The design of these milestones, triangular with a pyramid top and a rectangular base, was popular on roads in the Western Division of the county in the mid - 19th century. It was used on later turnpike roads and on non-turnpike roads made Main Roads before they were taken over by the new County Council. What is so unusual

SW899630
St Columb 508254

SW885623
St Columb 508253

SW904623
St Columb 507800

SW896612
St Columb 508252

SW871602 A392
Colan 71016

SW871602 A392 Colan 71016
Colan parish milestone dated 1852.

about these milestones is that they are not on a turnpike road or a road that was ever made a Main Road. They mark the mileage on parish roads.

The small size and poor quality of the granite stone and the poor quality and shallow depth of the inscription are in marked contrast to the milestones in this style used on the Main Roads of the Western Division. The authority that was responsible for roads in St Columb Major and Colan parishes from 1835 was the St Columb Highway Board.

The best of this group of milestones is the milestone at Mountjoy on A392 to Newquay (SW871602). It is the same style and of a similar poor stone to the rest, but stands taller. On the left face it carries the legend **ST COLUMB 4**

COLAN CHURCH 1 and in a smaller font **FIR HILL 1½**. The right face reads **QUEENS 3¼ ST MICHAEL 4¼ TRURO 11¼**. The Fir Hill was a mansion just north of Colan Church, destroyed by fire in the 20th century. 'Queens' refers to Indian Queens, and 'St Michael' is the ancient borough of Mitchell. This stone is inscribed with the date 1852. It would seem likely that the whole set of parish road milestones was erected at this date.

GUIDESTONES

In 1864, newspaper article singled out the area around St Columb Major as being well supplied with 'Directing Posts':

> In some parts of our county you may ride for miles and not see one of these silent monitors. Last summer I had occasion to travel over a great part of Trigg, Pydar and Powder West, and except in St Columb, and the turnpikes of course, a directing post was scarcely to be seen.[14]

A rich variety of distinctive granite directing posts or guidestones survive to this day around St Columb:

SX091876 This very tall granite pillar has inscriptions running vertically down three faces in very large capital letters to **LANSON**, **TINTAGEL** and **CAMELFORD**.

SX099824 This is a neatly faced triangular guidestone. The wooden direction arms repeat the carved inscriptions on the three faces of the stone pillar.

SW911704 This guidestone is so attractive that it has been listed by St Issey and St Ervan parishes independently! It has bevelled edges to the top and arrows on two faces pointing in four different directions.

SW892676 Bevelled edges to the top and

SX091876
Trevalga 68885

SX099824 A39
Camelford 68535

SW911704 B3274
St Issey 397127
St Ervan 396940

SW892676
St Ervan 396939

SW937683 A39
St Issey 397126

*SW942617
Tresaddern turn, left face.
St Columb 71156*

*SW942617
Tresaddern turn, right
face. St Columb 71156*

*SW926632 Tregatillian,
St Columb 71155*

*SW908647 St Columb
71153*

four arrows on two faces pointing in three directions. St Issey is just painted on, but the other destinations are carved as on the other similar stone.

SW937683 This rectangular guidestone has a curved top and just one arrow.

SW942617 Most of the guidestones around St Columb are triangular in cross section and stand at forks in the road, rather than crossroads. This one is triangular with a pent top, and unusual spelling of Tresaddrn with a missing **e**, and the alternative version of St Austle for St Austell. It has four arrows, but has St Columb on both inscribed faces, since both directions will take you there.

SW926632 A slender triangle of stone has been heavily damaged by turning traffic at this Y-junction. There are three arrows for four destinations. **Trewolves** was Trevolvas and is now Trewolvas.

SW908647 There were three guidestones on the hill just north of St Columb Major. Sadly, only this rather battered slender triangle survives. Arrows point in the three directions with four destinations named. SW901630 West of St Columb Major where four roads meet is a five sided guidestone with inscriptions and distances

on four sides, but no arrows. It stands next to Cross Putty, the town goal in the annual St Columb hurling competition.[15]

South of St Columb Major the road through White Cross and Gummow's Shop was the main route to Mitchell before the turnpike was made. The turnpike took a wider sweep to avoid the steep valleys, passing through Black Cross and Fraddon to reach Mitchell. There are no milestones on the pre-turnpike route, but there are guidestones.

SW907624 This guidestone is south of the modern southern by-pass of St Columb, with direct access north to the town only possible to walkers now. The stone has a rectangular top giving the distance to St Columb as 1 mile. Below this is a triangular section. On one face an arrow points east towards the Haleworthy Trust turnpike for Bodmin, Truro and St Austle (St Austell). The other face has an arrow pointing the other way for Trebadannon (Trebudannon) 1 mile, Newlyn with no distance, Crantock 9 miles and Cubert 10. This stone has a rectangular base, joined to the triangular section by triangular pyramid stops. It is altogether a magnificent specimen.

SW907625 Immediately north of the

*SW901630 A3059
St Columb 71160.
Left side*

*SW901630 A3059
St Columb 71160. Right
side*

*SW907624
St Columb 508477*

*SW907625
St Columb 71161*

SW896613
St Columb Major

SW896612
St Columb 71151

SW870580
Newlyn East 63993

SW803570 A3075
Rejerrah Hill
63962+63652

SW820529 B3285
St Allen 63917

elaborate stone just described is a slender and battered triangular stone, inscribed **St Columb ½** on one face and **Newquay 7** on the other. Again the stone has been made redundant by the St Columb by-pass, and now gives information of value only to walkers.

SW896613 The first turning to Trebudannon has the place name and an arrow on a stone set into the wall below an old cast iron letter box. The current letter box is on a wooden post on the opposite side of the road.

SW896612 The next turning is Trebudannon Lane and the guidestone has an arrow pointing towards Colan. An arrow points along the main route to **Newlyn** or St Newlyn East. This stone has a rounded top, thicker, square section middle and a narrow octagonal section base.

SW870580 Continuing on the same route, this guidestone stands in the fork of the road north of Gummow's Shop, marking where the roads for Newlyn and Mitchell divide. It has a massive base, tapering to a triangular top. There are three arrows and three destinations.

SW803570 The chamfered top edges of this guidestone recall the design near St Issey and St Ervan. There are no arrows, but there are four destinations inscribed on two sides. A bent over iron stud in the top of the stone may once have

supported a post with wooden arms – a fingerpost.

SW820529 At the crossroads of B3285 and the road south from Newlyn East is a tall rectangular guidestone with a worn pyramid top. The shape is similar to the very early milestones on the A30 spine road from Mitchell to Hayle which rushes past a few metres to the south. There are inscriptions on two faces with carved pointing hands, the only example of a pointing hands stone in this part of Cornwall.

SW918590 On the junction in Indian Queens is a solid granite pillar with neat but shallow carving, similar in style to the carving on the Newquay Highway Board milestones.

SW871602 At Mountjoy this slender, fragile stone has been referred to earlier because of the date 1852 carved on the top surfaces. It gives distances to three destinations along the minor road to the north through the hamlet of Mountjoy. It does not indicate Newquay at all. The distances on the second face suggest that the traveller is directed via White Cross to reach St Michael (Mitchell) and then Truro, while Queens refers to Indian Queens, 3½ miles away.

While it is possible to group small numbers of these 17 guidestones together, it is their variety and idiosyncrasy, as well as their remarkable survival, which is their appeal.

SW918590 Indian
Queens, St Enoder
71311

SW871602 A392
Colan 71016

Polson Bridge and Launceston, J FARINGTON. ENGRAVED BY W WOOLNOTH.
CORNISH STUDIES LIBRARY

CHAPTER SIX

LAUNCESTON AND NORTH CORNWALL

HALL DRUNKARD

The post road from Launceston to Truro went through Egloskerry and followed the high ground to the north of the River Kensey as far as Halworthy. In 1675 Ogilby describes Halworthy as 'Hall-Drunkard alias Halworthy, a noted inn affording as good entertainment as any on the road.'[1] The place is marked 'Haleworthy alias Halldrunkard' on Thomas Martyn's county map of 1748. Black's Guide to Cornwall in 1895[2] calls it 'Hallworthy, scandalously known as 'All drunkards' inn'. This shows that the alternative name lasted for over two hundred years.

William Wynne followed the post road in his 1755 visit. He crossed into Cornwall over Poulson Bridge on 2 August, but the post road took him to St Stephens, not up the long steep climb to Launceston Castle. His road to Egloskerry was over the downs where a horse race was to take place the following month. This means that he climbed due north out of St Stephens and turned left at the top of the hill to follow the northern edge of what is now a golf course. From Egloskerry he crossed more downs to 'Hallsdrunkard' along the post road north of the River Kensey. Note that he separates the inn of Hallsdrunkard from the 'town' of Hallworthy, and that the roads were good 'for a Coach'. He writes:

> …we came to St Stephens, an antient Burrough town which is very small though it sends two members (to Parliament); left Launceston, Castle and town on our lefthand, which is a pretty large Burrough and Market town and sends two members, and is as it were the Key of Cornwall and has the remains of a very Large Castle which is now the County Gaol.

> We thought it more suitable to our journey for the day to dine at Egleskerry a small village but a bad Inn and very bad accommodation but a pretty good Church. 'Tis 8 miles from Lifton and done in 2 hours, great part Lay over the downs, where there were horse races in the September following and afforded a pleasant and extended prospect of the towns of Launceston, St Stephens, Sir William Morices

(Werrington House) and the adjacent Country.

> From Egleskerry we passed over downes to Hallsdrunkard which is a tolerable Inn on the Downes 5 miles of. But the town is a distance and is sometimes Calld Hallworthy or Hallsdrunkard and from thence to Camelford about 5 miles further. In all that day 27 miles and good roads for a Coach.[3]

PRE-TURNPIKE MILESTONES

An alternative route from Egloskerry to Hall Drunkard was revealed by a slip of paper inserted in one of the binders of the Philbrick Collection[4] which reads:

> Egloskerry to Tregear Rd. By Badharlick Farm – rough granite M.S. 47 inches x 10 inches sq. on top of hedge.

Following this on the ground led to the discovery of a milestone with the inscription **XI To Cam** – eleven miles to Camelford – in the hedge on top of a high bank just west of Egloskerry (SX265863). This was not on the post road to Hall Drunkard, but on a route that crossed the River Kensey on a county bridge at Badharlick, to join what was to become the turnpike road to Halworthy at Cold Northcott.

The route can be picked out on Thomas Martyn's county map of 1748 which shows an enclosed road (between hedges) from Egloskerry to Badhallick (Badharlick), then an unenclosed road to Tregear, an enclosed section south of Bedgale (Badgall) to a crossroads, after which there is a stream crossing on Badgall Downs and the road splits into three unenclosed routes across the moorland. Following this route on the ground reveals a well-made single arch bridge at the stream crossing (SX228861) and a second milestone in the hedge beside a farm track (SX214864). This milestone reads **VIII To Cam** – eight miles to Camelford – and is three miles, measured on the map, from the first milestone. Apart from the slip of paper dating from the 1970s, no written record of these milestones has been found.

It should be noted that 200 yards west of the **XI to Cam** milestone is a county bridge stone

SX214864
Treneglos pre-turnpike milestone

Badharlick Bridge Stone, Egloskerry SX267862

SX265863 Egloskerry pre-turnpike milestone. Disappeared 2010

SX265863 Egloskerry. Replica milestone 2012

(SX267862), near Badharlick Bridge over the River Kensey. This unusual slate county bridge stone was discovered lying in a ditch near the bridge and was re-erected the regulation 300 feet west of the bridge under the supervision of Egloskerry Parish Council in 2009.

With the evidence of the two milestones, the county bridge stone and county bridge and the second bridge on Badgall Downs, this road must have been important before the Launceston Turnpike Trust established a different route to Camelford in 1760.

Sadly, the milestone at Badharlick disappeared at the beginning of 2010. Despite a determined search it could not be found. Eventually a decision was taken by the local community to make a replica replacement. Fortunately a local artist had made an accurate sketch and taken measurements of the missing milestone. A redundant granite gatepost of very similar dimensions was donated and the artist carved a new **XI to Cam** milestone, which was re-erected with a secure concrete foundation in March 2012.

LAUNCESTON TURNPIKE TRUST

The Launceston Turnpike Trust was established in 1760 (33 GII c.lix) for 'amending, widening and keeping in repair several roads leading to the Borough of Launceston'. In other words, the Trust was set up, not to make new roads, but to improve the most important of the existing roads.

Launceston, CYRUS REDDING 1842

'Whereas the Highways or Roads

1...leading from Coomb Bow Bridge (SX485879) in the Parish of Thrustleton, through the several parishes of Thrustleton, Lewtrenchard, Maristow, Stowford and Lifton in the County of Devon, Lawhitton, Saint Mary Magdalen, the Town and Borough of Launceston, Southpetherwin, Saint Thomas the Apostle, Trewen, Laneast, Treneglos and Davidstow, to Halworthy (SX180878) in the parish of Davidstow in the County of Cornwall;

2. And from a certain Place called Pennigillam Pool in the Road aforesaid in the Parish of St Mary Magdalen, through the Parishes of Saint Mary Magdalen and Southpetherwin to a certain Place called Trekellearn Bridge (SX300798 Trekelland Bridge) in the Parish of Southpetherwin;

3. And from the Borough of Launceston in the Road aforesaid through the Parishes of St Mary Magdalen and Lawhitton and Lezant to Greston Bridge (SX 368803). (This road took a higher route to the modern road, passing through Hexworthy to reach Greystone Bridge. This is the route shown on Greenwoods' 1 inch county map of 1827.)

4. And from a certain Place called Laburnick Cross (SX351816) in the said Road and Parish of Lawhitton to a certain Place called Jonas's Shop in the Parish of Lezant; (Jonas's Shop has not been identified, but the turnpike road is shown going south-west to Lezant churchtown (SX338790) then south-east to Beals Mill Bridge (SX358770) on Greenwoods' 1 inch county map of 1827. This would avoid the very steep descent and climb at Lowleybridge on the alternative pre-turnpike route.)

5. And from a certain Place called Page's Cross (SX336839, by St Mary's Hospital) in the Road aforesaid in the Parish of St Mary Magdalen to a certain Place called Hurdon Water (SX335819) in Saint Mary Magdalen;

6, And from Launceston to the village of Bennacott (SX298920) in the Parish of Boyton;

7. And from Launceston to the village of Sutcot (SX360909 Sitcott) in the Parish of St Giles in the Heath;

8. And from Launceston to the Village of Egloskerry (SX272866) in the counties of Cornwall and Devon;

Are in ruinous Condition, and in many Places narrow and incommodious,

And so on in the standard language of Turnpike Acts.

The Trustees, who would support the running of the Turnpike Trust as a charity and probably support it financially, were listed in order of importance:
Sir John Molesworth Baronet
James Buller Esquire
Sir William Courtney Baronet
Sir Richard Warwick Bampfylde Baronet
Sir Richard Vyvyan Baronet
Sir John St Aubyn Baronet
Humphrey Maurice
Richard Burrell
John Lee
The Mayor and Aldermen of Launceston, followed by a further 87 names.

The Trustees proposed to turnpike the main east to west route through Launceston from a point well over the Devon border, controlling the road beyond Polson Bridge on the River Tamar as far as Combebow Bridge (SX485879) 10½ miles from Launceston, where it linked with the Okehampton Turnpike Trust. At the east end of Combebow Bridge is a stone 23 inches tall, inscribed **END OF OKEHAMPTON TRUST**. On the wide verge on the long climb east of Combebow is the **OKEHAMPTON 8 MILES** stone of the Okehampton Turnpike Trust (SX489880). The Okehampton Turnpike Trust in Devon was established in the same year, 1760, as the Launceston Trust.[5] To the west of Launceston, the turnpike did not follow the post road used by William Wynne, but ran through the parishes south of the Kensey valley to link with the Haleworthy Turnpike Trust of the previous

chapter, which was also established in 1760. In addition to this main route, there was:

A road south-west to Trekelland Bridge – the route to Liskeard

A road south-east to Greystone Bridge – the route to Tavistock

A road south to Beales Mill – the route to Callington

A road south to Hurdon Water – the route to St Germans

A road north to Bennacott – the route to Kilkhampton

A road north to Sitcott – the route to Holsworthy

Greston or Greystone Bridge on the road to Tavistock SX368803

SX307861
Launceston to Egloskerry,
St Stephen 68031

SX291861
Launceston to Egloskerry,
St Stephens 68034

SX276865
Launceston to Egloskerry,
Egloskerry 67933

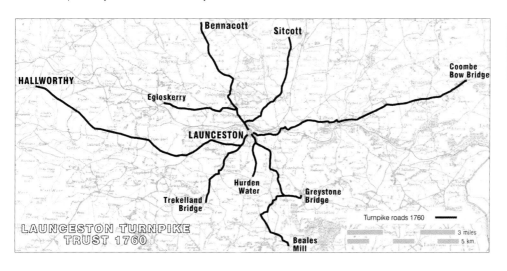

LAUNCESTON TRUST MINUTE BOOK – THE FIRST FIVE YEARS

Study of the minutes of the meetings of the Trustees shows how toll gatherers' wages were established and modified in the initial months, and how the work of improving the roads progressed during the initial five years of the Trust. Four minute books survive for the Launceston Trust, giving a wealth of information about the running of one of Cornwall's most important turnpike trusts.

Extracts from the first Minute Book are given here for the first five years of the Trust, with a summary of the work undertaken shown in the table below. This is followed by some comments on the extracts and a summary table.[6]

First meeting of Launceston Turnpike Trustees

Tuesday 17 June 1760
Tollgatherers:
John Edgcumbe – Dutson Cross (SX338856).
Samuel Smith – Saint Stephens.
Thomas Lenn – Pages Cross (SX336839).
William Carthew – the Buddle.
At wage of 5s per week.

3 July 1760
Extra 1s per week added to wages until proper houses be built for them at the several toll gates.
Samuel Mayfield & assistant to survey:
• Launceston South Gate (SX332845) to Polston Bridge (SX355849)
• Launceston West Gate (SX330844) to Trebursey Tree (SX306845) by way of Pennigillam Pool
• Launceston Southgate to Twimaways
• Launceston Northgate for Newbridge, Yeolmbridge and the Village of Egloskerry
• Road from Launceston Southgate to Polston Bridge be carried on by way of Lower Bamhouse Lane and not by the way of Bullsworthy Lane.
Toll gatherer:
Richard Carpenter Graves and Mills
Joseph Deacon Lane near Westgate
Allowed threepence for every Shilling they collect.

8 July 1760
Samuel Mayfield appointed Surveyor at 10s per week.
Toll houses and toll gates to be erected at
• Saint Stephens
• Dutson Cross
• Pages Cross
• Chapple (SX328842)
To be finished by 30 October next. Joseph Beard of Launceston, Carpenter, to oversee.

23 July 1760
Toll houses and toll gates ordered at:
• St Stephens adjoining the house of John Abbot
• Where the Direction Post stands at Dutson Cross

• Where the Tollgate & Box now stands at Chapple
• Where the ground is marked at Page's Cross
• Near Polston Bridge in the field near Bamham Mill.
The road from Bamham Leat to Polston Bridge be carried through the said fields.

11 August 1760
Samuel Dunn appointed Surveyor from John Geeks house without Southgate to Bamham Leat.

8 September 1760
Samuel Dunn appointed Surveyor of road:
• Northgate to Yeolmbridge (SX318873)
• Westgate to Pennygillam Pool (SX325837)
• Southgate to Pages Cross (SX336839)
John Harris appointed Surveyor of road –
• White House at Newport to Newbridge (SX348867).

15 December 1760
John Harris to make a road proper for Carriages and Travellers to pass to and from the Turnpike Road towards the Buddle leading to St Stephens.

19 January 1761
John Harris appointed Surveyor at 10s-6d per week
Samuel Dunn discharged as Surveyor from Southgate to Pages Cross.

3 February 1761
Samuel Mayfield appointed General Surveyor for all the Turnpike Roads.

20 May 1761
• Hendra Lane to Pennigillam Pool
• Southgate to the Red Post in Bamham Lane
• Northgate to bottom of St Stephens Down leading to Yeolmbridge
Be measured by Samuel Mayfield & Samuel Dunn.

25 November 1761
Pay John Harris for 20 yards of road made by him beyond Dutson Tollgate.
Pay Walter Turner for building Tollhouses and Tollgates at St Stephens and Dutson.

10 March 1762
Samuel Dunn Surveyor of roads from:
• Polston Bridge to Tinney (old) Bridge (SX293854)
• Tremeale Water (SX319832) to South Petherwin Church Town (SX310819).

3 June 1762
Inspected and properly finished:
• Southgate to Polston Bridge
• Northgate to Yeolmbridge.

19 January 1763
Road from South Petherwin Churchtown to beyond Tregillas Lane End South Petherwin (SX304814) and thence to Honiton Lane End

South Petherwin (SX303806).
Road from Pennigillam Gate to the Barn Lake Hoggats is repaired by Samuel Dunn.
Proposal for repairing road from Kenners House (SX287830) to Pipers Pool (SX259841) (at four score pounds a Mile to be completed by Michaelmas next – 9 February 1763).

2 March 1763
Road from Western End of St Stephens Down as far as the Turnpike (gate) in Egloskerry Parish.

30 March 1763
Samuel Dunn contract for road from end of road already finished beyond Dutson Toll Gate to New Bridge, St Stephens, and thence to Dobbles Thorn as far as the lane that leads to Druxton Bridge, Werrington, Devon (SX354875).

18 May 1763
Samuel Dunn forming, stoning and gravelling One Mile of road from Tinney Bridge, Lifton towards Port Gate (SX418858), Sowford, Devon.

1 June 1763
Inspection of roads from
• Tremeal Water to Honiton Lane South Petherwin
• End of St Stephens Down to Egloskerry Churchtown (SX272865).

15 June 1763
Samuel Dunn to make road from the end of the mile from Tinney Bridge to Haynes Gate leading into Newton Down.

22 June 1763
John Harris to make a road from Hurdon Gate to Hurdon Water (SX334819).

6 July 1763
Road from Honiton Lane End to Trecrogo Gate (SX303811) South Petherwin is repaired by Samuel Dunn at 6s-6d per yard.

5 October 1763
Contract with John Harris for road from Pypers Pool to the Entrance of the Downs leading to Hallworthy at 4s-6d per yard to be completed by 1 November next.

25 January 1764
Treasurer to pay no more money to Samuel Dunn because he has not finished the work, that he be dismissed and any money owing to be used to complete the work he started.

29 February 1764
Contract with William Spowder for road from eastern end of Low Fronthard Down to where the County work ends at the western end of Coomb Bow Bridge (SX484879).
Contract with Bartholomew Howe of Saltash for road from Lawhitton Cross (SX357817?) where the County work ends at Greston Bridge

(SX368803), Lezant to be completed by Michaelmas.

23 May 1764
Pay John Harris the balance for making the Road from Pypers Pool to the Entrance of the Downs towards Hallworthy and for making the road over Hurdon Down.

30 May 1764
Contract John Harris of Illogan Yeoman for making road from place commonly called Sweetwell Corner, Laneast a half mile eastward leading towards Launceston.
Contract Bartholomew How for making road from North end of Yeolmbridge to Lady Cross (SX320882), Werrington, Devon and from Tiphill Lane, Werrington to ½ mile 1 furlong towards Haggaton Green, St Giles in the Heath (Haukadon Green SX358891).

19 September 1764
Bartholomew How appointed Surveyor for road from Dobbs Thorn to Peters Finger (SX358885) and Yeolmbridge to Ladys Cross.
John Harris of Illogan repairing road from West end of St Stephens Down to Egloskerry Church Town, and road from Peters Finger ¼ mile one furlong towards Huggaton Green.

14 November 1764
The Marsh or Hollow under the House on Hallworthy Down called Cold Knorth (SX204864) to be forthwith repaired the same being very founderous – contract with John Harris. The said road to be formed 20 feet wide and furzed stoned and gravelled 16 feet wide.

30 January 1765
John Harris to repair and widen road from Chapple Turnpike Gate to Trecrogo Gate, South Petherwin and –
Pennigillam Pool to 20 yards beyond Trebursey Tree (SX306840), South Petherwin and –
Launceston Northgate to the Milestone near St Stephens Church (Milestone is now at SX322861).

6 June 1765
Contract for making road from Newton Down Gate to Lew Down (near Haynes Gate) and for Repairing road from Tinney Bridge to Newton Down Gate.
Contract with John Harris of Illogan for making Road from Cold Knockit Hollow to Hallworthy (SX180878) at 6s per yard to be made 20 feet wide in the clear and finished by 1st November.
Notice be given for making a road from Horrells Gate (SX310888), Werrington to the next water beyond Stendalls Lane, North Petherton.

4 July 1765
Pay Bartholomew How for making:
• Lawhitton to Greston Bridge
• Yeolmbridge to Lady Cross

• Dobles Thorn to Peters Finger.
That Bartholomew Howe be discharged from being Surveyor for those roads.
Contract for making and erecting Mile Stones on the eastern and western roads and the same be started as soon as conveniently may be.
Pay John Harris for making:
• Sweetwater Lane to Cold Knockit Hollow
• Peters Finger to Huggarton Green
• West end of St Stephens Down to Egloskerry.
Contract for repairing road from Launceston West Gate to Chapple Turnpike Gate and from South Gate to the Red Post leading to Lawhitton.
Contract with John Harris of Illogan, Tinner for making Road from next Water beyond Standalls Lane, North Petherwin one Mile towards Launceston at 7s per yard.

COMMENTS

Toll gatherers were hired and paid a wage, which was later changed to a fraction of the tolls collected (threepence for every shilling, that is to say 25%). Later it became standard practice for the Trusts to advertise the toll gathering each year to be competed for by sub-contractors, with the bidding based on the previous year's toll income.

A series of Surveyors were hired for different sections of road. Samuel Dunn took on a lot of

work from 1760 onwards, but was dismissed in 1764 for failing to complete work on time. Bartholomew How or Howe was appointed in September 1764 and discharged in July 1765 after completing his work successfully. At this early date, surveyors were not professionally trained. John Harris, who worked for the whole of the five year period studied, was described as a Yeoman from Illogan (near Redruth) and later as a Tinner.

Few details of the techniques used for road repair are given. The lengths of road repaired suggest that some were easier to put in good order than others. The marsh at Cold Northcott, called 'Cold Knorth' and 'Cold Knockit Hollow' in the minute book, was filled with cut furze and given a top dressing of stone. There is no mention of an attempt to drain the marshy area.

The summary table shows how the work was divided between the different routes radiating from Truro. The main road from Okehampton to Camelford (Combebow Bridge to Hallworthy) had the most work, while the road to Callington, via Beales Mill and Stoke Climsland was not mentioned at all in the first five years of the Trust. The sections of road mentioned in the Minute Book are not always contiguous,

Launceston Trust minute book summary.

	Combe Bow Bridge	Hallworthy	Trekelland Bridge	Greston Bridge	Beales Mill	Hurdon Water	Bennacott	Sitcot	Egloskerry
1760	Pages Cross toll gate. Survey to Polston Bridge via Lower Bamham Lane	Survey to Trebursey Tree via Pennigillam Pool	Chapple toll gate	Survey South Gate to Twimaways			St Stephens toll gate. Survey to Yeolmbridge	Dutson Cross Toll gate. Survey to Newbridge	Survey to village of Egloskerry
1761	Measure from South gate to Red Post in Bamham Lane.	Measure Hendra Lane to Pennigillam Pool.					Measure North Gate to bottom of St Stephens Down. St Stephens Toll House finished.	Dutson Toll House finished. Pay John Harris for 20 yds beyond Dutson toll gate.	
1762	Samuel Dunn surveyor from Polston Bridge to Tinney Bridge. South Gate to Polston Bridge finished.	Hendra Lane to Pennigillam Pool finished	Samuel Dunn surveyor from Tremeale water to South Petherwin churchtown.				North Gate to Yeolmbridge finished.		
1763	Sam Dunn making 1 mile from Tinney Bridge towards Port Gate.	Pennigillam Gate to Barn Lake Hoggarts repaired by Sam Dunn. Propose Kennars House to Pipers Pool by Michaelmas. John Harris contractor for Pipers pool to entrance to Downs.	S.Petherwin Church Town to Honiton Lane End repaired by Sam Dunn. Inspect Tremeal Water to Honiton Lane. Honiton Lane End to Trecrogo Gate repaired			John Harris to make road from Hurdon Gate to Hurdon Water.		Sam Dunn contractor beyond Dutson toll house to New Bridge, Dobles Thorn to lane to Druston Bridge.	West end of St Stephens Down as far as turnpike in Egloskerry. Inspect St Stephens Down to Egloskerry churchtown
1764	Contract Wm Spowder Low Fronthard Down to west end of Coomb Bow Bridge.	Pay John Harris for Pipers Pool to entrance to Downs. Contract for Sweetwell Corner for half mile east. John harris contract to repair marsh at Cold Knorth.		Contract Bart Howe Lawhitton Cross to Greston Bridge to finish by Michaelmas.		Pay John Harris for making road over Hurdon Down.	Contract Bart. How north end of Yeolmbridge to Lady Cross.	Contract Bart How for Tiphill Lane 5 furlongs towards Haggarton Green. Bart How surveyor Dobbs Thorn to peters Finger. John Harris repair Peters Finger 5 furlongs towards Huggaton Green.	John Harris to repair west end St Stephens Down to Egloskerry churchtown.
1765	Contract to make road Newton Down Gate to Lew Down and repair Tinney Bridge to Newton Down Gate. Contract for South gate to Red Post leading to Lawhitton.	John Harris repair Pennigillam Pool to 20yds beyond Trebursey Tree. John Harris contract Cold Knockit Hollow to Hallworthy by 1 Nov. Pay J Harris for Sweetwater lane to Cold Knockit Hollow	John Harris to repair Chapple toll gate to Trecrogo Gate. Contract for Launceston west Gate to Chapple toll gate.	Pay Bart How for making Lawhitton to Greston Bridge.			John Harris to repair Launceston N gate to milestone near St Stephens church. Notice of road from Horrells Gate to beyond Stendalls Lane. Pay Bart Howe for Yeolm Bridge to Ladys Cross	Pay Bart Howe for Dobles Thorn to Peters Finger. Pay J.Harris for Peters Finger to Huggarton Green. Contract J.Harris Standalls Lane one mile towards Launceston.	Pay John Harris for St Stephens Down to Egloskerry.

suggesting some sections of road did not need major repair. Work was concentrated on the bottlenecks, just as it is today.

The Callington Trust was not set up until 1764, and did not include the road from Callington to Beales Mill until 1785. This route did not prove successful, as a major new route was created by the Launceston Trust in 1835 with a new bridge at Wooda to the west of Beales Mill.

19TH CENTURY IMPROVEMENTS

Renewal Acts in 1781, 1801 and 1815 maintained the same roads as the original Act of 1760.

In 1824 a new bridge was built on the road between Lawhitton and Lezant at Landue Bridge (SX346797). This was on the original route to Callington via Bealsmill which was to be radically redesigned in the 1835 Act. A subscription was raised to pay for the bridge. This is commemorated by a plaque in the parapet on the north side of the bridge.

EXPANSION NORTH AND SOUTH

The Act of 1835 (5&6 WIV c.lxv) saw the road over New Bridge to Sitcott extended through Holsworthy to Woodford Bridge (SX398125) in the parish of Milton Damerell, a distance of some 15 miles. The aim was to improve communications between North Devon and Plymouth[7], linking with the Bideford Trust

Higher New Bridge on the road to Holsworthy with a milestone above the central cutwater SX348866

SX348866 A388 St Stephen 68030

at Woodford Bridge. A toll gate is recorded in the census of 1841 and again in 1871 at Deep Lane Head, Holsworthy (SS344042). This would have been on the Launceston Trust's road to Woodford Bridge, called in the Act 'the Holdsworthy District of Roads'.

A new route was built to the south, incorporating the 1824 Landue Bridge and crossing the River Inny on the newly built Wooda Bridge which carries a commemorative plaque reading **R WISE Lanson 1836** and continuing to Taylor's Shop (SX347729). The route by-passed Lawhitton, Lezant, Beals Mill and Stoke Climsland. This is the line of today's A388, except for a realignment in 1980 which left Landue Bridge on the now quiet road to Lezant. The original descent from Treburley to where Wooda Bridge was to be built can still be followed running parallel to the new turnpike then diving beneath it through a high-arched tunnel. The tunnel and approach embankments are a much more unusual engineering achievement in the early 19th century than the bridge at Wooda.

An improved line was made on the approach

THIS BRIDGE was BUILT BY SUBSCRIPTION AD 1824.

SX348798 Landue Bridge was on the old and the new turnpike route to Callington

Wooda Bridge. The plaque behind the steel barrier reads R WISE LANSON 1836. There was no bridge and no road here until then. A388 Callington road (SX347769)

Turnpike flyover built in 1835 over the green lane to Bealsmill. SX349773 A388 Treburley; Treburley end of the turnpike flyover. SX349773

to Greystone Bridge – the modern A384 at about this time. This is not mentioned in the Act, but appears as the turnpike road on the 1860s Ordnance Survey 1 inch map, superimposed on the old road.

Improvements were made to the main east-west route, easing the gradients at Lifton.

The new road north of Sitcott, through Holsworthy to Woodford Bridge does not appear in the 1867 Act. It seems to have been handed over to the Holsworthy District Highway Board by this time.

The new road south of Wooda Bridge to Taylor's Shop is also missing from the 1867 Act.[8]

An improved line was made on the approach to Greystone Bridge SX368803.
Cyrus Redding 1842

THE MINUTE BOOKS AND MILESTONES

The surviving Launceston Trust Minute Books mention work on milestones on a number of occasions. In general, making, erecting and maintaining milestones was a small part of the cost of a turnpike road. Any mention in the minutes is rare.

1765 Treasurer to contract with some persons for making & erecting Milestones on the Eastern & Western roads & the same be erected as soon as conveniently may be.

1807 Direction Post at Langdon Moor (SX304899) with fingers to Launceston, Stratton & Mary Week Road.

1833 Milestones erected on Launceston to Camelford road and new TP house at Hallworthy.

1839 Milestones between Launceston and Woodabridge to have distance to Callington added.

Milestones on Okehampton road to be arranged at the end of each mile

1843 Milestones to be set right on Camelford & South Petherwin roads, measuring from Centre of Broad Street Market.

1848 Letter from Mr Francis Rodd representing the variation between the Post Office measurement and the Milestones between Coombe Bow Bridge, Launceston and Okehampton of one mile and a quarter, but Milestones correct between Launceston and Coombe Bow Bridge.

£11-5s-0d allowed for fixing milestones to Coombe Bow Bridge.

1856 Direction Posts to be painted and new ones erected at Cross Roads - £15 allowed.

1858 Milestones between Launceston and Coombe Bow Bridge to be painted when weather permits.

1858 Milestones on Tavistock Road, from Mr Deacon:

2 at £1-3s-0d each – 'Launceston, Tavistock'

SX191873 A395 Treneglos 68091

SX204864 A395 Treneglos 68092

SX217854 A395
St Clether 68389

SX231848 A395
Laneast 68352

GONE 2012
SX246843 A395
Laneast 68353

SX262840 A395
Pipers Pool, Trewen
432429

SX275831 A395
South Petherwin
68412 and St Thomas
393844

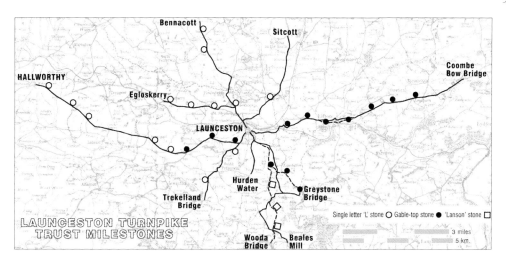

2 at £1-8s-0d each – 'Launceston, Tavistock, Callington'

1873 Direction posts to be repaired and renewed where necessary

Direction posts were required at all cross roads on turnpike roads. They were painted wood on the Launceston Trusts roads, and no original direction posts have been identified.

The Launceston Trust milestones that remain fall into three design groups:

• Tall tombstones with rounded tops, with a large **L** for Launceston above a single number. Examples of this type are on B3254 south to Trekelland Bridge - **L 1**(SX321833), **L 2** (SX312822) which disappeared in 2009 and **L 3** (SX303811) and on B3254 north to Bennacott - **L 1** (SX323861), **L 4** (SX303899) and **L 5** (SX298915). On both these roads the one mile stone has an old style one written as **J**. The **L 5** stone at Bennacott has additional inscriptions

SX321833 B3254
Launceston
503130

GONE in 2009
SX312822 B3254
South Petherwin
68411

SX303811 B3254
South Petherwin
503129

SX323861 B3254
St Stephen 68033

SX303899 B3254
North Petherwin
67973

SX298915 B3254
Boyton 67895

SX345808 A388
Callington road,
Lawhitton 68405

SX347793 A388
Callington road,
Lezant 393596

SX348779 A388
Callington road,
Lezant 393597

SX345823 A388
Lawhitton 503134
Hedge slasher
damage 2009.

SX358817 A384
Dewcombe,
Lawhitton 68399

SX367804 A384
Lezant 393587

Okehampton 8 Miles.
Milestone of Okehampton
Turnpike Trust SX489880
E of Combebow

End of Okehampton Trust
stone and county bridge
stone. SX 485879 East
end of Combebow Bridge

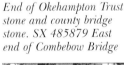

Launceston Turnpike in
Devon SX485879 E end
of Combebow Bridge

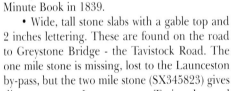

following the adoption of the entire road to Kilkhampton as a Main Road in 1890 – an unusual example of re-carving. The same tall tombstone with a rounded top is used on the A395 Camelford road. All but one of the milestones survive beyond the Kennard's House turn from the A30 Bodmin road. The same design of milestones continues beyond the limit of the Launceston Trust at Haleworthy and into Camelford itself. The last milestone, **L 16**, being just north of Camelford Bridge (SX109839).

• Tall tombstones with rounded tops, with distance to **LANSON**, the old spelling of Launceston, and a distance to **CALL** (Callington) added below. **LANSON** is written in an arc above the distance. Three of these milestones are on the A388 north of Wooda Bridge (SX345808, SX347793 & SX348779). They match the description of the milestones mention in the Minute Book in 1839.

• Wide, tall stone slabs with a gable top and 2 inches lettering. These are found on the road to Greystone Bridge - the Tavistock Road. The one mile stone is missing, lost to the Launceston by-pass, but the two mile stone (SX345823) gives distances to Launceston, Tavistock and Callington, while the three (SX357816) and four (SX367804) mile stones give distances to Launceston and Tavistock only, matching the description of the milestones ordered from Mr Deacon in the minute book for 1858 at £1-8s-0d and £1-3s-0d each, respectively. This style of milestone also exists on the pre-bypass line of the A30 west from Launceston, and on the old A30 east of Polson Bridge as far as Combe Bow Bridge.

It is difficult to be certain of the age of each group of milestones.

If the minute books are to be relied on, the first design with the single letter **L** was used in 1833 when milestones were 'erected on Launceston and Camelford road'. Does this mean that the milestones on the road to Trekelland Bridge and the road to Bennacott are of the same date? Perhaps 1833 was the last time this design was used, and the Trekelland Bridge and Bennacott milestones are earlier than 1833, as suggested by the archaic **J** for one mile.

The Wooda Bridge milestones fit the description in the Minute Book for 1839 so exactly they must date from this period.

In a similar way, the Tavistock road milestones match the entry for 1858, when Mr Deacon was paid for four milestones. Perhaps this fixes the date of the new line of road to Greystone Bridge shown on the 1860 1inch OS map.

Can we deduce that the similar design used from Launceston to Combebow Bridge, with two destinations were erected in 1848, when the minute book entry reads '£11-5s-0d allowed for fixing milestones to Coombe Bow Bridge'? Ten years later, Mr Deacon was paid £1-3s-0d per milestone with two destinations. There would be 10 milestones. At Mr Deacon's price this would have been £11-10s-0d. Is this a good enough match to date the milestones to Combebow

SX465868 Lobhill Cross guidestone, a few yards from a missing Launceston Trust milestone

SX451869 Launceston 8. East of Lewdown

SX435863 Launceston 7. Royal Exchange, Stowford

SX420859 Launceston 6. Postgate

SX389851 Launceston 4. East of Lifton

Bridge to 1848? Six of the ten Launceston Trust milestones survive on this road, all on the Devon side of the Tamar.

AFTER THE TURNPIKE TRUST

LAUNCESTON DISTRICT HIGHWAY BOARD

The Launceston Trust was wound up on 7th November 1879.

The Trust's roads were handed over to the Launceston District Highway Board, which had been established in 1863, with other similar Highway Boards throughout Cornwall to maintain the parish roads.[9]

The Launceston District Highway Board was responsible for roads in fifteen parishes:

Altarnun
Northill
South Petherwin
Lezant
Trewarlett Hamlet
Lewannick
St Stephen by Launceston
Egloskerry
Lawhitton
St Thomas the Apostle
Trewen
Laneast
Tremain
Tresmeer
Boyton

The parishes of Werrington and North Petherwin were in Devon in 1863, though they are now part of Cornwall.

Each parish within a District Highway Board appointed a Waywarden, who was supervised by the District Highway Board Surveyor. The Surveyor could claim the cost of road maintenance by levying a Highway Rate on properties within his District. Glen's text book for highway surveyors instructs:

In order to raise money for carrying the several

purposes of the Highway Acts into execution, it is enacted that a rate shall be made, assessed, and levied by the survetor upon all property at the passing of the Highway Act, 13th August 1835, liable to be rated and assessed to the relief of the poor.[10]

However, the roads taken over from expired turnpike trusts were deemed to have importance and related running costs beyond the local district, so these 'Disturnpiked Roads were to become Main Roads, and half the expense of maintenance to be contributed out of the County Rate'.[11] So, although the District Highway Board Surveyor took on the extra responsibility of maintaining the busy disturnpiked Main Roads, he was given considerable financial help from the County Rate.

In addition, if a District Highway Board had other roads which it felt should be main roads, it could apply to the county for these to be made Main Roads, and so have half the cost of maintenance met from the County Rate.

Where it appears to any highway authority that any highway within their district ought to become a main road by reason of its being a medium of communication between great towns, or a thoroughfare to a railway station, or otherwise, such highway authority may apply to the county authority for an order declaring such road to be a main road; and the county authority....shall cause the road to be inspected, and, if satisfied that it ought to be a main road, shall make an order accordingly.[12]

When the new Cornwall County Council was set up in 1889, it was inundated with requests to have roads made up to Main Roads. Cornwall County Council Highways Committee was unique in insisting that any road to be adopted as a Main Road must have milestones. The evidence for this stands by the roadside

SX372853 Launceston 3. A388 East of Liftondown

SX358848 Launceston 2. A388 Polson Farm, east of Polson Bridge

SX180764
Launceston 12
Bodmin road A30
Altarnun 68301

SX224806
Launceston 8
Bodmin road
Altarnun 68312

SX242803
Launceston 7
Bodmin road A30
Altarnun 68240

SX256803
Launceston 6
Bodmin road
Lewannick 430668

SX266812
Launceston 5
Bodmin road
Lewannick 503128

SX288832
Launceston 3 Bodmin
road Kennards House,
St Thomas. Re-erected
2012

SX304841
Launceston 2
Bodmin road west
of Trebursye Oak, St
Thomas 393842

SX320837
Launceston 1
Bodmin road
Tresmarrow Road,
Launceston
503131

today. Throughout the Launceston District Highway Board's area, the Main Roads have milestones of a similar design to the last design of the Launceston Turnpike Trust – wide, tall stone slabs with a gable top and neat, 2 inches lettering. These survive beside the Launceston to Bodmin road (A30) as far as Bolventor, the limit of the Launceston District Highway Board, where a different design of milestone takes over.

B3254 from Trekelland Bridge as far south as Botternell has the Launceston design.

The road from Plusha to the North Hill parish boundary near Clampit Farm (B3257) was a Main Road linking Callington to the A30. It was within the Launceston Highway District so it has Launceston design milestones.

A loop of road through Trebartha and North

Railway milestone. By the entrance to Berrio Bridge House is a milestone moved from the 1858 Kilmar Railway, later Liskeard & Caradon Railway, to Kilmar Tor. SX273756

Hill churchtown must also have been made a Main Road, since it too has milestones, including a remarkable double width stone near Trebartha Barton (SX264776).

Beyond Clampit Farm on B3257, and south of Botternell on B3254, the Callington Highway Board adopted the Launceston design on its sections of Main Road.

Berrio Bridge date stone 1640 SX273757.
Plaque on west side reads WIDENED 1890

SX298797 B3254
Trekelland,
Lewannick 430699

SX286788 B3254
Slipperhill, North
Hill 431718

SX280773 B3254
North Hill 431719

SX274759 B3254
East Berriow,
North Hill 431720

SX278745 B3254
Botternell, North
Hill 431723

SX299764 B3257 North Hill 431729

SX288776 B3257 North Hill 431726

SX278788 B3257 Lewannick 430672

SX266796 B3257 Lewannick 1406859

Guidestone for the North Hill loop SX281776 B3254 North Hill 431698

SX277776 North Hill 431715

SX266770 North Hill 431710

SX291928 B3254 Boyton 67894

SX284943 B3254 Boyton

The parish boundary stone by the stream at Botternell divided Launceston Highway Board from Callington Highway Board. SX278744

SX264776 Trebartha Barton, North Hill 432410

The B3254 north of Launceston retained its turnpike milestones in Werrington parish which was then in Devon. The L5 turnpike milestone in Boyton parish was re-carved with the additional distances to Bude and Kilkhampton to match the two new 1890 milestones further north in the same parish.

STRATTON DISTRICT HIGHWAY BOARD

North of Boyton, all the way to Kilkhampton, the same Launceston Trust design was used by the Stratton District Highway Board on its part of B3254. Where the Launceston Highway Board milestones showed the distance to Bude above the distance to Kilkhampton, the Stratton Board stones all have the distance to Kilkhampton above the distance to Bude. The road dipped back into Devon in the parish of Bridgerule, which is still in Devon. The 1907 Ordnance Survey map has a milestone shown here, but there is no surviving Devon milestone on the ground. All the Stratton Highway Board milestones are intact.

The Stratton Board used the same design for the Main Road north of Stratton (A39) as far as the Devon border north of Woolley Barrows. All

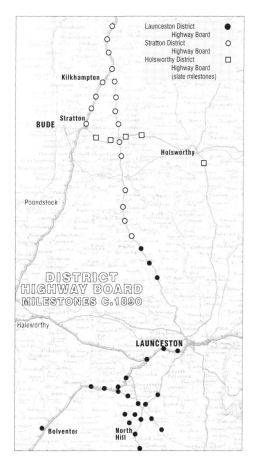

SX274955 B3254
North Tamerton

SX269970 B3254
Whitstone

SX266986 B3254
Whitstone

SS268002 B3254
Whitstone

SS265033 B3254
Launcells

SS264049 B3254
south of Red Post,
Launcells

SS264064 B3254
Launcells

SS260079 B3254
Launcells

SS262095 B3254
Kilkhampton

SS260110 B3254
Kilkhampton

these milestones survive, but north of the border, in Devon, no milestones are to be found.

The Stratton Highway Board had battled for years to have some of its roads made main roads.

In 1880 the County's Eastern Surveyor had passed a total of 95 miles for adoption as main roads, and refused 21 miles, while the Western Surveyor had passed 62 miles and refused 26 miles.[13] In April 1880 it was reported that the County's Committee on main roads would accept no new main road applications at present, and that the Stratton District was particularly badly hit, since it had never had any turnpike roads it now had no main roads at all.[14]

In July 1890, the proposed main roads in the Stratton area had been put in satisfactory repair and were to be taken over from the first of the month.[15] While no route was specified, the priority road was the A39 north from Stratton to Woolley Barrows. The road from Bideford in Devon to the county boundary near Woolley Barrows had been a turnpike and so was now a Devon main road. The Cornish part of the road had never been a turnpike, which was why the

SS230068 Townsend, Stratton

SS236082 Stratton

SS242096 A39 Kilkhampton

SS250109 A39 Kilkhampton

SS260122 A39 Kilkhampton   SS256137 A39 Kilkhampton   SS255153 A39 Morwenstow   SS262166 A39 Morwenstow

Stratton Highway Board had struggled to have it adopted. The 1880 Ordnance Survey map shows no milestones on the road between Stratton and Woolley Barrows, while the 1907 Ordnance Survey map shows a full set of milestones, set up in 1890 when the road was adopted.

In November 1890 Stratton District Highway Board was successful in having 2 miles and 2 furlongs from Kilkhampton towards Launceston made main road.[16] This is the first stretch of B3254 from the junction with A39 in Kilkhampton to the crossroads near Hersham. In February 1892, 5 miles and 2 furlongs from Dolston to Red Post was made a main road.[17] This linked the Stratton part of what is now the B3254 with the Launceston District Highway Board's section at Dolsdon (SX277950) at the boundary of Boyton parish. The two mile stretch between these two sections, from Red Post north to Hersham crossroads, must also have been adopted during the same period, since the run of milestones is complete and the milestones are all the same design.

SLATE MILESTONES

Most Cornish milestones are made of granite, but there is one set of slate milestones. These run from Bude on the coast of North Cornwall to Highampton in Devon, nearly 19 miles to the east. They were erected in the 1870s by the Holsworthy District Highway Board. Holsworthy lies 9½ miles from Bude, midway along the road to Highampton. Nine Devon milestones were shown on the OS 1:25000 map in 1983 of the original 14 in Devon. In 2010 only three Devon milestones could be found. The Cornish milestones in Bude and Stratton have gone, but three survive, near Launcells (SS239054), Thurlibeer (SS254049) and east of Red Post (SS269052), forming a run of four milestones at one mile intervals with the first of the Devon milestones (SS284054).

The slate milestones in Cornwall are 18 inches wide and only a couple of inches thick. They carry inscriptions on two faces at a very shallow angle to each other, almost flat. The left hand face gives a distance to **HOLSy**. (Holsworthy) and

SS239054 A3072 Launcells   SS254049 A3072 Thurlibeer   SS269052 A3072   SS284054 A3072
503533 Slate milestone   503535 Slate Milestone   east of Red Post, Launcells   Tamarstone, Devon.
                                                              Slate Milestone   Pancrasweek 91952
                                                                                            Slate Milestone

the right face gives distances to **BUDE** in large capitals and **STRATTON** in smaller capitals to allow the two words to fit in the same width of stone.

A similar slate milestone also survives one mile south of Holsworthy on the A388 Launceston road (SS350024). Here **HOLSy**. Is on the right face, but the left face has been badly damaged and the legend, giving the distance to Launceston has gone. Milestones at 2, 3, 4 and 6 miles are marked on this road on the 1:25000 OS maps of 1983 and 1989, but none survive on the ground now. The First Series Ordnance Survey 1 inch map of 1884 shows a full set of milestones on this road, one every mile between Launceston and Holsworthy. However, the milestones south of Sitcott are labelled with a distance to Launceston only – **1**, **2**, **3** and **4** miles respectively, because these are the Launceston Turnpike Trust milestones, though the two in Devon (**L3** and **L4** are gone), while those north of Sitcott are labelled on the map with distances to Holsworthy and Launceston, to match the Holsworthy Highway Board milestones which once lined this road.

LAUNCESTON TURNPIKE
Tolls to be taken in pursuance of The Act of Parliament
Passed in the Fifth Year of the Reign of His Majesty
King William the Fourth. 1835
PENNYGILLAM GATE

	£	s	d
For every Horse or other beast of draught drawing any Coach, Chariot Stage coach, Barouche, Sociable, Phaeton, Break, Diligence, Omnibus, Berlin, Landau, Chaise, Curricle, Calash, Chair, Caravan, Van, Hearse, Litter, Car, Gig or other such like Carriage, the sum of	0	0	6
For every Horse or other beast drawing any waggon, wain or cart or o-ther such like Carriage the sum of Sixpence except when employed in carrying or conveying fuel or lime as hereinafter mentioned	0	0	6
For every Coach, Barouche, Chaise, or other carriage with four wheels, affix to any Waggon or Cart the sum of	0	1	0
For every carriage with two wheels affixed to any Waggon or Cart the sum of	0	0	6
For every Horse or other Beast if more than one drawing any timber Car-riage upon three or four wheels of a less breadth than six inches at the bot-tom or soles thereof the sum of	0	0	9
For every Horse, Mule or Ass, laden or unladen and not drawing th sum of	0	0	1½
For every drove of Oxen, Cows or neat Cattle, the sum of one shilling and three pence per score and so on in proportion for any greater or less number	0	1	3
For every drove of Calves, Goats, Swine, Sheep or Lambs the sum of Ten pence per score and so on in proportion for any greater or less number	0	0	10
For every Horse or other beast drawing any Carriage laden or unladen when solely employed in carrying or conveying coals, wood for fuel, or fuel of any other kind, the sum of	0	0	3
For every yoke of Oxen drawing any Waggon, Cart or other Carriage when solely employed as last aforesaid, the sum of	0	0	4
For every Horse, Mule or other beast drawing any Carriage laden or unladen when solely employed in carrying or conveying lime to be used as manure if the fellies of the wheels of such Carriage shall be of less breadth than four and a half inches, the sum of	0	0	1
For every Carriage moved or propelled by steam or machinery by any other power than annual (sic) power, the sum of	0	1	0
For every Waggon, Wain, Cart or other such like Carriage having the nails of the tyre of the wheels thereof projecting more than one quarter of an inch a-bove such tyre, any sum not exceeding the sum of	0	10	0

This Gate frees all others except Polson, Lifton Down, Lifton Town, Tinney Lane, Coombe-bow, and Bullsworthy lane Gates.

Chr, L, Cowlard
Clerk.

Transcription of Pennygillam Gate Toll Board pictured opposite. LAWRENCE HOUSE MUSEUM, LAUNCESTON

LAUNCESTON TURNPIKE

Tolls to be taken in pursuance of The Act of Parliament,
passed in the Fifth Year of the Reign of His Majesty
King William the Fourth. 1835

PENNYGILLAM GATE.

	£	s	d
For every Horse, or other beast of draught drawing any Coach, Chariot, Stage coach, Barouche, Sociable, Phaeton, Break, Diligence Omnibus Berlin, Landau, Chaise, Curricle Calash, Chair, Caravan, Van, Hearse Litter, Car, Gig, or other such like Carriage, the sum of	0	0	6
For every Horse, or other beast drawing any waggon, wain, cart, or other such like Carriage the sum of Six pence, except when employed in carrying or conveying fuel or lime, as hereinafter mentioned	0	0	6
For every Coach, Barouche, Chaise, or other Carriage with four wheels, affixed to any Waggon or Cart, the sum of	0	1	0
For every Carriage with two wheels affixed to any Waggon or Cart the sum of	0	0	6
For every Horse, or other Beast, if more than one, drawing any timber Carriage, upon three or four wheels of a less breadth than six inches at the bottom or soles thereof the sum of	0	0	9
For every Horse, Mule or Ass, laden or unladen and not drawing, the sum of	0	0	1½
For every drove of Oxen, Cows, or neat Cattle, the sum of one shilling and three pence per score and so on in proportion, for any greater or less number.	0	1	3
For every drove of Calves, Goats, Swine, Sheep or Lambs, the sum of Ten pence per score and so on in proportion for any greater or less number.	0	0	10
For every Horse or other beast, drawing any Carriage, laden or unladen when solely employed in carrying or conveying coals, wood for fuel, or fuel of any other kind, the sum of	0	0	3
For every yoke of Oxen drawing any Waggon, Cart or other Carriage when solely employed as last aforesaid, the sum of	0	0	4
For every Horse, Mule or other beast, drawing any Carriage laden or unladen, when solely employed in carrying or conveying lime to be used for manure, if the fellies of the wheels of such Carriage shall be of less breadth than four and a half inches, the sum of	0	0	1
For every Carriage moved or propelled by steam or machinery or by any other power than animal power, the sum of	0	1	0
For every Waggon Wain Cart or other such like Carriage having the nails of the tire of the wheels thereof projecting more than one quarter of an inch above such tire, any sum not exceeding the sum of	0	10	0

This Gate frees all others except Polson, Lifton Down, Lifton
Town, Tinney Lane, Coombe-bow, and Bullsworthy lane
Gates.

Chr. L. Cowlard.
Clerk.

Bodmin to Liskeard Turnpike road over Respryn Bridge and Bofarnel Downs (SX116633). Replaced by A38 in 1835.

CHAPTER SEVEN

BODMIN

BEFORE THE TURNPIKE TRUST
MILESTONES ON THE JUDGES' ROAD

In 1716 Bodmin gained the privilege of hosting the Assize Court. The Courts had always been held at Launceston, on the border between Devon and Cornwall, but the government was persuaded that the Summer Assize should be moved to a more central location within the county. The judges would be travelling by coach, and the road between Launceston and Bodmin would need some improvement if they were to make the journey, even in summer. The winter Assize Court remained at Launceston until the 1830s.

A letter sent to the Town Clerk of Bodmin in 1716 sets out the requirements:

> The Bill for removing the Assizes being now passed, and the Judges having nominated Bodmyn for the place where they designe to hold the same this summer, his Lordship would have you and the Mayor to apply to the Bishop of Winchester (Trelawny) if in the country, and other Justices of the Peace, that they ... take some effective care, that the roads and ways, from Launceston to Bodmyn, be levelled and the trees and hedges be cut fit for travelling with coaches, etc. You are also to observe that both the Judges are to lye in one house, and that bedding, furniture and other accommodations are to be provided accordingly. [1]

This is one of the earliest references to road improvement in the county and was to ensure that the road around the northern edge of Bodmin Moor, via Camelford was fit for carriages.

Ogilby's strip maps of the post roads in 1675 [2] show a route north of the moor, avoiding Bodmin town, but in 1703 a Warrant was issued by the Treasury to the Post Master General 'to settle a new post for the midland Towns' in Cornwall.[3] In 1707 the Postmaster at Bodmin was paid an annual fee of £54 to receive and distribute the Royal Mail. At this date the post road ran from Camelford to Bodmin and then to St Columb and Truro. The route from Camelford to Bodmin in 1707 used the existing

Bodmin church CYRUS REDDING 1842

lanes. It left the St Teath road at Valley Truckle, stayed to the east of 'Michael Stow' and 'Hengarr' and crossed the River Camel at 'Wenvir Bridg', then the De Lank River at 'Key Bridge'. It went through 'Merry meting' and stayed to the west of 'Coldrinnick' and to the east of 'Lancar' onto 'Bodmin Down', dropping into Bodmin town itself from above the church. All this is shown, with the place names as indicated, on a beautiful map of Cornwall published in 1699 by Joel Gascoyne.

This is the road the judges must have used in 1716 – Valley Truckle to Wenfordbridge, Keybridge, Merry Meeting, Racecourse Downs and Old Callywith Road into Bodmin. Remember, the post was carried by postboys on horseback. This is why the special Warrant needed to be sent to the Justices in Bodmin to make sure the route was made fit for carriages.

The milestones still remain on this pre-turnpike route to Bodmin. At least some of them do. The milestones were erected in the middle of the 18th century, probably before the Bodmin Turnpike Trust was established in 1769. The 2, 3, 4, 5, 9 and 10 mile stones survive. 1, 6, 7 and 8 are missing and were replaced by granite replicas in 2013 as part of a locally funded project.

SX082673 Bodmin 1 This replacement milestone was made in 2013 as part of the Judges' Rosd project. It replaces a later turnpike milestone lost in 2000.

SX091697 Bodmin 2 appears to have been rcarved at some time in the past Cardinham 507019

SX088715 Bodmin 3 showing evidence of hedge trimmer damage Helland 507021

SX089729 Bodmin 4 Tresarrett Blisland 76313

SX086743 Bodmin 5 at Penpont, St Breward was buried under rubble until 2013

SX082757 Bodmin 6 All the replacement milestones were made at nearby De Lank Quarry, St Breward in 2013

SX082774 Bodmin 7 replacement St Tudy

SX084787 Bodmin 8 replacement Michaelstow

SX090802 Bodmin 9 B3266 Advent 68462

SX096816 Bodmin 10 B3266 Advent 68461

This road continued to be important in the 19th century. When the Royal Albert Bridge was opened in 1859, the Royal Mail came by train to Bodmin Road station. The mail then travelled <u>north</u> by cart along the route from Bodmin to the Postmaster at Camelford.[4]

MILESTONES ON THE PATHLESS MOOR

In the early 18th century there was no defined road across Bodmin Moor, as John Wesley found to his cost. He became lost in the dark on the 'pathless moor' and was only saved by hearing the sound of a bell, possibly the curfew bell, being rung in Bodmin.

His journal entry for September 1743 reads:

> Mon.29 – We rode forward (from Exeter). About sun-set we were in the middle of the first great pathless moor beyond Launceston. About eight we were got quite out of the way; but we had not got far before we heard Bodmin bell. Directed by this, we turned to the left, and came to the town before nine.

Wesley did not make the same mistake twice.

When he returned to Cornwall in the spring of 1744, he used a local guide to cross Bodmin Moor. On this and subsequent visits to Cornwall, he stayed with a family in Trewint, near Altarnun, before tackling the worst of the Moor. Their cottage is now a museum to Wesley and Methodism.

His journal entry for April 1744 reads:

> Mon. 2 – I preached at five (in the morning at Sticklepath), and rode on towards Launceston. The hills were covered with snow, as in the depth of winter. About two we came to Trewint, wet and weary enough, having been battered by the rain and hail for some hours. I preached in the evening to many more than the house would contain, on the happiness of him whose sins are forgiven. In the morning Degory Ishel undertook to pilot us over the great moor, all the paths being covered by snow; which, in many places, was driven together, too deep for horse or man to pass. The hail followed us for the first seven miles; we had then a fair, though exceeding sharp, day.[5]

Pre-turnpike milestones were set up on the 'pathless moor' by a public spirited inn-keeper from Bodmin. He was able to advertise the fact in 1754. The following article appeared in the *Western Flying Post* in October of that year:

> We are assur'd from Cornwall, that Mr Lewis, Master of the White Hart at Bodmin, has at his own Expence, erected Mile Stones for twenty two Miles over the large Moors, that lay between Launceston and Bodmin; the road over which was so difficult before, that those not acquainted with it, used to choose to take a Circuit of 33 Miles, to pass from the one Town to the other, tho' the Way over the Moors is no more than 24 Miles. He has likewise indicted several parishes so that many Roads which were before almost impassible are now putting in good Order.' [6]

The newspaper editor commented:

> A very noble and laudable Example this; worthy of being imitated and deserving the Notice and Acknowledgements of all Travellers who pass that Way, as it must give everyone Pleasure, as well as be of vast use to all that are Strangers in those Parts.'

None of these milestones survive.

THE BODMIN TRUST

While John Lewis of the White Hart may have erected milestones and put pressure on parishes to improve their roads, he built no roads and none of his milestones appear to have survived. However, The Bodmin Turnpike Trust used the same central route across the moors to Launceston as the key route in its new network, and this is still the main trunk road (A30) into Cornwall today. Work began on the Bodmin to Launceston moorland road in 1756. [7]

In 1769 an application was made to parliament for an Act for 'repairing and widening the roads leading to Bodmin'. Although a number of routes were mentioned in the Act which would link the new Bodmin turnpikes with the existing Haleworthy turnpike to the north, controlling the existing road links, it was the new roads to the east across Temple Moor to Jamaica Inn and to the west across Goss Moor to Indian Queens that would make Bodmin a pivotal point in the growing turnpike network through Cornwall. These two roads were later to become part of the A30 spine road.

The 1769 Act (9 GIII c.lxix) specified the following roads:

1. Kennards House in the parish of South Petherwin, over Hicks Mill Bridge through the parishes of Lawanack, Alternon, St Neot, Cardinham, Temple to Bodmin.

2. From Bodmin, thro' the parishes of Lenevet, Luxilian, Roache, St Columb Major as far as Higher Fraddon at the W. End of Fair Mile Common in the parish of St Enoder.

3. Roads through Bodmin and parishes of

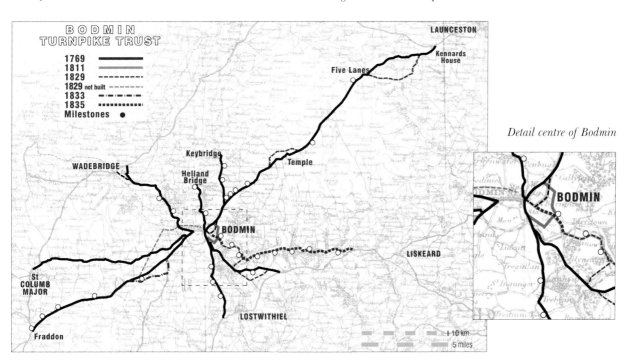

Detail centre of Bodmin

Lanhydrock and Lanlivery as far as No Mans Land

4. Also thro' Bodmin, Lanhydrock over Respryn Bridge then parishes of St Winnow and Broadoak as far as where Bodmin road near the Four Burrows joins the Lostwithiel to Liskeard road

5. Roads leading from Bodmin over Dunmeer Bridge thro' parishes of Bodmin and Egloshayle to Trenair Lane End where it joins the Camelford to Wadebridge road

6. Also from Bodmin to Helland Bridge

7. Also from Bodmin thro' parishes of Bodmin, Helland, Blisland to Key Bridge

8. Also from Bodmin thro' parishes of Lenevet, Withiel, St Wenn & Columb Major to East end of St Columb

1. This is the new road to the east of Bodmin across Temple Moor, from the Launceston Trust's turnpike at Kennard's House (SX287830), but it leaves the modern A30 at Holyway Cross (SX273823) descending to the River Inny at the old bridge at Hick's Mill below Polyphant. This was the route of the turnpike until the 19th century when a diversion was built via Two Bridges.[8] The road forked left at the top of the hill (SX252822) where a granite guidestone with a triangular granite capstone is carved **LAUNCESTON RODE**, **BODMYN RODE** and **CAMELFORD** on the three faces of the capstone (SX253822). It descends to cross Penpont Water over Trerithick Bridge and climbs to the crossroads at Five Lanes (SX224806). The Kings Head Hotel at Five Lanes was built in 1622 and is the oldest inn on Bodmin Moor. The turnpike runs through Trewint, picking up the modern road near the **B**

Trerithick Bridge is on the original Bodmin to Launceston turnpike route (SX243819). The 1821 route from Five Lanes to Holloway Cross became the A30.

13 milestone (SX212800). The toll house at Palmer's Bridge (SX041689) and the adjacent milestone were lost when the Jamaica Inn by-pass was built in the 1990s.

The present Jamaica Inn was built in 1750. It was named in memory of members of the Rodd family of Trebartha who were governors of Jamaica. The first dwelling here was built about 1547. In the past it has been both a smugglers retreat and a temperance house, but today it is famous for the novel by Daphne du Maurier by the same name. The hamlet of Bolventor at Jamaica Inn did not exist until 1844. Originally called 'Bold Venture', it grew up around the coaching inn and the church, which was built in 1846.

From Jamaica Inn, the road went past Fourhole Cross (SX171749), one of a series of wayside crosses marking the medieval route to Temple. Temple was founded as a hospice on the moor by the Knights Templar in the 12th century, with causeways to carry the roads across the marshy headwaters of the Bedalder on either side. Temple Bridge (SX150737) was built and the causeways rebuilt for carriages by the turnpike trust in 1769.[9] Peverell's Cross is the next medieval waymark (SX125721).

The London Inn stood near Pounds Conce (Greenwood county map 1827) and from here to Praise (Preeze) Cross the land was enclosed as shown on Thomas Martyn's county map of 1748. The turnpike then ran across the open ground of Racecourse Downs before entering Old Callywith Road which becomes Castle Street and drops down Tower Hill to the centre of Bodmin beside the parish church.

LAUNCESTON rODe
inscription on very early capped guidestone SX253822 Altarnun 68232

Temple Old Bridge, built by Bodmin Turnpike Trust

This route was altered considerably during the life of the Bodmin Trust, as will be described later.

2. The pre-turnpike route east of Bodmin towards Truro is difficult to identify. No places are named in the 1769 Act, except the destination – 'the W. End of Fair Mile Common in the parish of St Enoder', where the hamlet of Indian Queens has grown up around the inn of the same name.

Joel Gascoyne's county map of 1699 shows a road branching south from the main Bodmin to St Columb route to the west of St Lawrence, which joins another road from 'Lepery' (Reperry) at a place named 'Pedtye' (Redtye), but this does not match any modern road , lane or even footpath. From Redtye, Gascoyne's road crosses unfenced ground south of 'Collibigon' (Colbiggan) before reaching an enclosed lane at a place named Lane End on the modern map (SW974617) near 'Belovedy als(o) Belowsey', which is named as Belowda on the modern map, but known locally as Belovely. From here the Gascoyne route joins an unfenced road from the eastern flank of Castle an Dinas, possibly the modern footpath past Castle Farm, then heads straight for 'High Fradham' (Higher Fraddon).

Thomas Martyn's county map, published in 1748, shortly before the turnpike act, shows a road from the west end of Bodmin past Levedden (Laveddon House SX053661), crossing a stream to Lamorick (SX036645) and then over unfenced ground to Red Tye, where it joins the road from Reperry, as shown on the Gascoyne map. From Red Tye, an unfenced road runs to East Lane End, Belovely, along a fenced section to West Lane End, then over unfenced ground all the way to Fraddon.

Greenwood's county map of 1827 shows the turnpike road, picked out by a heavy line along one edge, from Bodmin to Fraddon.[10] There is a toll booth or bar, marked as T.B., at the west end of Bodmin, which matches the site of the Town End Toll-house (SX062670) described by Patrick Taylor.[11] Greenwood shows the road passing Leveddin (Leveddon House) and crossing a stream just north of Lanivet (at Lamorick). It then runs across open moorland to the north of Red Tye (which is marked), on the line of a road now called the Old Coach Road on modern maps. It runs north of Gregland (Griglands) and south of Brin (Brynn), then, significantly, well south of Belovely across Goss Moor to Indian Queens at the west end of Fraddon.

From the study of these maps, it would seem that, while the road to the east of Bodmin was largely an improvement of an existing road, much of the road to the west, between Bodmin and Fraddon, especially between Lamorick and Fraddon, was built from scratch by the Turnpike Trust.

A description of a journey by coach from Launceston to Indian Queens in 1795 is contained in the diary of an unknown gentleman, travelling with his wife and daughter on a journey to Land's End. It shows that the Bodmin Turnpike Trust had done a good job on this its principal toll road:

June 12th Fryday. Launceston to Five Lanes. Eight miles of good road over several mountains – quite barren, nothing but heath. Views of distant mountains right and left. The road sparkles when the sun shines, it seems to be all spar. Five Lanes has a single house (presumably the Kings Head), only a makeshift, but good stabling.

Five Lanes to Bodmin – 13 miles of good road over several mountains, which are quite barren, with scarce a tree or hedge.

The original turnpike road through Temple

SX099634
Respryn Bridge,
Lanhydrock carried the
main road from Bodmin
to Liskeard until 1835

In Bodmin the writer stopped at 'the White Hart, a good inn'.

Bodmin to the Indian Queen – 11 miles of most excellent road mostly upon a level. All moorland, not a tree to be seen on this road.

The Indian Queen, a single house, keeping post chaises but only a make-shift upon an emergency.[12]

The writer stayed overnight at the Indian Queen, but pressed on to the Plume of Feathers in Mitchell for breakfast on Saturday.

Returning to the list of roads in the turnpike act of 1769:

3. Bodmin to No Mans Land. This is the road south from Bodmin, through Sweetshouse to meet the existing St Austell to Lostwithiel turnpike road at the medieval cross at No Mans Land (SX089590), the high point on the hill above Lostwithiel. Today this road is numbered B3268 as far as Sweetshouse and then B3269. This was the main route from Bodmin to Liskeard and Plymouth.

4. 'Also thro' Bodmin, Lanhydrock over

Respryn Bridge then parishes of St Winnow and Broadoak as far as where Bodmin road near the Four Burrows joins the Lostwithiel to Liskeard road.' The medieval Respryn Bridge crosses the River Fowey just south of the splendid grounds of Lanhydrock House. This was the main road to south-east Cornwall from Bodmin, meeting the Lostwithiel to Liskeard turnpike road on the high ground to the north of Boconnoc at SX143631. Today, 'Respryn Road' branches off the B3268 (the road to No Mans Land) near Bodmin School. It crosses the modern A30 Bodmin by-pass on an elegant suspension bridge, suitable for walkers and cyclists only. South of the by-pass the road can be driven as a quiet country road. One milestone survives at Higher Bofarnel (SX116633), four miles from Bodmin. 5. 'Roads leading from Bodmin over Dunmeer Bridge thro' parishes of Bodmin and Egloshayle to Trenair Lane End where it joins the Camelford to Wadebridge road.' This has become A389 the Bodmin to Wadebridge road. Over the years the route has been altered a number of times, most recently by the Wadebridge by-pass of 2006. This by-pass took the road away from the village of Egloshayle on the north bank of the River Camel, but the road through the village is not the original turnpike road. Greenwood's map of 1827 has the turnpike climb away from the river to the east of Egloshayle along Higher Lane to Above Town, then past Trevarner to meet the Haleworthy Trust turnpike at SX998729.

6. The road to Helland Bridge climbed north from Bodmin along Berry Lane past Berry Tower, then dropped down to the ford at Clerkenwater before climbing again past Pimligoe and Furzey before descending steeply to Helland Bridge. Helland Bridge is an early 15th century bridge on the site of an older bridge.[13]

SX080639 B3268
Lanhydrock 67541

SX082624 B3268
Lostwithiel 70797003

SX090610 B3269
Lanlivery 70767

SX116633 Higher Bofarnel,
St Winnow 1409033

SX041688 A389
Lanivet 67579

SX033701 A389
Egloshayle 67652

SX070686 Helland 507024

SX065712 Helland 67533

7. This road branches off the main (A30) turnpike on Racecourse Downs, turning north across the open moorland. Keybridge crosses the De Lank River to give access to St Breward. Although the turnpike stopped at Keybridge, this is the southern end of the pre-turnpike 'Judges' Road' described above and the three surviving milestones on this section are probably pre-turnpike milestones.

8. 'Also from Bodmin thro' parishes of Lenevet, Withiel, St Wenn & Columb Major to East end of St Columb.' This was the postal route west from Bodmin to St Columb Major, but the construction of the turnpike route over Goss Moor to Indian Queens so eclipsed the postal route that the trust left it alone.

This first Bodmin Turnpike Act required 'milestones and direction posts to be set up', which was the standard wording used in turnpike acts. All the roads described above, apart from the last mentioned, do have milestones of a similar design still surviving, but not in complete sets. They are substantial rectangular granite blocks with semi-circular rounded tops. The dressed face has a single capital **B** for Bodmin above or below the distance in Arabic numerals. There are no milestones on the network of lanes between Bodmin and St Columb Major.

An Act of 1786 (26 GIII c.cxxxix) allowed the erection of more toll gates, and 'hedges, rails and ditches may be erected on commons and wastes near toll bars' to stop travellers dodging round the toll gate. Unusually, this Act lists three sections of road which 'have not been repaired by the Trustees':
- Pimligoe (SX069694) to Helland Bridge (Road 6 above).

- E end of Callynough Downs in Helland (SX091704) to Key Bridge in Blisland (Road 7).
- From E end of Laningle Downs in Lanevet to E end of St Columb (Road 8).

These seem to have been given the lowest priority of the Trust's roads, but the sections of roads 6 and 7 mentioned here both have surviving milestones of the original style.

The 1811 Act (51 GIII c.clix) added a sort of southern by-pass to the list of turnpike roads 'from Callywith Turnpike Gate in Bodmin (parish)over Cookland Common to Priors Barn Turnpike, to Carminow Cross (SX088657) and to the turnpike road from Bodmin to Liskeard' - the road over Respryn Bridge. It is difficult to see how such a road would help the people of Bodmin town, since it allowed travellers to avoid the inns and shops that would have benefitted from their custom. Perhaps this was an existing short cut, and by adding it to the list of toll-paying routes there would be no advantage to travellers in avoiding the town in this way.

A TIME OF ROAD IMPROVEMENTS
In the later 1820s and the 1830s, when William McAdam and then his son, Christopher McAdam were active in Cornwall, considerable improvements were undertaken on a number of Bodmin roads.

1829
The 1829 Act (10 GIV c.xix) proposed:
- Replacing the last section of the Wadebridge road (road 5) from Clapper (SX004717) to Trenant Lane End with the road through Egloshayle to the north end of the bridge at Wadebridge.

SX089688 old A30 Racecourse Farm, Cardinham

SX098701 A30 Cardinham 507027005

SX103704 A30 Cardinham 507022

SX112709 A30 Blisland 67312

Fallen four mile stone on A30 April 2008 SX112709

Turnpike milestone repaired and re-erected July 2008 SX112709 A30 Blisland 67312

- Three new sections on the Launceston road (road 1)

(i) ... a new Piece of Road commencing at the Brewery Lane, through Priors Barn Lane, and through certain Inclosures adjoining the said Lane, to and over Cooksland Common, to join the present Turnpike Road at or near the One Mile Stone from Bodmin to Launceston.

The 1 mile stone would have been at SX084680 on the original turnpike road. The junction now contains a highway storage depot. The new route was longer, but avoided the steep climb of Castle Street when leaving Bodmin. This is now called Launceston Road, while its predecessor is called the Old Callywith Road. A milestone stood on Launceston Road until 2000, when a new Asda superstore was built beside it and the milestone

Both parts of the fallen milestones were recovered to Tolpetherwin Depot for a stainless steel dowel repair

disappeared. The top was damaged, obscuring a possible letter **B**, but there was a clear **J**, an old-fashioned **1** and a bench mark on this round topped stone. The style of this milestone suggests that it was the original 1 mile stone re-used at the new location on the longer route.

The 2 mile stone survives, by the entrance to Racecourse Farm. It was moved 600 yards towards Bodmin from its original position at SX091693 near where the turnpike road joins the modern A30 dual carriageway.

The 3 mile stone could not be moved, because it was at a road junction and served a dual purpose. It was both a milestone and a guide stone, giving the direction and distance to Blisland, carved as **Blifland**, along the minor road (SX103704). It survives, and 600 yards nearer Bodmin on the same north side of the A30 dual carriageway, the eastbound lane, is a unique design of replacement milestone. It is triangular in plan with **B 3** on the right face, but **L XIX** (Launceston 19) on the left face. This is the only Bodmin Trust milestone with Roman numerals (SX098701).

(ii) 'a new Piece of Road diverging from or near the Five Mile Stone from Bodmin to Launceston, through the Estate of Greenborough and Menacrin Marsh, to or near to the Seventh Mile Stone, to join the present road from Bodmin.' This avoided the causeways on each side of Temple, using the line of the modern dual carriageway. The reference to milestones shows that they were in place before the Act, but is confusing, since they would have to be reset, since all the improvements to ease the steep gradients would increase the distance from Bodmin to Launceston.

(iii) ... a new Piece of Road from the present Turnpike Road at Five Lanes, over and through the present Highway leading from Five Lanes to Plasha (Plusha) Cross, and from thence through certain Inclosures over Two Bridges to or near to Holloway Cross Turnpike Gate in the Parish of Southpetherwin to join the present turnpike road from Hick's Mill Bridge to Launceston.

This wide sweep to the south of the original route avoided the steep hills at Hicks Mill Bridge and Trerithick Bridge, but again, increased the total distance. The dual carriageway Plusha By-pass makes the 1829 route hard to follow. Start in Five Lanes at the cross roads (SX225816), not on the pre-dual carriageway Five Lanes by-pass of the later 20th century a few yards to the south. This gives four 'layers' of road-making side by side at this point. Just east of the crossroads, where it joins the old by-pass is a pent-topped milestone of the Launceston Trust style (SX224806), though this was always a Bodmin Trust road. Join the dual carriageway, but pull in to the lay-by one mile ahead to find the next milestone, again gable-topped. Leave the modern A30 by turning right towards Callington on B3257, but fork left at Plusha to keep on the 1829 road. On the north side of the road, a few yards west of the turn to Trevell, set at the back of a very wide verge, is the next pent-topped milestone (SX256803). The last part of the 1829 road is now a slip road off the westbound carriageway of the A30. Coming from Plusha this will be a dead end, but the last gable-topped milestone can be found immediately east of where the turnpike and the modern road meet (SX266812).

The 1829 road and the Two Bridges are now part of a lay-by complex on the east side of the modern A30. The milestone just east of Holyway Cross was lost during the dual carriageway construction, but the medieval cross survives.

The five pent-topped milestones all lie within the Launceston District Highway Board's group of parishes. The most westerly pent-topped milestone is at Bolventor (SX180764). There are no pent-topped milestones in the Bodmin District Highway Board's group of parishes.

Just west of Trewint, beside the eastbound lane of the dual carriageway is a round-topped Bodmin turnpike milestone, **B 13** (SX212800). This would suggest that the Launceston District Highway Board erected their gable-topped milestones only where the old Bodmin turnpike milestones had disappeared.

• A new Piece of Road from Carminow's Cross, over the Common near to Black Pool and down the Valley under or near Dreeson Ball to Resprin Bridge, to join the present Turnpike Road from Bodmin to Liskeard.

Carminow's Cross (SX088657) stands in the centre of the roundabout on the Bodmin side of the A30 trunk road where the A38 Plymouth road begins its descent of the Glynn valley. Dreeson Ball (SX107647) below Dreesonball Wood is where an existing road shown on Greenwood's 1827 map ran gently down to Respryn Bridge. This long detour avoided the steep gradient on the Bodmin side of Respryn Bridge,

• A new Piece of Road commencing at the Place where Polmawgan Lane joins the present Bodmin Turnpike Road, and through the said Lane to some Inclosures in the Possession of James Stephens and others, and over the Common to join the present Turnpike Road at or near the Five Mile Stone from Bodmin to Liskeard.

Polmaugan Lane branches off just south of Respryn Bridge at SX102634. This would avoid the long climb to the surviving fourth milestone on Bofarnel Downs (SX116633). The fifth milestone has not been found. Mentioned again in a later Act, this 'new Piece of Road' was never constructed.

• A final complex of roads to improve the western approach to Bodmin from Truro was never built: '

... a new Piece of Road diverging from the

SX172750 A30
St Neot 504622

SX212600 A30
Altarnun 68241

Holyway or Holloway Cross (SX273823) marks where the 1821 turnpike road (A30) joins the 1769 turnpike road.

SX013624 old A30 Luxulyan 70910

SW913584 old A30 St Enoder 50776

SW925595 old A30 St Columb 507729

January 2006 Milestone spotted in debris of hedge removed during road improvements SW939602 A30 St Columb

(right) July 2007. The restored milestone was the centrepiece of the opening ceremony of the Bodmin to Indian Queens Road Improvement. SW939602 A30 St Columb

present Turnpike Road near Townsend Turnpike Gate, through Dark lane, crossing the Turnpike Road to Dunmeer at or near the One Mile Stone from Bodmin, down the Valley to Boscarne Bridge, and passing near to Nanstallon Mill, over Mulberry Downs, through Tremoor and Rosewarrick to Colbiggan Corner, to join the present Bodmin to Truro, with a new Piece or Branch of Road from Nanstallon Mill to Polbrock; and also a new Branch from the said new Piece of Road, commencing at the Western end of Dark Lane, through and over certain Inclosures in the possession of James Webb, to a lane or highway leading from the town of Bodmin to Tan Wood, and from thence through the said lane to the County Gaol of Bodmin.

While the work proposed by this Act for the route eastwards towards Launceston was completed, the new lines proposed for the Liskeard and Truro links were superseded by better plans in two later Acts.

1833

In 1833 the Act (3&4 WIV c.lxxxix) repeated the proposals for three of the new roads in the 1829 Act, which had not yet been built –

> The Dreeson Ball route to Respryn Bridge;
> The Polmawgan Lane route;
> The Dark Lane to Dunmeer section

However, the Act proposed a much simpler alternative to the route towards Truro, which is still the main access to Bodmin via Lanivet – 'A new line from Town End TP Gate, past Launddon (Laveddon), Laninval (House), Forda, St Bennetts (Priory)to Colbiggan (SX009629) Corner near the Five Mile Stone on Truro Road.' This road was built, and 5

milestones existed on it at one mile intervals in the 1970s.[14] However there is now only one survivor, the five mile stone (SX013624). The five mile stone was recovered during construction of the 2007 dual carriageway and reinstalled at the completion of road works on what was now a *cul-de-sac*, accessible from the Roche Lane underpass, just below a lay-by on the dual carriageway. SX013624 old A30 Luxulyan 70910

The 1833 road was longer, and so the milestones had to be moved to match the new distance to Bodmin. A new milestone was needed **B 12** at the most western point on the Trust's road. This was a triangular design and stands near the bus stop in Fraddon (SW913584). SW913584 old A30 St Enoder 50776 One mile away, the **B 11** milestone is an original design at the eastern end of Indian Queens (SW925595) on the line of the turnpike, but no longer on the A30 which sweeps past a few yards to the south. SW925595 old A30 St Columb 507729

£93 MILLION MILESTONE

The **B 10** milestone was almost lost in the 2007 road improvement scheme. It was spotted when a hedge was grubbed out during road construction. Unfortunately the stone was damaged by the hedge grubbing machinery. However it was recovered, inverted and re-carved, and was used to mark the completion of the £93 million road improvement when it was unveiled together with a large granite plaque before a crowd of dignitaries and well-wishers on 11 July 2007. The milestone did not cost £93 million pounds, but the new by-pass did.

The **B 9** milestone is missing. There is a triangular 8 mile stone west of the railway bridge on the old line of the A30 (SW970611). The lettering is painted, not carved, on two faces. The new dual carriageway was built in 2007, largely to avoid the not infrequent accidents involving

SW939602 old A30
St Columb 71165

SW970611 old A30
Roche 70967

SX086662 A38
Triangular milestone
design used on the Glynn
Valley turnpike route built
in 1835 Bodmin 504619

SX099655 A38
Cardinham 504618

SX107646 A38
Cardinham

SX121648 A38
Cardinham 50463

SX137651 A38
Broadoak 504562

SX153652 A38
Broadoak 504561

SX166649 A38
St Neot 62251

SX195649 A38
Dobwalls 504560

high vehicles and the low iron bridge.
1835
The 1835 Act (5&6 WIV c.cv) sorted out the problems with the Liskeard route by proposing the modern line of the A39 from Dreeson Ball down the Glynn Valley to Dobwalls. A survey map of the new route is held in the County Record Office in Truro.[15] This road had a new, triangular design of milestones, with the distance to Liskeard (**L**) on one face and the distance to Bodmin (**B**) on the other face. Almost all these milestones survive. They are on the left side of the road coming from Bodmin and give distances to Bodmin in whole miles, with the odd half mile added to the Liskeard distance. Both these points reinforce the fact that these are Bodmin Trust milestones, not Liskeard Trust milestones.

The 1866 Act (29&30 V c.CXI) showed all the major routes still being maintained, including the Hellandbridge Road as far as Pimligoe. Two minor improvements were proposed on the Wadebridge roads, easing the gradients. These can be seen just north of Dunmere Bridge, where the old road went straight up the hill and the new 1866 road sweeps round to the right (SX047679 to SX046681) and in Treveigan Wood where a wider sweep is taken again (SX029710 to SX026712).

The Bodmin Trust expired in November 1874 (37&38 V c.xcv).

MILESTONES ON NON-TURNPIKE ROADS

A further route, north from Bodmin towards Camelford, carries milestones of the Bodmin Turnpike Trust design – rectangular in plan with a rounded top and an inscribed **B** and Arabic number, but this route was never maintained by the Bodmin Turnpike Trust. B3266 leaves the Bodmin to Wadebridge turnpike at Mount Charles, just north of the **2 B** milestone (SX041688). There is a continuous run of six milestones along the B3266. All have a **B** above a number, but there are some differences in style. The first two, **B 3** (SX046705) and **B 4** (SX055716) have large letters and numbers on relatively slender stones. **B 5** (SX058732) had a very elaborate **5**, but disappeared before 2003. **B 6** (SX065745), **B 7** (SX072759) and **B 8**

SX046705 B3266
Egloshayle 67653

SX055716 B3266
St Mabyn 67737

SX065745 B3266
St Tudy 67783

SX072759 B3266
St Tudy 505709

SX074774 B3266
Michaelstow 505710

SX064746 St Tudy
67782

SX065762 St Tudy

SX046633
Reperry Cross, Lanivet
67575

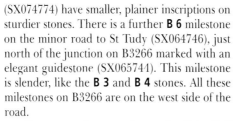

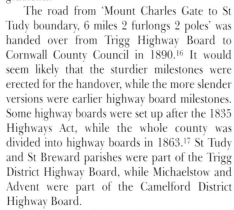

SX046633
Reperry Cross, Lanivet
428374

(SX074774) have smaller, plainer inscriptions on sturdier stones. There is a further **B 6** milestone on the minor road to St Tudy (SX064746), just north of the junction on B3266 marked with an elegant guidestone (SX065744). This milestone is slender, like the **B 3** and **B 4** stones. All these milestones on B3266 are on the west side of the road.

Almost exactly one mile north of the **B 8** milestone is another eight mile stone. This is a modern replica milestone on the pre-turnpike route described at the start of this chapter – the Judges' Road. The **B 9** (SX090802) and **B 10** (SX096816) on B3266 are on the east side of the road, as are all the milestones on the Judges' Road further south. This confirms that these two milestones belong to the Judges' Road set of pre-turnpike milestones and not to the B3266 set of 19th century milestones. The discrepancy in distance is not a measurement error. The B3266 route via Mount Charles is just over a mile longer than the Judges' Road route via Key Bridge, but it does have much easier gradients.

The road from 'Mount Charles Gate to St Tudy boundary, 6 miles 2 furlongs 2 poles' was handed over from Trigg Highway Board to Cornwall County Council in 1890.[16] It would seem likely that the sturdier milestones were erected for the handover, while the more slender versions were earlier highway board milestones. Some highway boards were set up after the 1835 Highways Act, while the whole county was divided into highway boards in 1863.[17] St Tudy and St Breward parishes were part of the Trigg District Highway Board, while Michaelstow and Advent were part of the Camelford District Highway Board.

There is one further milestone in St Tudy village (SX065762) which has the inscription **BODMIN 7**. It is one mile north of the B 6

milestone on the minor road mentioned above. The carving is crisp, suggesting a late date. The style of inscription is unique.

GUIDESTONES

Not only does this part of Cornwall have a fascinating collection of milestones, but it also has the largest collection of guidestones (direction stones at road junctions) in the county. There are a number of striking individual designs and a group of stones with carved capstones unique to this area. It is difficult to link the surviving guidestones to a particular date, with one exception, but a number seem to be linked to a Will. In 1697, in the reign of William and Mary, Justices in Highway Sessions were authorised to require Surveyors of Highways to set up 'direction stones or posts' at 'cross highways' (8&9 WIII c.XVI). A number of subsequent exhortations were issued. The first Bodmin Turnpike Act of 1769 called for 'Milestones & Direction Posts to be set up'.

The guidestone at Reperry Cross (SX046633) south of Bodmin is the only dated guidestone in the area. It is a tall, square granite pillar with a pyramid top. The names of the destinations are broken up into several lines of writing on each face – for example, Lostwithiel becomes **LOST**, new line, **WITH**, new line **IEL**. Below this is the date, 1776.

Just across the road is another guidestone with a hand like a car headlight beam pointing towards Lanivet, which is inscribed **LANI** with a dot over the capital **I** and then **VT** set above, to give **LANIVT**. SX046633

At the same location is the celtic cross, Reperry Cross itself, which is in effect a medieval guide stone. SX046633 Reperry Cross

THE WILL OF HENDER MOLESWORTH

The Courtney Library of the Royal Institution of

SX046633 Reperry Cross, Lanivet 67575

SX057721 B3266
St Mabyn 67733

Cornwall in Truro holds a copy of the Will of Hender Molesworth Esquire of the Middle Temple, made on 18 September 1731. After all the usual bequests made by a wealthy man to members of his family and staff, there is the following, perhaps unique bequest:

I give unto my beforementioned friend Hugh Gregor the sum of forty pounds of lawfull money of Great Britain in trust that he the said Hugh Gregor shall by and with the approbation and consent of my executor hereafter named dispose and lay out the same in erecting posts in cross lanes within the county of Cornwall for the better directing of travellers the road.

The executor of Hender Molesworth's will was his brother, Sir John Molesworth of Pencarrow House, just north of Bodmin. Forty pounds was a considerable sum in 1731. If it was invested wisely, the interest might pay for a whole series of direction posts.

On the roads around Pencarrow House, particularly the B3266, stand guidestones of a design unique to the area. They consist of a tall granite pillar with a large capstone, usually rectangular, with destinations carved into the edges of the capstone. The style of pillar, the thickness of the capstone and the style of lettering varies considerably, but all are of the same basic design found nowhere else in the county.

Closest to Pencarrow House is a guidestone with a rectangular capstone on a slender octagonal pillar (SX057721). This stone is described and illustrated in *Famous Milestones*, where it is described as 6 feet tall.[18] The pillar has fractured close to the ground and the guidestone is now only 2 feet tall, but still records the directions to seven destinations with all the names written in full.

At the next crossroads to the north

An OLD CORNISH STONE
near ST. TUDY, CORNWALL

A RARE design to be seen in Cornwall is this 6 ft. granite post with its rectangular head. Motorists in this duchy must have noticed the delightful vagueness of some of the Cornish stones, with only the initial letter of the nearest town engraved upon them.

This stone lies between Bodmin and Helland and quite near to St. Tudy.

THE SPIRIT FROM BRITISH COAL
"National" contains British Benzole produced by the coal, steel, iron and gas industries of this country. When you run your car on "National" you are helping to keep British labour employed.

SX057721
FAMOUS MILESTONES

SX060733 B3266
St Mabyn 67751

SX072759 B3266
St Tudy 67784

SX073774 B3266
Michaelstow 505710

SX068699 Helland

SX090704
Helland 508685

(SX060733), beside a medieval cross at Longstone, is a 4 feet tall rectangular section pillar with a capstone carrying a total of eight destinations.

At the crossroads west of St Tudy (SX072759), the guidestone has a rectangular capstone on an oval section pillar almost 7 feet tall. The capstone has four destinations on its edges, including **LISKD** (Liskeard), 15 miles away. It directs the traveller to Liskeard via Keybridge, but the traveller to Bodmin is directed along B3266 to Mount Charles.

At the junction north of St Tudy (SX073774) beside a medieval cross head, an oval granite pillar supports a capstone with writing on three edges for just three destinations.

A rectangular pillar stands at the junction (SX068699) north of Pimligoe on the Bodmin to Hellandbridge road. Photographs from the 1980s shows a square capstone with inscriptions on three faces.[19] but the capstone disappeared in 1991.

Two capped guidestones with rectangular section pillars stand on the Bodmin to Keybridge road. At the crossroads south east of Helland (SX090704) the capstone gives directions to four towns, but no villages.

At Merry Meeting (SX089731) the four inscriptions have each place name split onto two lines, even **BOD – MIN** is broken in two. Blisland is spelt **BLISS – LAND**.

A few yards beyond Key Bridge, there is a third guidestone of a similar design, with a rectangular section pillar and heavy capstone with destinations on three faces (SX087738). However, there is a long square section iron stud rising from the centre of the capstone, with a threaded top section carrying a square nut. In 2009 a replacement wooden fingerpost was mounted on this stud, restoring this unique combined fingerpost and guidestone.

There is one outlier, miles to the north-west of all the rest, beside the pillar of a medieval cross at Long Cross between Port Quinn and Port Isaac (SX989797). The land here belonged to the Molesworth estate. This stone has a rectangular pillar and a four-sided capstone with destinations on all four edges.

The triangular guidestone on Priors Barn Road in Bodmin (SX076667) has **LANSON**, the old form of Launceston, and **LISKEARD** carved neatly on the edges of the capstone and **TO STATION** with a carved pointing hand on the pillar below the Liskeard edge.

SX089731
Merry Meeting,
Blisland 67361

SX087738
St Breward 67434

SW989797 St
Endellion SM24282

SX076667 A389
Bodmin 368043

SX253822
Altarnun 68232

SX086617 B3269
Lanlivery 70759

SW997624
Roche 70959

SX118724 Blisland

SX065713
Helland 67525

SX066774
St Tudy 67770

To the east of Bodmin, on the line of the original turnpike route to Launceston to the west of Polyphant, is a guidestone with a triangular cap, inscribed on its edges, **BODMYN RODE**, **LAUNCESTON rODe** and **CAMEL FORD** (SX253822). The style of inscription and the spelling of 'rode' rather than 'road' suggest this guidestone is older than the original turnpike. The Launceston Old Cornwall Society was responsible for the repair and re-erection of this stone in 1958.[20] The guidestone was again repaired and re-set in the spring of 2005.

Other unusual guidestones, but without capstones, exist:

- At Sweetshouse (SX086617) on the turnpike to No Man's land and Lostwithiel, where Bodmin is spelt with a **Y - BODMYN**.
- At the Withiel turn (SW997624) on the Truro turnpike, where the guidestone reads simply **WITHIEL**
- At Higher Penstroda on Bodmin Moor (SX118724) a boulder is carved **BODMIN**.
- At Hellandbridge (SX065713) a crisply carved late 19th century guidestone must once have stood in the middle of the road since it is carved on three sides. It is now set beside the bank, less vulnerable to damage, but with the direction to Bodmin obscured.
- At a quiet crossroads (SX065774) north of St Tudy the guidestone has an unusual bronze benchmark insert. It gives directions to five destinations, including Penvose, a manor house nearby.
- At the St Tudy turn on B3266 (SX064744) a slender triangular guidestone separates the old and newer routes both with non-turnpike **B 6** milestones as mentioned above.
- The oldest stones are often the hardest to spot. Over the centuries they have merged with their surroundings. The guidestone at Wenfordbridge has **Bodmin Rode** in neat but ancient script on its main face, with **Cam Rod(e)** squeezed onto one edge. It stands beside an excellent example of a 20th century cast iron fingerpost. Most fingerposts were removed in the 1960s when new reflective aluminium sign boards were introduced.

GRANITE FINGERPOSTS

Wooden posts with wooden arms to point the way, usually called fingerposts, have been a feature of the English landscape for many years. These were the usual form of direction post erected in response to the 1697 Act of William and Mary. Wood is not as durable as stone, and it would be difficult to find an ancient wooden fingerpost today.

In mid-Cornwall it was the practise to mount a wooden post with wooden arms on a granite pillar. These are mentioned in the mid 19th century, where the wooden post worked loose on the granite pillar, allowing it to turn with the weather. The letter quoted in an earlier chapter, bemoaning the lack of direction posts except around St Columb, goes on:

SX064744 B3266
St Tudy 67771

SX085751
Bodmin Rode
guidestone at Wenfordbridge, St Breward 67431

20th Century fingerpost and 18th century guidestone at Wenfordbridge, St Breward SX085751

Nor is this all: Even where posts are erected they are but seldom painted not unfrequently you find only on side of the hand with letters on it, and some posts are so placed on the granite pedestal as to swing round with the wind. On Friday last I observed a post giving what I thought from my knowledge of the country must surely be a false directory, and on examination the timberwork was found inserted in a granite pillar and the hole so large as to allow the wood work a rotary motion.[21]

Many of these granite fingerposts survive around Bodmin Moor. Where the wooden parts have worn out, they have been replaced by County Highways or in some cases by the initiative of the Parish Council. Most have a wooden post mounted on a long wrought iron stud set into the granite base, an improvement on the method described by the newspaper correspondent quoted above.

Examples of this type can be found at:

SX084751 in Wenfordbridge with new wood in 2001, oval pillar

SX111766 on Lady Down, oval pillar
SX128675 near Cardinham, spelt **CARDYNHAM** on arm, square pillar

Some have more elaborate supports:

SX075754 west of Wenfordbridge has a wrought iron band round the oval pillar attached to the wooden top.

SX135683 on Treslea Downs has a wrought iron band and long curved brackets supporting the wooden arms high above the square granite pillar.

SX143680 west of Mount has an inverted wrought iron tripod to support the three wooden arms

SX118674 south of Cardinham has aluminium arms, made as a copy of the original wooden arms mounted on a single central stud.

The granite capstone guide post at Keybridge (SX086738) has an iron spike through the capstone which carries a three-armed wooden fingerpost, as mentioned above.

The granite guidestones at Valley Truckle (SX099824) and at Tich Barrow (SX145880), both on A39, have metal spikes for wooden fingerposts as well as carved inscriptions.

SX111766 Granite fingerpost on Lady Down, St Breward

SX135683 Granite fingerpost on Treslea Downs Cardinham 428371

On the A30 at Temple crossroads (SX136736) is a granite pillar with the date 1893 carved in large numbers running up one face. A photograph in the Courtney Library.[22] shows this pillar with a four armed wooden top supported on curved wrought iron brackets in the 1970s.

A modern direction post on the Camel Trail cycle path draws on the old design, using wooden arms on a slender steel support, mounted on a cylindrical granite pillar just south of Tresarrett (SX089730).

Other granite fingerposts survive on the eastern edge of Bodmin Moor and south of Bodmin, near Luxulyan.

SX280696 at Tokenbury Corner on B3254 has been waiting some years for new arms on its tall iron spike

SX294698 has been given an ugly metal framework and plastic arms in the heart of Pensilva

On Goonzion Downs just west of St Neot are four nicely restored examples at SX179678, SX174680, SX174677 and SX174669

The Luxulyan examples are at SX044591 and SX055579

Granite pillars with the broken stub of a wrought iron spike are found in numerous other locations and await further study.

CHAPTER EIGHT

ST AUSTELL, LOSTWITHIEL, LUXULYAN AND ROSELAND

ST AUSTELL AND LOSTWITHIEL
TURNPIKE TRUST

In 1760 a turnpike trust was set up to improve the 'road leading from the Eastern End of the Borough of Grampound through St Austell and Lostwithiel and to East End of Western Taphouse Lane.' (1 GIII c.xxvii) The preamble to the Act for this trust declares – 'No gates to be set up within two miles of St Austell or one mile of Lostwithiel' and 'Roads to be measured and Mile-stones erected'. The line of this turnpike is now the A390. It linked the well established Truro turnpike which came as far as the bridge to the west of Grampound and the Liskeard Trust which came to the east end of West Taphouse Lane.

The route of the turnpike was along existing roads which were to be improved by the trust. From Grampound, the first toll gate was to be at Teague's Gate (SW964497 Hewas Water). Teague's Gate is a name older than the turnpike. It is marked on Joel Gascoyne's map of 1699. The road here has been extensively altered in modern times and a toll house cannot be

SX009522
West Bridge, St Austell;

SX009522 *Bridge plate dated 1895, West Bridge, St Austell. Silvanus Jenkin's name is misspelt.*

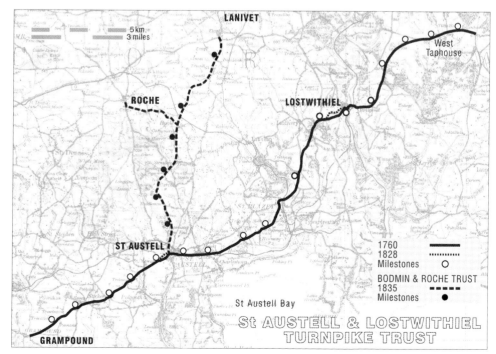

St Austell Bay

ST AUSTELL & LOSTWITHIEL
TURNPIKE TRUST

123

SX106598 Lostwithiel Bridge

SX107597 The Toll House at Lostwithiel has a commemorative plaque beside the front door

identified, though there is a milestone set back from the present road on the original route. The road ran through Sticker, now by-passed, and through St Austell along Ledrah Road, over the 16th century West Bridge[1] and up West Hill to Fore Street. It left the town via East Hill and Holmbush to St Blazey Gate, which was named after the toll gate there. The next toll gate was to be at 'Pelyn Mill Pool' (SX086588) but there is nothing to mark the spot today. The road ran through the centre of Lostwithiel and over the 15th century bridge, with a toll house on the east side (SX108598).[2] The last toll house is at the west end of West Taphouse (SX151633) and was incorporated in the late Victorian primary school when this was built.

MILESTONES

In 1764 the trustees ordered milestones to be sct up between Grampound and Lostwithiel[3]. Distances were to be calculated from the last milestone of the Truro Turnpike Trust, the 8 mile stone. This would mean that distances to St Austell would have an odd half mile. Distances are indicated on the milestones in Roman numerals, with the half mile as a half size I. All have St Austell spelt with one I, i.e. **St Austel**.

The milestones west of St Austell survive, including a half mile stone on the outskirts of the town. All but one of the milestones between St Austell and Lostwithiel survive. Sadly the milestone at Trevorry (SX082577) was knocked over by a car in 2001. The stone was recovered to the nearby Highways depot, but has since been lost.

An unusual and much later milestone, late 19th century, stands in Alexandra Road, St Austell, opposite a row of shops. Perhaps it replaced an original turnpike milestone. It has the same basic shape as the old milestones, but a much finer inscription – **ST AUSTELL** (with two Ls and in an arc above the distance) ½ **MILE** , then a dividing line **TRURO XIV MILES** in three

SW952489 A390 Grampound 71356

SW964497 off A390 Creed 71355

SW980502 St Mewan 71425

SW992512 A390 St Mewan 71426

SX006520 A390 St Austell 507031

SX034524 A390
St Austell 507028

SX049531 A390
St Austell 478839

SX061537 A390
St Austell 506699

SX069551 A390
St Austell 506700

SX078561 A390
St Austell 506701

SX082577 A390
Lanlivery GONE

SX089591 A390
Lostwithiel 70798

SX103597 A390
Lostwithiel 70881

SX018523
St Austell 1407574

different size fonts, then a dividing line, and a huge bench mark near the base.

In 1766 the trustees ordered milestones east of Lostwithie.[4] Walter Treleavers was to be paid 17s (seventeen shillings) delivered per stone. There were five milestones in this group, showing distances to Lostwithiel and Truro. Lostwithiel was shortened to **LOSTW** with a final **L** added above the **W** rather as an afterthought. The last stone in the series, east of West Taphouse and five miles from Lostwithiel has a slightly different form of lettering, as if it was carved by a different hand to the same basic design. All five milestones are still in place.

IMPROVEMENTS
In 1808 some improvements were made to ease the gradients on hills at St Austell, Cliney and Sticker.

In 1828 new routes were proposed to avoid hills. The entrance to St Austell from the west crossed a new bridge along 'Truro Road'. The road into Lostwithiel from the west took a wider sweep at the very steep hill there.

NEW ROAD
In 1835 a new turnpike trust was set up, called the Bodmin and Roche Trust, to build a new road running north from St Austell towards

SX119602 A390
Lostwithiel

SX124617 A390
St Winnow 60650

SX133628 A390
Broadoak 60527

SX149632 A390
Broadoak 60528

SX162635 A390
Broadoak 60532

This milestone was moved and re-erected when the Bodmin bypass was built in the 1980s, but disappeared in 2006

The Bugle Inn was built to serve the new turnpike road from St Austell to Bodmin. The china clay village grew around the inn. SX015588

The sign reflects the origin of the inn and later the village at Bugle. SX015588

Bodmin (5&6 WIV c.cv). The road was to follow a newly surveyed route from the General Wolfe, St Austell up the St Austell River valley and over the moors to Lanivet on the Bodmin turnpike, with a branch north-west to Roche. The General Wolfe Inn stood at the apex of the road junction of what are now called Truro Road and Bodmin Road respectively. In 1785 Samuel Pentecost left the inn and malting stock in trade to his son Samuel in his will. In 1798 Joseph Gawler was the proprietor. He left the inn in trust for his wife in 1803.[5] The General Wolfe continued as a public house into the early years of this century when it closed and was incorporated into the adjacent pram and toy shop.

As the infant china clay industry developed and expanded, villages grew along the new turnpike road and traffic expanded from the growing open cast pits to the ports of St Austell on the south coast. The village of Bugle, halfway between St Austell and Bodmin, grew up around the Bugle coaching inn.[6] In the 19th century, china clay was made into blocks or packed in large casks to be transported to the docks for shipment to the potteries of Staffordshire and

elsewhere. Sturdy wagons pulled by three horses in a line could carry up to three tons of clay at a time down the road to the coast. A return load of coal for the clay driers needed six horses to tackle the climb.

Milestones on this road were triangular in plan, with chamfered corners and a top sloping upwards towards the back of the stone. **St A** stood for St Austell on one face and **B** stood for Bodmin on the other face. The distance was given as a large Arabic numeral.

Six of the original seven milestones survive but the most northerly milestone four miles from Bodmin, only survived after a battle. When the A30 Bodmin bypass was built in the 1980s, this milestone was moved onto the new line of the A391 St Austell to Bodmin road from its original 1835 location, despite being Grade II listed. Then in 2006 it disappeared. It was rediscovered in a pile of discarded granite kerb stones in the Highways Depot at Callywith Road to the north-east of Bodmin in 2008. Negotiations took place and consent was eventually obtained to return the milestone to its original 1835 location in 2011 (SX035622).

SX012539 A391
Treverbyn 478900

SX005553 A391
Treverbyn 478897

SX011566 A391
Treverbyn 478899

SX014581 A391
St Austell 507054

SX018597 A391
Treverbyn 507030

SX035622
Newgate, Luxulyan 79011

The milestone found in Callywith Road Highways Depot in October 2008

The milestone was re-erected in its original 1835 location in 2011. SX035622

Wood Gate toll house where Mrs Ann Matthews was Toll Collector in 1878 (SX010529)

A toll house was built at the St Austell end of the turnpike road, at Wood Gate (SX011529). Today it is overshadowed by the viaduct of the railway main line to Penzance. Faced in dressed stone with gothic windows, it was restored as a private house in the 1990s. Kelly's Directory of 1878 lists Mrs Ann Matthews as the Toll Collector at 'Bodmin Road gate'.

CREED AND ST JUST TURNPIKE TRUST

An Act of 1761 (2 GIII c.lxvi) was to turnpike the roads 'from Lostwithiel Turnpike Road, on Western side of Teages Gate (Creed Parish) where the Tregony and Grampound roads divide through the Borough of Tregony to parish of Ruan Lanihorne and from the Truro Turnpike at Dennis Water (Probus parish) to 3 hundred yards on the south side of Trethim Mill (St Just parish)'.[7]

This would link inhabitants of the Roseland peninsula with the main through route to the east and to the west of the county. The St Austell Trust had a toll house at Teages (Teague's) Gate as mentioned above. Dennis Water is Denas Water (SW87468) where the Truro Turnpike crosses a tributary of the Tresillian River. The junction at Denas Water was radically altered when the Probus by-pass was built in the 1990s. The by-pass chopped up the Creed and St Just turnpike route, leaving sections of it to the north and south of the modern road as far as the Tregony turn near Trevorva. One of the Trust's milestones is to be found hidden by a corner on the road to Tresawle, where the old turnpike now ends in a farm gate into a field (SW892465).

SW892465
Probus 508988.
Creed and St Just Trust milestone hidden in a corner near Tresawle after the Probus bypass chopped up the old road.

SW917451
Tregony 508365

SW921432 A3078
Ruan Lanihorne 508359

From Trevorva to Tregony the turnpike took the direct route with a steep descent and climb past Freewater, past the turn to Cornelly Church (SW916451), where another Trust milestone survives, and through a steep, twisting cutting made in the rock to the bridge below Tregony town. The gentle gradient and sweeping curves of the A3078 from the Freewater turn to Tregony look like the work of a turnpike engineer, but this section of road was built new in the 1920s.

The bridge over the River Fal at Tregony is mentioned in the Trelawny Deeds in 1382.[8] The medieval bridge was unchanged by the turnpike trust, though there were complaints about its narrowness. In 1863 a Tregony resident wrote to the local paper to complain that the width of the bridge was affecting his business:

> Sir, I have many times wished that some people would take it upon them to urge the necessity of widening the bridge at the bottom of Tregony town spanning the River Fal, the present bridge being only 8½ feet wide, and what still makes it worse, there are blocks of granite fixed to protect the sides of the bridge which are placed directly opposite each other, so that if any implement drawn on its own wheels should

exceed 7½ feet, it is impossible to pass without lifting one wheel on the granite coping, which takes three or four men to perform. [9]

The writer manufactured hay making machinery in Tregony, and he had to make a detour of four miles via Grampound and Probus to avoid the bridge. A new bridge was built late in the 19th century, which today's traffic now finds too narrow.

In the early days there were two toll gates, called Higher and Lower. The renewal Act of 1827 (7&8 GIII c.lxxiii) set up four gates in total, at Freewater (SW906459), Veryan Bridge (not located), Cuby (SW955473, at Fair Cross, on the parish boundary with Creed) and at Bessie Beneath (SW923423, the Veryan turn). The Fair Cross toll house still stands, but looks like just another cottage. A granite block with two horizontal holes, in the bank opposite the toll house, marks the location of the toll gate.

The road to Ruan Lanihorne is mentioned in the 1827 renewal Act, but Greenwood's county map of 1827 does not highlight it as a turnpike. The part of this road nearest to Tregony runs alongside the river and suffered from flooding and surface erosion. There are no milestones on this road.

There are no milestones on the Creed to Tregony road, but to the south of Tregony the road into the Roseland has five surviving stones of various designs.

1 mile. The first milestone south of Tregony is built into the stone hedge opposite Hay Cottage (SW921432). It has a mixture of lightly carved upper and lower case lettering, which reads **VeRYaN 3 TREGONEY 1**. This is the only milestone to spell Tregony with an 'e'. 'Tregoney' appears on maps from the late 19th century onwards, where the maps are 'based on the Ordnance Survey'. All earlier maps use 'Tregony', including earlier Ordnance Survey maps. Guide books use 'Tregony'.

The turning to Veryan at Bessie Beneath is less than two miles from Tregony. A milestone on the Veryan road three miles from Tregony is marked on the1:25000 Ordnance Survey Explorer map (Sheet 105, Revised 1997) at SW931405. It is now missing. No two mile stone has been found on the Veryan road.

2 miles. The second mile stone on the turnpike road is at a road junction and carries inscriptions on two adjacent faces of the rectangular stone (SW920420). Facing the main route, lightly carved, in a mixture of upper and

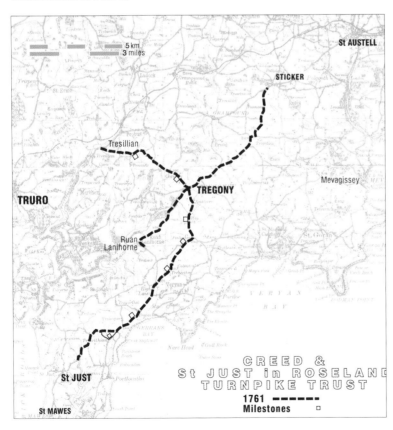

SW920420 A3078
Veryan 508357

SW909405 A3078 Veryan 508358
*This milestone appears to be in a
ditch, but is on the original line and
elevation of the road.*

SW890382 A3078
Gerrans 509240

SW878372 A3078
Gerrans 509241

lower case script, it reads **ST MawES 8 TReGoNY 2**. Facing the side turning in a larger script, it reads **RUAN 2**, the distance to Ruan Lanihorne along a very twisty lane with steep hills.

3 miles. The third milestone appears to be in a ditch several metres to the west of the metalled road, but this is a result of road improvement (SW909405). The milestone has not moved, but the road has. The milestone is tombstone shaped, again with a mix of upper and lower case script, but more clearly carved to read **ST MAWeS 7 TRegoNy 3**. There is no consistency in the choice of upper and lower case between this and the previous stone.

4 miles. The fourth milestone was found and photographed in 1970 [10] but cannot be located today. The inscription was all in capitals, **ST MAWES 6 TREGOИY 4**, but the 'N' in Tregony was reversed.

5 miles. The fifth milestone uses capital letters but Roman numerals – **ST MAWES V TREGONY V** (SW890382).

6¼ miles. The next milestone takes the same form as the others, with capital letters, Arabic numerals and no fraction lines, reading **ST MAWES 4¾ TREGONY 6¼**. This milestone is in the hamlet of Trewithian, which was by-passed by the original turnpike road (SW878372) Greenwood's 1827 map shows the turnpike running to the north of Trewithian in what is now a sunken green lane between arching trees which meet overhead. This is a public bridleway. The gradient of the green lane is surprisingly steep in places, and it may be that the loop though Trewithian was primarily to give an easier gradient. The loop is not one mile longer than the original green lane route, as suggested on the milestone, which has increased the distance between Tregony and St Mawes from 10

miles to 11 miles.

No trace has been found of the last milestone in this series.

The turnpike ended 300 yards south of Trethem Mill, beyond the parish boundary. This was probably to ensure that the bridge and its approaches were maintained by the Trust, even though the remainder of the road through St Just parish to St Mawes was not to be improved.

THE ROAD TO PENTEWAN

On the B3273 is a rectangular milestone with a rounded top and an inscription on one face reading **ST A 1** (SX011509). The B3273 runs south from St Austell along the valley of the St Austell River to its mouth at Pentewan. It was never a turnpike road. Neither Joel Gascoyne's county map of 1699, nor Thomas Martyn's county map of 1748 show any road south of London Apprentice. C & J Greenwood's 1 inch county map of 1827 shows a road from St Austell to Pentewan which matches the modern B3273. This map also shows a pier at Pentewan.

The road was probably constructed in about 1820.

Between 1818 and 1826 Sir Christopher Hawkins rebuilt the harbour at Pentewan.[11] He planned to compete with the new harbour at Charlestown, built by Charles Rashleigh in 1791 and to make money from the rapidly expanding china clay trade. The gentle gradient of the river valley provided an easy passage for the heavy china clay wagons, once a modern, well-drained road surface had been made. The project was successful. In 1824 two ships entered, two in June and thirteen in July. New technology was coming in, and in 1825 it was proposed that a horse-drawn railway should be built alongside the road. The railway opened in 1829.

SX011509 B3273
St Austell 507524

There is only one milestone in Cornwall giving a distance to Heligan. SX008479 B3273 St Austell 508306

SX025524 St Austell 507035

SX028510 St Austell 478835

The harbour continued to function off and on for a hundred years, but it was frequently out of action. Waste material from the china clay industry and from the older tin works were washed down the St Austell River and would block the harbour entrance with sand.

THE HELIGAN MILESTONE

There is no sign of a two mile stone on this road, but just north of Pentewan, is a triangular milestone giving the distance to **HELIGAN 1 ¾** on one face and **ST A 3** on the other face (SX008479).

John Hearle Tremayne was squire at Heligan House from 1829 to 1851. He was responsible for the creation of the long drive which comes up from Pentewan. This was supposedly built to bring in coal to the estate, as the incline on the public road south of Pentewan was too steep for wagons. The Drive was lined with ornamental trees and a magnificent avenue of Cornus capitata planted from seedlings in 1832.[12] The different number three on the two inscribed faces would suggest two masons if not two dates for the inscriptions on the milestone.

The Lost Gardens of Heligan have become a major tourist attraction in Cornwall, since their re-discovery in 1990. The Heligan milestone holds special significance in this context, since it, too, was lost. The milestone was discovered by David Stark, Area Surveyor for Cornwall County Council, where it 'had sunk into the ground, probably due to vibration from passing traffic, to the extent that only the top was visible'.[13] Mr Stark arranged for the stone to be raised and refurbished.

PENRICE MILESTONES

On the road to Penrice House from St Austell stand two milestones SX025524 & SX028511). They are triangular in cross section with flat tops. They give the distance to St Austell, spelt **ST AUSTLE** and to the country house of **PENRICE**.

The first stone gives the distance to Penrice as **2 MILE** with an **S** added on the apex of the triangle to correct the local grammar to Standard English. Stockdale writes, 'Penrice which is two miles from St Austell, is an antient mansion, but has lately undergone a complete modernization by its worthy proprietor, Joseph Sawle, Esq.'[14] Note that Cyrus Redding in his *Itinerary of the County of Cornwall* published in 1842 also spells St Austell as 'St Austle' throughout his book, including the appendix listing the turnpike roads, i.e. 'St Austle and Lostwithiel Trust'.[15] It would seem likely that the milestones and house improvements were of the same date, the 1830s.

TREGOTHNAN

Milestones to private estates are a distinctive feature of Cornwall's milestone heritage. They exist at Mount Edgcumbe, Trelowarren, Penrice, Heligan and here on the road to Tregothnan. Tregothnan House has been the home of the Boscowen family since the 14th century. In 1335 John de Boscowen Ros of St Buryan married heiress Johan de Tregothnan and moved from Penzance to Tregothnan. The house was sacked in the Civil War. All that remains of the original house is now the entrance doorway to the kitchen garden. The core of the present house was built in the time of the Protectorate. The date 1652 is carved in stone over the side door.

In 1698, Celia Fiennes approached Tregothnan from Tregony:

> I crossed the water on a long stone bridge and so through dirty stony lanes 3 mile and then I came into a broad coach rode which I have not seen since I left Exeter; so I went 3 mile more to Mr Bescawens Trygoltny (Tregothnan) a Relation of mine; his house stand on a high hill in the middle of a parke with several rows of trees with woods beyond it; the house is built all of white stone like the rough coarse marble and cover's with slate.[16]

The 'dirty stony lanes' were on the line of the

SW884464 Probus 508993

SW876452 St Michael Penkevil 508992

SW868437 St Micheal Penkevil 508990

SW858428 St Michael Penkevil 508989

SX044571
Luxulyan 70915

SX050558
Luxulyan 70916

SX056545
St Austell 506702

SX043593
Luxulyan 70914

SX039609
Luxulyan 70913

SX036621
Luxulyan parish milestone before cleaning and repainting in 2008

SX036621
*Luxulyan after cleaning and repainting in 2008
70912*

Creed and St Just turnpike, which in 1698 was yet to be built, and the 'broad coach rode' must be the ridgeway route to Tregothnan which is now lined by four milestones giving the distance **FROM TREGOTHNAN**. The shape and style of the milestones and their lettering is the same as that used by the Truro Turnpike Trust established in 1754.

In 1811 Edward Boscowen decided to build a new house, and designs for the house and landscaped gardens were drawn up by designer Humphrey Repton. Unfortunately Repton died in 1818. The architect William Wilkins took over, re-facing and re-roofing the old manor house, which was embodied in the new and enlarged Tregothnan family home. In 1821 Edward Boscowen was created Earl of Falmouth.

In 1895, Black's *Guide to Cornwall* mentions 'the long entrance drive opening miles away at Tresillian Bridge'.[17] This drive still exists and runs along the banks of the Tresillian River from a grand entrance gate by Tresillian Bridge. The private drive passes under the public road at Merther Bridge before approaching Tregothnan House through woodland. The long entrance

There are four milestones on the public road to Tregothnan House. All are older than the private drive from Tregothnan Lodge, Tresillian

drive is not shown on C & J Greenwood's 1 inch map of Cornwall in 1827. The four milestones stand, not on the private drive, but on the public road through St Michael Penkevil.

It seems that there was competition between Cornish gentry in the mid 19th century to build the longest serpentine drive. Many of these, including the one at Tregothnan, feature milestones.

LUXULYAN PARISH MILESTONES

On the roads north and south of Luxulyan village there are six similar milestones, three to the north and three to the south. The three milestones to the north are similar to each other and uniform in inscription. The three to the south are more idiosyncratic.

One could speculate that they were all carved by the same person who steadily improved his skills with practice. His first milestone was one mile south of the village, where he missed off the last letter of Luxulyan and had to add it above the main inscription (SX044571). On the second milestone to the south he got the whole name, **LUXUlyAN** in correctly but used lower case **l** and **y** with an upper case **A** and **N** the same size (SX050558). On the third milestone south he put the village name in an arc above the distance, but still had a lower case **y** (SX056545). By the time he started work to the north of the village he had achieved a design everyone was happy with – all capital letters and with the village name in an arc. No proof of this hypothesis exists.

In 1863 Luxulyan was grouped with Fowey, Lanhydrock, Lanlivery, Lostwithiel, Saint Blazey, Saint Sampson, and Tywardreath to form the Tywardreath Highway District.[18] None of the other parishes in this District have milestones, except on the turnpike roads. This suggests that the Luxulyan milestones were set up before 1863.

The Treffry Viaduct (SX057572) was built between 1839 and 1842 by J. T. Treffry to

131

SW910576
My Lord's Road,
St Enoder 71309

SW917500 Probus

SW915484 Probus

provide a direct rail link between the china clay pits around Bugle and the new port at Par (SX075530). Before the railway was built, china clay wagons with their teams of horses stretched in a single line in front would have been hauled along the parish roads of Luxulyan to meet the Liskeard turnpike at St Blazey Gate. The milestones mark the least hilly route to St Blazey Gate.

THE ROADS TO GRAMPOUND ROAD

The railways brought an end to long distance road travel, but created a need for good local roads. The Cornwall Railway opened through for passengers on 4 May 1859 from Plymouth to Truro, crossing the Tamar by the Royal Albert Bridge, and connecting Cornwall with Plymouth, Exeter and London. A station was opened at High Lane (SW916505) to serve Grampound and, being two miles from the town, was called Grampound Road station. Road traffic feeding the station at Grampound Road prompted the upgrading of the roads to the north and south from parish roads to Main roads, repaired at the county's expense.

The road north from 'Grampound Road to Scarcewater Hill' was proposed to be made Main by West Powder Highway Board to link with the turnpike road network that converged on the neighbouring hamlets of Indian Queens and Blue Anchor, both places named after coaching inns. The road south from 'Stopgap Freewater Hill to Grampound Road railway station' was proposed by Tregony Highway Board. Stopgap (SW911456) was a side gate on the Creed and St Just turnpike at the top of the hill to the west of Tregony.[19]

Both Highway Boards set up milestones as part of the road improvements required for adoption as Main roads by the county. At first sight the two sets of milestones look the same. They are both triangular granite blocks on rectangular bases with cast iron plates carrying the destinations. However, while the Blue

Anchor stones to the north had a conventional triangular pyramid top, the Tregony stones had a massive rectangular top, the same size as the base, a design unique to this road.

At the Blue Anchor end of what is known locally as 'My Lord's Road' there is a guide stone giving directions to **GRAMPOUND ROAD** and to **TRURO** (SW910575).

There are now only three surviving milestones on the road north to Blue Anchor, and only the one in Grampound Road had a surviving cast iron plate. On the road south to Tregony all four milestones survive and the stone nearest Grampound Road has both its original plates. These plates were used as patterns to cast new iron plates for the other three milestones in the series in 2011, so the Tregony milestones now look as they did in 1890.

Responding to the publicity for the re-plated Tregony milestones, local resident Mike Hearn

New cast iron plates for the milestones north of Grampound Road

SW918469 Probus

SW911456 Tregony

SW920534 Ladock

SW920518 Ladock

SW915504 Ladock

SW916549 Ladock.
Too late to have new plates. This milestone was
destroyed by a vehicle collision in 2007.

dug out a mile plate from one of the Blue Anchor milestones which he had picked up at the roadside many years ago. With this as a pattern, new plates were cast for the three milestones

GUIDE STONES

There is a line of granite guide stones along the network of lanes north of St Ewe churchtown running from Mevagissey on the coast to Grampound. No two stones are the same. Inscribed place names are usually broken in two in a variety of ways. The surviving stones are in several parishes and cross the boundary between two Highway Districts. It is possible that these are the survivors of a wider network of guide stones in this area.

SX011463 Granite guidestone St Austell
478860 and a remarkable cast iron fingerpost
made by Charlestown Foundry

Taking the stones in order from east to west:

SX011463 near Tregiskey Farmhouse is a rectangular stone with inscription on three faces – **TO GRAM POUND** has the **GRAM** in an arc; **TO MEVAG ISSEY** has **MEVAG** in an arc; **ST AUST ELL** is in straight lines. Sharing the site is a cast iron fingerpost with a single arm. It has a three dimensional pointing hand and a serrated top edge to the arm, identifying the maker as Charlestown Foundry.

SW991471 is the most elaborate stone in this group. It is triangular with concave cut outs at the top corners. There are inscriptions on all three faces – **GRAMPOND AND TREGONY** has Grampond without a **U**, **GRAMPOND** arcing above **AND**, with **TREGONY** in a concave arc below. **MEVAGIS** arcs above a straight **SEY** to read Mevagissey. **ST** is above an arcing **AUSTELL**.

SW984471 is rectangular, partly buried in the bank. It has inscriptions on two adjacent faces – **ST EWE** and **GRAM POUND**. The end of a metal bolt surrounded by three holes on the top suggests that a wooden fingerpost may have been mounted on the stone in the past.

SW972473 near Trudgian Farm is triangular, set against a low stone hedge. Inscriptions on two faces read – **GRAMP OUND** below a benchmark with a metal pin on the top face, and **St AUSTE LL** in three lines.

SW957473 is a misshapen rectangular block with inscriptions visible on two adjacent faces. The left edge shows considerable traffic damage, which may explain why the A of St Austell has perhaps been re-carved above the main name – **ST A USTELL** has a benchmark below. The adjacent face has **TO GRAM POUND and TREG** with the **ONY** possibly buried. Before it was repainted, some had read this as **TO GRAM POUND AND TRURO**.[20] The carved inscription is very faint. This stone is a few hundred yards east of the toll house at Fair Cross.

SW953469 is south of Fair Cross. This is another misshapen block with four sides but a triangular pyramid top. It had inscriptions on three faces, but indented areas show where most of the inscriptions have been chiselled off. This was probably done in 1940 as a wartime defence measure. The remaining inscriptions read – **TO** blank line **NT** blank line; **TO** blank line **AND** blank line; **TO** blank line above a benchmark. At present no information about the missing inscriptions has been found.

Three guide stones have been identified further south in Veryan parish.

SW932410 is rectangular with two adjacent

SW991471
St Ewe 71506

SW991471
St Ewe 71506

SW984471
St Ewe 71505

SW972473
St Ewe 71504

SW957473
Grampound 71535

SW953468 B3287
Cuby

SW932410 Veryan

SW932404 Veryan

SW924401 Veryan

SW908445
Tregony GONE

dressed sides. A faint inscription on one face may read **S AUSTL**.

SW932404 is rectangular with three dressed faces. Photographs taken in the 1960s by a local resident show inscriptions **Gorran** on the left face, **Austle**, **Tregony** and **Truro** on the front face and **Veryan** on the left face.

SW924401 is rectangular with two adjacent dressed sides. The front edge has been damaged by turning vehicles.

One guidestone stands on the road to Fowey surrounded by hoardings (SX087582). It needs pointing hands but none can be traced on the stonework. Note that the Fowey road is to the left side of the stone and the Par road is to the right of the stone.

One more guide stone used to stand on the 1920s stretch of A3078 west of Tregony, at SW908446. It marked where two adjacent private drives left the public road through one gateway and promptly divided. The stone was a narrow isosceles triangle in plan, with a pyramid top and a rectangular base. It was neatly dressed and carved in very small writing to read **TRELASKER** on the left face and **TREWARTHENICK** on the right face. Sadly, in 2002, only the rectangular base remained. The triangular section had been snapped off, presumably by a vehicle cutting the corner too sharply.

SX087582 B3269
Lanlivery 70760

CHAPTER NINE

LISKEARD AND LOOE

Liskeard is a considerable town, situated on the side and at the foot of a rocky hill, and is one of the oldest in the county, having been made a free borough by Richard, Earl of Cornwall, in 1240.[1]

While Liskeard's importance through the centuries cannot be denied, the principal road to Liskeard has changed more times than for any other Cornish town. The 17th century route from the Devon border to Liskeard ran through Callington. In the 18th century the Liskeard Turnpike Trust built a link to the Cremyll Ferry at the mouth of the Tamar. It was the road to the ferry at Torpoint which became the main road to Liskeard during the 19th and first half of the 20th century. When a new road bridge at Saltash was built in 1961 the route now designated A38 switched from the Torpoint crossing to Saltash.

PRE-TURNPIKE ROADS

In 1675, John Ogilby mapped the post road into Cornwall from Plymouth, crossing the Tamar at Crimble (Cremyll) Passage. This by-passed Liskeard completely, sending the traveller along the coast as far as Looe and then on to Fowey.[2] Celia Fiennes followed Ogilby's route in 1698, so she gives no mention of Liskeard in her journal. She gives a colourful description of the ferry crossing at Cremyll, which she calls Cribly. This was a route for intrepid travellers only.

> From Plymouth I went 1 mile to Cribly Ferry which is a very hazardous passage, by reason of 3 tydes meeting; had I known the Danger before I should not have been very willing to have gone it, not but this is the constant way all people goe, and saved severall miles rideing; I was at least an hour going over, it was about a mile but indeed in some places, notwithstanding there was five men row'd and I sett my own men to row alsoe I do believe we made not a step of way for almost a quarter of an hour, but blessed be to God I came safely over. [3]

Ogilby does put Liskeard on a secondary route from Exeter to Truro which he describes as 'an indifferent good road, being everywhere furnished with good inns of accommodation.' This secondary route comes 'over Dartmoor to Tavistock exceeding bad, being hilly, boggy and stony without any accommodation', then across Gunnislake New Bridge (built about 1520) to Callington and St Ive churchtown, then through:

> ...Combrow a small village. A furlong beyond you cross Combrow Water a small river and ascend four furlongs and at the top pass through Merrymeet a small village, 7 furlongs further you cross another small river, whence an easy ascent conveys you to Liscard or Liskerd[4].

Combrow or Coombe Row is an important landmark in trying to trace the roads which were to be turnpiked by the Liskeard Trust, as we shall see.

Gascoyne's map of 1699 shows Saltash on the River Tamar with a network of roads that can be linked to Liskeard, but not on the line of the modern A38. Going west from Saltash and crossing Notter Bridge, (SX384608) Gascoyne shows two ridgeway routes to Liskeard, one through Quethiock and one through Menheniot. Both involve some very steep gradients and both are no more than twisting country lanes today. Gascoyne does not mark Torpoint. It did not exist in 1699.

The 18th Century saw Britain's navy grow to dominate the world's oceans. With it grew a new naval base at Dock on the Devon side of the River

Liskeard from Beloytha Fields, HISTORY OF BOROUGH OF LISKEARD BY JOHN ALLEN, 1856

Market Street, Liskeard.

Tamar. Dock was to become Devonport and to continue as a major naval base into the 21st Century. On the Cornish shore, opposite Dock, a new town began to develop at Tor Point to service and supply the ships anchored in the Hamoaze, as this part of the river is called. At first the area was mainly commercial and industrial, but in 1774, Reginald Pole Carew of Antony House commissioned a grid-based design for the growing town, which can be seen today.

In January 1790 the Carew and St Aubyn families obtained an Act of Parliament for a ferry from Torpoint to the Devon shore. The far-sighted trustees of the Liskeard Turnpike Trust saw the potential to link their town to Torpoint and the growing town on the opposite bank. In 1760 they put a bill before Parliament for a turnpike road from Liskeard to Torpoint and the ancient ferry crossing at Cremyll Passage, and westwards from Liskeard to join the St Austell and Lostwithiel Trust's turnpike to give a route from Plymouth right through to Falmouth where the Post Office sailing packets were based.

Martyn's county map, published in 1748, marks 'Tore Point' and a road much along the line of the modern road from 'Crimble Passage' to Millbrook and beyond. Although this map was published just a few years before the first Liskeard Turnpike Act in 1760, it shows no continuous road to Liskeard from any of the entry points into Cornwall which match a modern road. The Trust tried to improve the existing roads, but later was compelled to map out new routes with better gradients.

THE LISKEARD TURNPIKE TRUST
An 'Act for repairing and widening the road from the east end of West Taphouse Lane, to the borough of Liskeard, and from thence to Coombe Row House; and also the road from the said borough to Crafthole, and from thence to Crimble Passage, Tar-Point, and to St Germans Beacon' was proposed in 1760 (1 GIII c.xxv).[5] West Taphouse Lane was an enclosed section of the pre-turnpike road to Lostwithiel. The same 'east end of West Taphouse Lane' is defined as the end of the St Austell and Lostwithiel Trust's turnpike road set up by Act of Parliament in the same year. The road to Liskeard from the west was more or less the line of the 20th century main road, but was altered considerably by the Dobwalls by-pass of 2009.

Note that the first road mentioned, and by implication the most important proposed route, ran through Liskeard and north-east to Coombe Row in the direction of Callington and Gunnislake New Bridge, the line of Ogilby's 'indifferent good road' from Exeter. To follow the line of the original turnpike, leave Liskeard along Pengover Road, cross the River Seaton on Stony Bridge and climb to Pengover Green to reach the River Tiddy near Coombe Row House. The road through Merrymeet was a late turnpike improvement.

The ferries at Cremyll Passage and Torpoint were rowing boats and a risky undertaking with a carriage. With classic understatement, one traveller described the ferry as inconvenient:

> June 25th 1795: Leskard to Tor-point. Sixteen miles, the shortest way to Plymouth Dock from here. We went by Tavistock to avoid crossing the Hamoaze to Plymouth Docks as it would not be convenient with a carriage.[6]

The road to the ferry crossings at Cremyll Passage and Torpoint went first to Crafthole (SX365542) but there was some concern in 1761 about which was the best route from Liskeard to Crafthole. A Petition was heard on 19 January 1761 in favour of a route through 'Hessingford' (SX307573):

> A petition from High Sheriff, JPs etc. having

occasion to travel the Great Road leading from Liskeard to Crimble Passage.

'To prove the allegations, Mr Joseph Johnson said that he knows the road from Crimble Passage to Liskeard and it is the usual way for both horses and carriages, is thru Hessingford and Crafthole, that he has travelled from Crimble Passage to St Germans to Liskeard; that the road thru Hessingford and Crafthole is the Post Road, that it is nearer and more level then the St Germans road and more easily repaired, though that part that lies between Hessingford Hill and Liskeard is too narrow and cannot properly be amended without buying land.

That the militia in their march from Liskeard to Plymouth went the Hessingford Road, and the carriages, which were pressed to carry the baggage went and returned that way.

That if he was asked the way from Crimble Passage to Liskeard he would direct persons this way and that St Germans is no thoroughfare from Plymouth to Saltash or Looe.

Being asked what judge he was of repairing roads he replied that he used to drive a carriage.

Being asked if the two hills on each side of Hessingford are not the worst on either road, he answered the negative.

Asked if he knew this was the nearest way he answered he judged so but never measured it.

'Mr Thomas Peeke said that he knows the road from Crimble Passage to Liskeard that he never travelled the St Germans road to Liskeard, that the road from St Germans to Crafthole is hilly and bad, that the Hessingford road is more level and easier for carriages, it is the common road and he never knew any person go the St Germans road.

That the road thru St Germans must be round about, that the road from Hessingford to Crafthole is very narrow, there being hardly room for a carriage in some places and a horse cannot pass a carriage.

Is this the Post Road, he said that it was as far as St German's Beacon, which is about 8 miles from Crimble Passage and 2 miles from Crafthole.

'Mr Samuel Way said that the militia used the way thru Hessingford and Crafthole, the St Germans road is not the common road and is more hilly than the road thru Hessingford.[7]

Despite these gentlemen's arguments, the fact that the Hessenford route was longer and there were very steep hills on either side of the Hessenford crossing of the River Seaton seemed to have favoured the St Germans route. However, the turnpike did not follow the line of the modern main road. Greenwood's map of 1827 shows a turnpike route, indicated by a heavily shaded edge to one side of the road, from Crafthole to Polsco (SX360552), over the hilltops to Polbathic (SX348569), past Treboul Cross

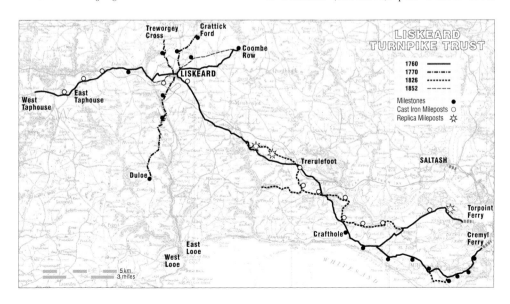

(SX346576) on Barn Hill to 'Trerule Foot', past Bake Lane End (SX323589) on the ridge route north of Wilton and south of Catchfrench Manor, crossing the River Seaton near Tresulgan and then to Maudlin and Liskeard. Only the section from Tresulgan to Maudlin is a modern main road. All the rest of this route is along what are now minor roads. Greenwood also shows as a turnpike a road from Crafthole along the coast to Cargloth then inland to Nackers (SX322599) and north to Bake Lane End where it joins the first road.

OTHER TURNPIKE ROADS

A second Act of Parliament in 1770 (10 GIII c.lxxxvii) added short sections of three roads to other destinations:

Lux Street to Crattick Ford (SX266671), two miles north-east towards Launceston

Bull Post to Treworgey Cross (SX244668), past Woodhill Manor, north towards St Cleer

Barn Street to Duloe Church (SX234581), a road through St Keyne to the south

A NEW ACT AND NEW ROADS

While Greenwood was preparing to publish his 1827 map, the Liskeard Trust had a new Act before Parliament (7 GIV c.lxxiv) to alter and improve much of its route to the Tamar, to form the basis of the modern roads from Trerulefoot to Torpoint and Cremyll Passage. This was 'An Act for more effectually making, repairing and improving certain Roads leading to and from Liskeard, and certain other roads therein mentioned, in the Counties of Cornwall and Devon (5th May 1826).

> And whereas a New Line of Road from Tresulgan Lake (SX297603) to Trerule Foot, in the Parish of St Germans, by the said Act directed or authorised to be made, has been commenced, and a considerable Part thereof has been made, and the making and completing of the whole thereof is now in Progress.

From Tresulgan the original turnpike climbed a very steep hill to reach the ridge route just south of Catchfrench Manor to Trerule Head (SX285588). The new line was to take the same valley route as the modern A38, with sweeping bends to ease the gradients. Road developments from 1967 – the Liskeard by-pass – straightened many of the turnpike's bends and took away several of its cast iron mileposts. As the extract from the Act says, this new road was already under construction in 1826. Greenwood shows both old and new roads.

> And whereas the Road comprised in the said Act leading from Liskeard to Torpoint and Cremill Passage, is in some parts narrow, steep, circuitous and incommodious, and it would be of much Convenience and Advantage to the Public if certain new Pieces of Road were to be made on the Line of the last-mentioned Road; (that is to say), a new Piece of Road diverging from Antony Green (SX400547), through Brockhole, along Whacker Lake (SX375548 to 389550), Trethill, Kerslake, and Sheviock (SX370550), to join the present Road near Stump Cross (SX362550).

Greenwood does not show this new road beside Wacker Lake in 1827, but marks the original turnpike route from Antony climbing south west along the line of the modern B-road to join the other branch of the original turnpike to Cremyll Passage at Tregantle (SX385535).

> A new Piece of Road diverging from Polscove (Polsco SX360553) by the Side of Scanner Lake, through Trewin and Scanner (Sconner SX365564), and along the side of Polbathick Lake, to join the present Road near Polbathick Lime Kilns.

An Ordnance Survey 1 inch map of the 1860s shows the turnpike linking Sheviock and Polsco on the north side of the valley, the present main road. It seems likely that the road builders under the 1826 Act may have built this section to avoid the climb up Horsepool Lane to Stump Cross and then back down again to Polsco. From Polsco to Polbathic lime kilns to Polbathic is the scenic route of the modern A374.

> A new Piece of Road from Polbathick up the Valley, through Treskelly, to join the present Road at Trerule Foot.

Treskelly (SX338575) is on the side of the hill. This new piece of road ran through the grounds of Treskelly and is the valley road section of today's A374 to the Trewhat roundabout.

> A new Piece of Road diverging at or from near Tresulgan Bridge (SX297603) up the Valley, and through North Trevido (SX275622), to join the present Road near the Quarry on the Eastern Side of Cartuther.

This section of road was never built. The modern road follows the route of the original turnpike

> A new Piece of Road diverging from the Farm

at Mount Edgcumbe (SX447526) along the shore of Millbrook Lake, across Inceworth Barton (SX427528), Penhale Lake (Penhale SX416532), and along the Shore of St John's Lake (St John SX408535) to Antony Green.

This ambitious low level route from Cremyll Passage to Antony was never built. The idea was taken up again in the 1852 Act (15 & 16 V c.cxxix) as 'a new line of road from Mount Edgcumbe to Antony Green, which road was authorized to be made by the Act of 1826 but was not made.' It was claimed that this would reduce the distance by a quarter mile to four and a half miles, but the cost of four and a half miles of completely new road was too high, and the Cremyll Ferry lost out to Torpoint.

A new Piece of Road...from and out of the said intended new Piece of Road leading from Polbathic to Trerule Foot, at or near Treskelly (SX338575), to Hessenford (SX307573).

This was the road recommended by the High Sherriff and JPs in their petition.

IMPROVING THE FERRIES
The ferries at Cremyll, Torpoint and at Saltash were all rowing boats until 1829, when a private company was formed at Torpoint and a twin-hulled steam boat was built. However this was not a success as the tides and strong currents were too much for the steam engine. Learning from the problems at Torpoint, the Saltash Ferry laid chains across the river, which passed over vertical wheels on their ferry, to keep it on course and to propel it forwards. A similar floating bridge was installed at Torpoint in 1834 and this became the main crossing point until the late 20th century.

In 1961 a new road bridge was opened at Saltash. This saw the end of the busy ferry at Saltash, but at Torpoint floating bridges still shuttle back and forth taking much of the rush hour commuter traffic to and from Plymouth each day.

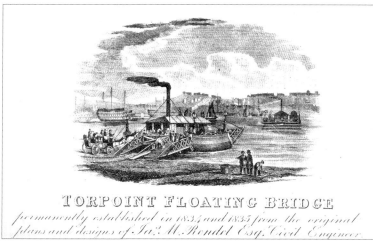

TORPOINT FLOATING BRIDGE permanently established in 1834 and 1835 from the original plans and designs of Jas. M. Rendel Esq. Civil Engineer

TURNPIKE MILESTONES
Milestones were erected following the original turnpike Act of 1761. With each new phase of road improvement new milestones were erected. A great variety of milestones survive, including two groups of cast iron mileposts. Cast iron mileposts are not uncommon in the clay areas of Britain, where good quality stone is hard to find, but in granite-rich Cornwall, cast iron mileposts exist only in east Cornwall.

Taking the roads radiating from Liskeard in order, clockwise starting with the main road from the west:

1. On A390 between Middle Taphouse and East Taphouse is the first cast iron milepost (SX178633). In raised, cast letters, with the place names arching over the distance, it records **Liskeard 5½** and **Lostwith 6**. This shows that mileages on this road were calculated from Lostwithiel. Similar cast iron mileposts stand at 4½ (SX191642) and 3½ (SX205648) miles from Liskeard. They are cast with two flat surfaces at ninety degrees, facing up and down the road, with a rounded top.

There is one stone milestone west of Liskeard. This was removed and reinstated in 2009 when the Dobwalls by-pass was built. It is

Torpoint Floating Bridge, HISTORY OF BOROUGH OF LISKEARD BY JOHN ALLEN, 1856

SX178633 A390 St Pinnock 60599

SX191642 A390 Dobwalls 504558

SX205648 Dobwalls 504559

SX220649 old A38 Dobwalls 61257

SX220649
Dobwalls 61257
Liskeard Trust milestone beside the old turnpike road with the modern bypass thundering past behind.

SX244642
Dean Street, Liskeard
382221

SX244659
Woodhill Manor, Liskeard
382095

on the slip road to the Moorswater industrial estate, immediately east of the bridge over the modern dual carriageway (SX220649). This is 2½ miles from Liskeard and is the only milestone to abbreviate the town's name to **Liskd**.

The original turnpike climbed into Liskeard from Moorswater, just east of Lady Park and entering the town along Old Road. New Road was built by the Liskeard and Looe Union Canal Company in 1831 to improve the link between the head of their new canal at Moorswater and Liskeard. This route was so much better than the original turnpike road that the Turnpike Trust paid a subscription to the Canal Company as so much traffic diverted to it. The road was finally handed over from the Canal Company to the Turnpike Trustees in 1881, just before the turnpike powers expired. [8]

The only cast iron milepost on the Canal Company road stands in Dean Street and records **Liskeard** arching over the distance – **½ mile to the Cross in Church Street**. Below this on the

same face **Torpoint** arches over **17 miles** (SX244642). The right face records **Lostwith 11 miles**. This is the only mile marker referring to **the Cross in Church Street**. Others take their reference point as the Parade, with one measuring from **the church gates**.

2. The road from Bull Post to Treworgey Cross. From the 18th Century until 1905 Liskeard market was held in the Parade, and a Bull Post and Bull Stone, used for tethering bulls for sale, stood where the Fountain is now. The road ran north past Woodhill Manor, where there is a milestone inscribed: **LISKEARD 1 MILE FROM CENTRE OF PARADE** in various sizes of script (SX244659). There were four one mile stones of this design all measuring distance from the centre of the Parade. Three survive.

Treworgey Cross (SX244668) stands on the boundary between Liskeard and St Cleer parishes. The road ahead to St Cleer, past Swallow Cottage, is an untarred track crossing St Cleer Downs. In 1761 it was the main route to St Cleer, but was superseded by a branch from the Launceston Road. The road west from Treworgey Cross leads to Canal Cross (SX237668) where there was a triangular guidestone, incised **LISKd**, **St CLEER** and **CANAL** on its three faces. Turn left, south, at Canal Cross

Canal guidestone near Treworgey manor.
M. J. MESSENGER

The Parade, Liskeard HISTORY OF BOROUGH OF LISKEARD BY JOHN ALLEN, 1856

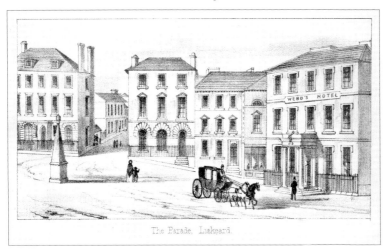

The Parade, Liskeard.

Found buried during excavations for a new house at Lux Cross, this milestone was replaced beside the road by a more elaborate design which has since been lost.

and the road descends to High Wood. From High Wood, the Canal Company built a new road, now a byway, to take traffic to the head of the canal at Moorswater. At the time of writing, the top section of the Canal Cross guidestone is at Treworgey Manor and negotiations are in progress to have it reinstated.

3. The road from Lux Street to Crattick Ford. Lux Street runs north from Market Street, the medieval centre of Liskeard, climbing steeply to cross Castle Street and become Higher Lux Street. At Lux Cross it branches from the Callington road and is designated B3254, the road to Launceston. There used to be another **LISKEARD 1 MILE FROM CENTRE OF PARADE** south of the turn to St Cleer (SX254659). This was listed (Grade II number 382240) in July 1981. It was still in place in November 1993, but has now gone.

In 2012 a builder clearing the site for a new house at Lux Cross uncovered a milestone and set it up in the back garden of the new house. It is inscribed **L 1** and appears to be the original turnpike milestone on the road to Crattick Ford that was replaced by the more elaborate design **LISKEARD 1 MILE FROM CENTRE OF PARADE**.

Crattick or Craddoc Ford is opposite Rosecraddoc Manor Lodge. This is the boundary of Liskeard Parish, marked with a granite boundary stone three feet tall, inscribed **B**. Fifteen yards from the boundary stone is the

original two mile stone of the Liskeard Turnpike Trust, carved with a large **L** for Liskeard and an elaborate, curly **2** (SX265670). There are milestones further north on this road, but they are beyond the reach of Liskeard Turnpike Trust.

4. The road to Coombe Row House and Callington. The Liskeard Turnpike met the Callington Turnpike at Coombe Row House. 'Comberow' is marked on Thomas Martyn's map of 1748 immediately east of the 'Tidi' river. Steart Cottage is now on the site of Coombe Row House. Opposite the entrance to Steart Cottage is a milestone with a sloping front and a rounded top, neatly carved in small, sans serif lettering: **LISKEARD 3 CALLINGTON 5½** (SX294661). The sloping front suggests that this is a Callington Trust milestone.

The original route from Liskeard to Coombe Row House was along Pengover Road, over Stony Bridge and through Pengover Green. This is the turnpike route shown on Greenwood's map of 1827. No milestones have been found on this route.

The modern route, A390, has a milestone (SX263655) near the Tremblaze crossroads above Hendra Bridge. This is inscribed **LISKEARD 1 MILE FROM CENTRE OF PARADE – CALLINGTON 7½** in the same style as the Woodhill Manor stone. This new route corresponds to a description by John Allen in 1856.[9] He writes that the road west from Coombrow was 'lowered' in 1850. This refers to the much improved gradients of the modern route via Merrymeet compared with the original turnpike route over Stony Bridge. This would link with the Renewal Act of 1852 (15 & 16 V c.cxxix). No two mile stone has been found near Merrymeet (SX278659).

5. The road to Torpoint. Cast iron mileposts were erected by the Liskeard Trust on the new line of its road to Torpoint, outlined in the 1826 Act (see above). They should have been in place for the opening of the floating bridge in 1834.

The A38 section of this road, as far as Trerulefoot, lost its cast iron mileposts when the road was made a dual carriageway in the 1960s. Token replacement steel posts were put up beside the westbound carriageway, **Liskeard 6 miles Torpoint 10 miles** at the turn to Catchfrench (SX316596), and **Liskeard 5 miles Torpoint 11 miles** (SX301600) before the Trebrownbridge turn. These rusted away and were replaced in 2005 with two new steel replicas. Unfortunately the opportunity was not

SX265670 B3254 Liskeard 382241

SX265671 B3254 Liskeard boundary stone beside the two mile stone at Crattick Ford.

SX263655 A390 Liskeard 382128

SX301600 A38
Menheniot

SX316595 A38
St Germans 62059

SX261640
Liskeard 503127

Re-erecting the cast iron milepost and parish boundary stone at Maudlin, Liskeard in 2006 SX261640

taken to correct the design or the distances shown, which do not correspond to the surviving original mileposts further east.

The original cast iron half mile post was rescued and re-erected beside a re-erected boundary stone on a new roundabout on the outskirts of Liskeard (SX261540) in 2006. It reads **TORPOINT 16** on one face and **LISKEARD ½ MILE TO THE CHURCH GATES** on the other face. The town names curve over the distance on both faces of the milepost. The back of all the cast iron mileposts is open – they have just two faces. All the survivors on the Torpoint road have pointed tops.

On the A374 between Trerulefoot and Torpoint all the mileposts survive except one.

The milepost in Antony (SX402547) has gone. The milepost opposite St Germans Quay (SX362566) was broken in two, but was welded together by Cornwall County Highways in 1985. The last milepost, one mile from the Torpoint Ferry is a cast replacement made in 1988 (SX429559).

6. The road to Cremyll Passage. The B3247 has a full set of mile stones and two half-mile stones, but they mark the distance to Mount Edgcumbe House not to Cremyll Passage. The stones are tombstone slabs with rounded tops. The inscription is unusual in that it uses lower case lettering, neatly carved, and with the **s** missing from miles to give a West Country accent to the distances, e.g. **4 Mile From Mot Edgcumbe** (SX408528).

Greenwoods 1827 map shows the turnpike climbing steeply from Millbrook towards Mount Edgcumbe. The **2 Mile From Mot Edgcumbe** stone (SX430515) is not on the climb, but just to the west of the point where this road joins the present road line. The 1860s OS 1 inch map shows the turnpike taking a wider sweep from Dadbrook along the present road line. This suggests that the Mount Edgcumbe milestones were erected after 1827 and before 1860.

With the opening of the 'Steam Bridge' at

SX453533 Toll Cottage at Cremyll Passage. The toll board would have filled the false top left hand window.

SX331589 A374
St Germans 62062

SX334575 A374
St Germans 62064

SX347569 A374
St Germans 62111

SX362565 A374
Sheviock 61943

SX360554 A374
Sheviock 61942

SX375548 A374
Sheviock 61944

SX389550 A374
Antony 61664

SX416555 A374
Antony 61667

SX430559 A374
Torpoint

Torpoint, as the floating bridge came to be known, in 1834, the oar driven Cremyll Ferry must have seemed an even more hazardous crossing in comparison.

7. The road from Barn Street to Duloe Church. Barn Street is the road south from the centre of Liskeard. It becomes Station Road, crossing over the A38 by-pass. Beyond the railway station, just before the road starts to drop towards the East Looe River, the toll house now called Tollgate House stands on the west side of the road. Few structural details are visible beneath the rendered surface of the walls, but there are heavy slate frames above the windows facing up and down the road, and a date stone with 1843 in raised numerals. Little more than a

Tollgate House 1843 at SX245634 on the Duloe road. Note the unusual slate inserts above the windows.

SX365543 B3247
Sheviock 61952

SX378535 B3247
Sheviock 61945

SX392529 B3247
Antony 61665

SX408528 B3247
Millbrook 61913

SX419519 B3247
Millbrook 61924

SX430515 B3247
Maker 61725

SX437518 B3247
Maker 61726

SX444520 B3247
Maker 61727

SX447527 B3247
Maker 61774

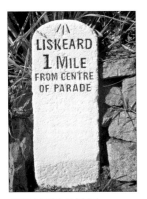

SX244632 B3254
Liskeard 382257

SX244619 B3254
St Keyne

SX241607
St Keyne GONE

SX236579 B3254
Duloe 60685

hundred yards down the hill there is a mile stone: **LISKEARD 1 MILE FROM CENTRE OF PARADE** (SX244632).

The zigzag bend in Lodge Hill and the bends climbing from Trussel Bridge to St Keyne were added to ease the gradient in 1842-3.[10] The two mile stone is just west of Trussel Bridge on a bend on the still steep climb (SX246619). It should read **L II**, but has been carved **L H**. It is a similar shape to the one mile stone.

The three mile stone stood just south of St Keyne church, at the road edge. It was four feet tall with the inscription in large letters – **L 3 M** - one above the other down its front (SX241607). In 2007 only a broken stump remained. The damage suggested a lorry strike had taken off the rest of this elegant milestone.

The four mile stone has not been found, though its location is still marked on the curent 1:25000 OS Explorer Sheet 107. The last milestone is south of Duloe churchtown. This is a sturdy tombstone, lightly carved **LISKd 5 M** (SX236579).

All the surviving milestones are of different designs, suggesting different dates. The style suggests that the one which might date from the first Turnpike Act of 1770 is the one in St Keyne destroyed by a lorry in 2007.

Duloe stands on a high finger of land pointing southwards between the deep valleys of the East and West Looe rivers. Links to any other roads are narrow and very steep. This was not a through route. Nor did it serve a large population. Greenwood's county map shows the turnpike continuing beyond Duloe church as far as Trenant Cross (SX235557), the entrance to Trenance Park, an estate which occupies the whole width of the ridge between the two rivers at this point. In 1770, Trenance Park was owned by Sir John Morshead, a friend of the Prince of Wales. Did he use his influence to have the road to his country estate made a turnpike? Later Morshead fell out of favour at court and sold the property to Sir Edward Buller, a distinguished naval captain, from the Buller family who lived across the East Looe at Morval House. The Bullers were instigators of a number of road improvements around Looe during the early 19th century, on roads that were not turnpikes.

East and West Looe, HISTORY OF BOROUGH OF LISKEARD BY JOHN ALLEN, 1856

NON-TURNPIKE ROADS
ROADS TO LOOE

The early southern route into Cornwall hugged the coast, crossing from East Looe to West Looe on the long, narrow medieval bridge. The bridge had fifteen arches, but was only six feet two inches wide, according to Dr Borlase in his Natural History of Cornwall. The bridge was as important as its north coast contemporaries at Bideford, Barnstaple and Wadebridge, but narrower. Wadebridge was built nine feet wide.[11] A stone on the quay at West Looe records in antique raised lettering that the bridge was **REPEARED BY THE COUNTY: 1689** (SX253534).

It was not the bridge that discouraged early travellers on this southern route but the road itself, filled with steep stony hills and dangerous muddy hollows. Celia Fiennes, riding side-saddle with great skill and experience, found this the hardest road in the west of England in 1698:

> I came down a very steep stony hill to Louu, 13 mile (from Millbrook), and here I cross'd a little arme of the sea on a bridge of 14 arches; this is a pretty bigg seaport, a great many little houses all of stone, from whence I was to ascend a very stormy and steep hill, much worse and 3 tymes as long as Dean Clapper hill, and soe I continued up and down hill. (This was West Looe Hill, the only road out at the time. Dean Clapper Hill, near Ashburton in Devon was described by Mrs Fiennes as very steep and made of bare rock steps. It was the standard by which she judged West Country hills.)

Things did not get better:

> Here indeed I met with more inclosed ground and soe had more lanes and a deeper clay road,

SX332570 A387
St Germans 62063

SX319574 A387
St Germans 62060

SX303574 A387
St Martin 60745

SX288576 B3253
Morval 60703

SX265558 B3253
St Martin 60746

which by the raine the night before had made it very dirty and full of water; in many places in the road there are many holes and sloughs where ever there is clay ground, and when by the raines they are filled with water its difficult to shun danger; here my horse was quite down in one of these holes full of water but by the hand of God's providence which has always been with me ever a present help in tyme of need, for giving him a good strap he flounc'd up againe, tho' he had got quite down his head and all, yet did retrieve his feete and got clear off the place with me on his back.[12]

She was following the post route mapped by Ogilby in 1675 through what is still today a maze of steep narrow lanes. Writing in 1842, Cyrus Redding was able to report the improvements to the roads since Mrs Fiennes' visit:

West Looe is situated at the base of a very lofty hill, over which, until a new road was made (A387 Polperro Road), the only outlet to the westward was almost inaccessible, from its steepness. New roads have been made in other directions, and these picturesque towns (East and West Looe) are now easily accessible from Torpoint, Liskeard or Fowey. [13]

MILESTONES TO TORPOINT

The road improvements around Looe were very recent when Cyrus Redding was writing. They predate the replacement bridge, which was built a hundred yards upstream of the old one. The foundation stone was laid on 16 June 1854 and the bridge was completed by the following year. It cost £2,984. [14]

A new and more level road from Looe via St Martin to No Man's Land and also via Sandplace was constructed between 1838 and 1839 chiefly through the exertions of J. Buller Esq. and W. Farwell, clerk[15]. The road, B3253, has

rectangular milestones with rounded tops. They give the distance to Torpoint and continue beyond No Man's Land, and along A387 through Hessenford to the junction with the A374 Trerulefoot to Torpoint turnpike with its cast iron mileposts. All four milestones survive between the A374 junction and Widegates on A387. The 10 mile stone (SX319574) appears to be a replacement, since it is inscribed **TORPOINT 10 MILES**, where all the other surviving milestones have an abbreviated **TORPT**. and no **MILES**. No milestones have been found on A387 beyond Widegates on the road via Sandplace to East Looe. The 13 mile stone at No Man's Land has been lost, and no 15 mile stone has been found on the Looe side of St Martin.

MAIN ROAD MILESTONES

In 1890, three roads put forward by Liskeard Highway Board were recommended to be made Main Roads by the County Council's Highways Committee:[16]

Looe to Liskeard

Looe to Menheniot railway station

Tokenbury Corner to Cradock Ford

The total length is quoted as 11 miles 7 furlongs and 23 poles, but there is only one surviving milestone. The road from 'Looe to Liskeard' and the road from 'Looe to Menheniot railway

SX288576
The milestone at Widegates stands beside a Diamond Jubilee Cross.

145

SX275679 B3254
St Cleer 503493

station' have not been positively identified, and none of the potential routes of these two roads carry milestones.[17] The road from 'Tokenbury Corner to Cradock Ford' is now part of the B3254 Launceston to Liskeard Road. Launceston Highway Board, Callington Highway Board and Liskeard Highway Board all applied to have their section of this road made Main. The Liskeard section ran from Cradock Ford, where the 2 mile stone marks the limit of the Liskeard Turnpike Trust, to Tokenbury Corner high on Fore Down, the boundary of St Cleer Parish, which was part of the Liskeard Highway Board's district. Just over two miles of road were to be made Main, so two milestones were required. Sadly the milestone on Fore Down disappeared some years ago and only the 3 mile stone near Higher Roscraddoc survives (SX275679). While the same size and shape as other 1890 milestones on B3254, the Liskeard Highway Board milestone and the Callington Highway Board milestones carry only the distance to Liskeard, while all the Launceston Highway Board milestones further north on the same road have distances to Liskeard and Launceston.

GUIDESTONES BETWEEN LOOE AND FOWEY

The roads between West Looe and Fowey have the most wonderful collection of guide stones to survive in the county. There are no guide stones in the parish of West Looe, but the parishes of Lansallos, Lanteglos, Lanreath, St Veep and Pelynt have eighteen.

All are square or rectangular in cross section with flat tops. Width and thickness is almost always between 10 and 12 inches. The style of inscription varies in quality, but is usually in Roman capitals with serifs. Spelling and abbreviations vary between guide stones. Looe is always spelt the same way, but Fowey can also be Fowe and Foy. One stone has Fowe on the front and Foy on the back. Two stones show evidence of re-facing. Eleven of the stones give distances, sometimes in Roman numerals, sometimes in Arabic numerals. One stone has Arabic numerals on two faces and Roman numerals on a third face. Two stones have pointing hands, but the general rule is that the inscription faces the place inscribed. In other words, if you are facing the inscription, the place will be behind you.

At first it was thought that the guidestones marked the Post Road described by Ogilby in his strip maps of 1675. Paul White traced out the post boys' route using Ogilby's map and accompanying note.[18] Half a dozen guide stones lie on the route, but others lie a mile or more to the north or south. The condition of most of the stones and the style of inscription suggests a 19th century date, with some being earlier than others, possibly later 18th century. By this time the post road would have been superseded by the east to west turnpike through Liskeard.

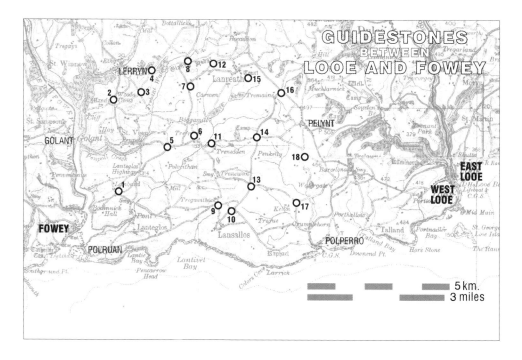

Moved to Polperro in 1940 to direct invaders over the cliff … Returned to Longcross in 2008. Lansallos 508369

In a farmyard since 1945… Returned to Bake Cross in 2008. Pelynt 508368

Placed upside down in a field in 1940… and still there!

All the guide stones are on minor roads. None are on A or B class roads. Not every road junction has a guide stone, but the pattern of surviving stones suggests that some have been lost down the years, rather than an original plan to sign only certain junctions.

In 1940, milestones and guide stones were removed, defaced or buried during the period after the Dunkirk evacuation when invasion by German forces was expected. Some guide stones never returned. Local knowledge shared with the author following a talk on milestones showed where three of the missing guidestones had gone. In the area between Looe and Fowey, three guidestones were out of position, presumably where they had been moved in 1940. One stone stood beside the road west out of Polperro (SX204510), but directed invading troops towards Looe to the south over the cliff and out to sea. After careful research, this guide stone was returned to its pre-war location at Long Cross (SX185530) in 2008. Another stone had been used as a gatepost in a farmyard near Pelynt. Research showed that it once stood at Bake Cross (SX186545). Negotiation with the farmer and the offer of a replacement granite gatepost saw this guide stone returned to bake Cross in 2008. A third guidestone was located upside down in the middle of a field in Lanreath (SX184569). Attempts to return this stone to its original location have not been successful.

The clue to the origin of the guide stones lies in their location in just five adjoining parishes. It seems most likely that the highway boards of the five parishes co-ordinated their efforts to way-mark the roads in their parishes by erecting

1. *SX137527*
Lanteglos 60594

2. *SX137560*
St Veep 504621

3. *SX146561*
St Veep 60610

4. *SX150568*
St Veep 60609

5. *SX157543*
St Veep 505803

6. *SX165545*
Lanreath 60542

7. *SX163564*
Lanreath 506697

8. *SX162572*
Lanreath 60541

9. *SX174523*
Lansallos 61472

10. *SX178522*
Lansallos 61467

11. *SX171543*
Lansallos 61473

12. *SX172571*
Lanreath 60540

13. *SX185530*
Lansallos 508369

14. *SX186545*
Pelynt 508368

15. *SX184569*
Lanreath

16. *SX196562 B3259 Pelynt 61619*

17. *SX200525*
Lansallos 61474

18. *SX203540*
Pelynt 61618

similar but not identical guidestones. The parishes to the north – St Winnow, Boconnoc, Braddock, Warleggan and Cardinham – have no guide stones, but they joined with the five parishes in 1863 to form the Trecan Highway District. This suggests that the guide stones were erected by the five parishes before 1863.

A journey to see the guide stones would take a curious traveller along some of the most picturesque roads in Cornwall. The sunken lanes and steep hills may be narrow and muddy in places, but the holes and sloughs filled with enough water to lose a horse are no longer a problem.

CHAPTER TEN

SALTASH AND CALLINGTON

SALTASH

The Valletorts of Trematon kept a ferry at 'Esse', the old name for Saltash, following the Norman Conquest, though there is evidence that the crossing is older than this.

In October 1356 the Black Prince, as Lord of Trematon, rewarded his porter, William Lenche, for his good service in the Battle of Poitiers, where Lenche had lost an eye, with a lease for life of the Passage of Saltash.[1]

In 1722 Daniel Defoe found the ferry crossing hazardous: 'The Tamar here is very wide, and the ferry boats bad, so that I thought myself well escap'd when I got safe on shore in Cornwall.'[2] The ferry overturned and sank with the loss of twenty lives in 1733.

In 1794, W.G.Maton found the road from the ferry so steep he had to walk his horse up: 'Saltash is situated in the declivity of a very steep hill, though the principal street, it is not easy to ascend on horseback'.[3] The principal street, Fore Street, was too steep for wheeled traffic even to descend, and horse drawn vehicles used to turn off along 'Back Lane' now called Culver Street to reach the foreshore along Tamar Street.[4]

THE SALTASH TURNPIKE TRUST

In December 1761, the 'Mayor, Burgesses and inhabitants of Saltash and gents travelling the

Saltash, River Tamar from the steep slope of Fore Street

road' sent a petition to Parliament about the 'ruinous, incommodious and dangerous' roads leading to the town. This was the standard procedure to establish a new turnpike trust and the Act was obtained. (2 GIII c.xliii)

The main route to be turnpiked was from Trerulefoot, where it joined the existing Liskeard

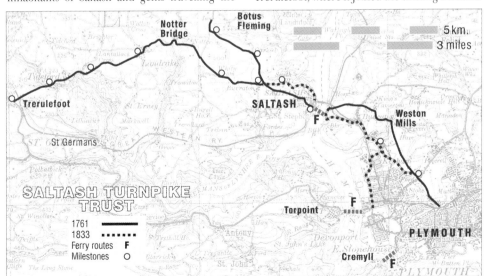

SALTASH TURNPIKE TRUST

1761 ——
1833 ••••••••
Ferry routes   F
Milestones   O

BST - Boundary of Saltash Trust. SX431586 Coombe Road &Culver Street, Saltash

Saltash Ferry from the Devon bank. By J Nixon, engraved by Lacy, published by J Asperen, Cornhill 1821. CORNISH STUDIES LIBRARY

turnpike, past 'Pole-marking' (Polmarkyn) over Heskin Bridge through 'Tiddeford' (Tideford) and Landrake over Notter Bridge to Boraton Lane End in the parish of St Stephen's next Ash (Ash was Saltash) to Culver Park Gate in Back Lane in the Borough of Saltash. There is a granite boundary stone at the junction of Coomb Road with Culver Street in Saltash carved with the initials **BST** for Boundary of the Saltash Trust (SX431586). This marks the limit of the turnpike along what was called Back Lane, avoiding the steepest part of Fore Street which was too steep for carriages.

After crossing Saltash Passage on the ferry, part of the western bank of the Tamar was until 1894 still in Cornwall, and the proposed turnpike ran 'from Saltash Passage thru' St Stephen's next Ash to Weston Mills in the Parish of St Budeaux by Swilly in Parish of Stoke Damerell to the corner of the meadow at the east end of the bridge by the Lower Grist Mill in Borough of Plymouth' which is near the present Central Library. This original road to Plymouth can be picked out from old maps. It climbed straight up the bank, heading due east from the ferry along what is now called Normandy Way, but which was called Passage Road.[5] This linked to Peters Park Lane. There was a milestone where Peters Park Lane becomes Weston Mill Road, labelled 'Saltash 1½' on the 1907 Ordnance Survey map, but no longer to be found. Weston Mill Road leads to Weston Mill Hill and the site of Weston Mill toll house by the Mowhay Road turn.[6] From the toll house, the turnpike ran along what was called Old Saltash Road, but is now North Prospect Road, to what was the entrance drive to Swilly House, then

along Alma Road to the Pennycomequick roundabout where there was another toll house.[7] It climbed the steep hill called Saltash Road to May's Cross, now called North Cross, and along Cobourg Street to the corner of a meadow which is now Drake's Circus.

Back on the Cornish side of the Tamar, the road to the parish church of Saltash which was outside the Borough of Saltash was to be a turnpike – 'from North Stile of Churchyard of St Stephen's next Ash by Cowders to the almshouses of Borough of Saltash'. This is now called St Stephens Road. The almshouses were at the west end of Fore Street.

The road to Callington and Launceston was also to be a turnpike for almost three miles – 'from Borraton Lane end thru' Carkeil in Parish of St Stephen's next Ash thru' Fighting Cocks in Parish of Botus Fleming.'

The first milestone on the road west, at Burraton Lane end (SX412594) is dated 1765. The western route took as its starting point an archway across the western end of Fore Street. Greenwood's 1 inch map of Cornwall, published in 1827, marks T.B. for toll bar at this point.

IMPROVING THE FERRY AND THE TURNPIKE

The steep approaches to both sides of the ferry at Saltash Passage were a deterrent to traffic. The new ferry crossing at Torpoint had easy approaches on both banks. When the Torpoint Ferry purchased a steam ferry boat in 1829, the worthies at Saltash knew they had to respond. A private consortium obtained an Act of Parliament in 1832 enabling them to purchase the ferry rights from Saltash Corporation and establish a steam powered 'floating bridge' (2 & 3 WIV c.VII). The 'floating bridge' was linked to two traction chains which ran from bank to bank along the river bed. The chains were picked up and ran over two steam driven cogged wheels on the vessel which pulled it across the river. The new vessel was constructed under the direction of J. M. Rendel, who had pioneered the chain traction ferry at Dartmouth.[8]

The new Turnpike Act was passed in the following year (3 & 4 WIV c.v 29 March 1833). This improved the road on the Plymouth side of the Tamar by building a 'New Line of Road' from Saltash Passage to 'near to the present entrance to Swilly House in the parish of Stoke Damerell'. The key feature of this new road, today called Wolseley Road for the whole of its length, was the new wooden bridge over Weston Mill Lake,

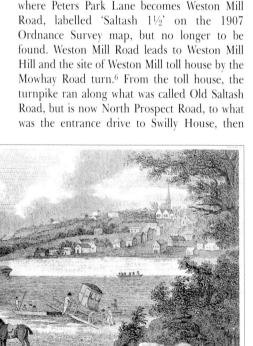

The Tamar road bridge at Saltash replaced the ferry at the same crossing point in 1961

which allowed a much lower crossing of the Weston Mill valley and greatly reduced the distance to the Borough of Plymouth. From the end of Wolseley Road the existing turnpike was followed to May's Cross where the turnpike now ended. The old road was dis-turnpiked between Ham Lodge (the junction of Peters Park Lane and Weston Mill Road) and 'a place called the Commons' in St Budeaux parish.

There was a toll house at St Budeaux (SX447581) and at Union Gate (SX455571).[9] Union Gate was where a new turnpike was built to link Morice Town and the Torpoint Ferry to Saltash Passage. This started at Union Terrace in Morice Town, which was on the corner of Albert Road and Keyham Road, and crossed Keyham Lake just north of the modern St Levan Road turn. There was a turnpike gate on the north shore of Keyham Lake, marked 'Keyham TP' on Ordnance Survey 25 inch to 1 mile map of 1889.

New milestones were set up, measuring their distance from May's Cross. Two survive to an unusual cylindrical design. The **1 MILE FROM PLYMOUTH** stone is just east of the Ford roundabout (SX465563) behind some railings on the north side of the road. The **2 MILES FROM PLYMOUTH** stone stands in Wolseley Road (SX453572). It has been painted black with white lettering by a local resident. A three mile stone stood just west of St Budeaux station[10] and a two mile stone stood near the Careswell Avenue turn on the Old Saltash Road (SX458576).[11]

On the Cornwall bank of the Tamar, a new

road was also constructed. The 1833 Act proposed 'to make a New Line of Road from the Western Landing Place of the Floating Bridge across the River Tamar, lying on the southward of Ash Tor Rock, to the place in the parish of St Stephen's next Ash (or Saltash) where the present Turnpike Roads leading to Liskeard and Callington join, commonly called Borraton Lane End'. A visitor to Saltash in the 1840s found the town rather mean, but praised the new road: 'The town of Saltash consists of one main street, so steep that a carriage cannot go up or descend. At the bottom of this principal street a mean-looking cross-street runs parallel with the Tamar. At the northern extremity the ferry-boat lands its passengers from the Devonshire side. A turnpike leads from the ferry along the river for some distance, perfectly level, and falls into the Callington and Launceston road'.[12] This was known as New Road until the Saltash road bridge was built in 1961 after which it changed its name to Old Ferry Road.

A milestone stands one mile from the ferry landing on New Road (at SX421594) inscribed **I mile To S**. Milestones on the Callington road at two miles, 200 yards north of the roundabout at the southern end of Carkeel, inscribed **II miles To S** (SX412603), and at three miles, south of Hatt, in the hedge on a fast bend, repeatedly shattered by heavy traffic (SX398611), were reset to match the route along New Road.

Milestones on the Liskeard road still took their starting point as the archway at the west end of Fore Street. This anomaly meant travellers to Liskeard using the easy ascent of New Road from the ferry passed two one mile stones, half a mile apart. Both the one mile stone in New Road and the one mile stone at Burraton Lane End have the same style of inscription, with the addition of the date, 1765, on the Burraton Lane End stone.

*SX465563
Ford Roundabout,
Devonport*

*SX453572
Wolsely Road,
Devonport*

*SX421594 New Road,
Saltash 503135*

*SX412603 A388
Saltash 60413*

*SX398611 A388
south of Hatt, Saltash
60414*

SX412594
Saltash 60447

SX398598 A38
Saltash 60450

SX372604
Landrake 62034

SX357600 A38
Landrake 503273

SX343595 A38 St
Germans 430028

SX328588
St Germans 62061
This unique Saltash
Trust Boundary stone at
Trerulefoot gives the
exact distance to the
nearest pole and yard.

The second milestone on the Liskeard road, the A38 trunk road, is in a lay-by on the north side of the road (SX398598). It is inscribed **2 M S**. The third milestone just east of Notter Bridge is missing. The fourth milestone is in the garden wall of a house in Landrake (SX373604) and is inscribed **4 M S**. The fifth milestone (SX357600) is inscribed **V miles To S**, in a style matching both of the one mile stones. The sixth mile stone has lost its **VI** which has been re-carved with an Arabic **6** to read **6 miles To S** (SX344597). The seventh milestone should be at Trerulefoot, but at the junction with the original Liskeard turnpike, now south-west of the modern Trerulefoot roundabout, set into the north bank, is a tall stone marking the boundary of the Saltash Turnpike Trust (SX328588). It gives the exact distance to the archway in Fore Street in miles, poles and yards – **7M 22P 1Y S B**, which is 7 miles 122 yards. Turnpike boundary stones are rare survivors in Cornwall, and this is a splendid example.

Before moving north to examine the area around Callington, there is one more stone which should be mentioned. This is a mile stone in the literal sense, since it does have the mileage to Landrake carved into its surface, but it is more properly described as a parish boundary stone.

On the lane to Lantallack, built into the parapet of a bridge over the stream which marks the boundary between the parish of Landrake with St Erney and the parish of St Germans, two dressed stones sit side by side to form the top half of a regular octagon. The left hand stone is inscribed **L 1½** and the right hand stone carries a large benchmark (SX354602).

GUIDE STONES

To the west of Callington is a collection of guidestones picking out routes much older than the turnpikes.

There is a granite guidestone in the hamlet of Gang (SX308682) a mile north of St Ive. The stone is not at a crossroads in Gang, but is set back from the road, opposite Gang Cottage. The stone has four irregularly shaped faces with inscriptions on three. The lettering is so large that the words on each face are broken into three or four fragments down the column, making them difficult to read at first. Joining the fragments together, the stone reads: **S - GER - MA - NS**, **CAL - LING - TON**, **LAUN - CES - TON**. Callington is four miles to the east of Gang and Launceston is ten miles to the north, while St Germans is a small village eight miles to the south.

SX354600 Parish boundary stone and milestone
Landrake 61999

SX308682 Guidestone at Gang, St Ive 50345.
The road to St Germans once ran through where
the barn now stands.

SX304687
St Ive 61345

SX301698
Charaton Cross, St Ive
61359

SX302740
Halwinnick Butts,
Linkinhorne 62148

SX318679 A390
Keason, St Ive 61359

There was a road junction here until at least 1880. It is marked on the First Series 6 inches to 1 mile Ordnance Survey map, which shows that there was a road branching from the lane on which the guidestone stands. The road ran behind the stone and southwards, not to St Ive Churchtown, but to St Ive Cross. The line of this lost road can be traced today by the line of the field boundaries. Beyond St Ive Cross it becomes a narrow lane, but a lane that can be followed almost all the way to St Germans.

Eight hundred yards north of Gang there is a fork in the road near Redland Farm, where another roughly shaped granite guidestone (SX304687) gives directions in a similar style to **RED - GAT - E**, **S - GER - MA - NS** and **LAN - CES - TON**. Taking the Launceston direction from here, a narrow lane comes to Charaton Cross in less than a mile where there is a third guidestone(SX301698), inscribed **S - GER - MAN - S**, **CAL - LING - TON**, **LAUN - CES - TON** and **LISK – EARD**. There is no guidestone at the next crossroads, but cross the River Lynher on the medieval Plusha Bridge and head northwards following the ridge of the land to the crossroads at Halwinnick Butts and here is another stone (SX302740), carved on four sides: **LAU - N - CES - TON**, **CAM - EL - FOR - DE**, **RED - GAT - E** and **LIS - KEA - RD**.

There is one more guidestone in this group. Going back to Gang and taking the turn east towards Callington, in just under a mile the hamlet of Keason is reached. The guidestone at the junction with the A390 (SX318679) reads: **LA - UN - CES - TON**, **LIS - KEA - RD** and **CAL - LIN - GT - ON** on three of its four sides.

Joel Gascoyne's map of Cornwall, published in 1699 shows relatively few roads. It shows the road from St Germans northwards all the way to Launceston. The road passes through St Ive Cross, not the churchtown. This is clear because the map is marked 'Cross' at the crossroads, and depicts a church with a spire to the west labelled 'S:IVE'. The road passes the location of the first guide stone at a place called 'Gang' where there is a turning in the direction of Callington. The next place north is called 'Redland', where the second guidestone stands. Then the road passes 'Charriton' where the third guidestone stands.

The guidestones and Gascoyne's map mark a route which probably pre-dates the Norman Conquest. It links the Anglo-Saxon priories of St Stephens at Launceston and St Germans, which was the residence of a Bishop until 1943. In the Middle Ages St Stephens Monastery was the richest in Cornwall and Launceston Castle was the headquarters of the Earl of Cornwall, while St Germans was an important port.

Another name shown on two of the guidestones is Red Gate. This is a crossroads on the southern edge of Bodmin Moor (SX227685) and was a landmark on the ancient road west to Bodmin and Lostwithiel.

When leaving Cornwall at the end of his visit in 1755, William Wynne and his family passed Red Gate in their coach on the way from Bodmin to Tavistock in Devon.

The next morning we left this place and passed by Red Gate which is a single tolerable Inn about 10 miles there are some tin works on these Downes. About 6 miles further we saw Kellaton or Callington on our right, a large Market town and a burgess town... and then

Callington,
CYRUS REDDING 1842

153

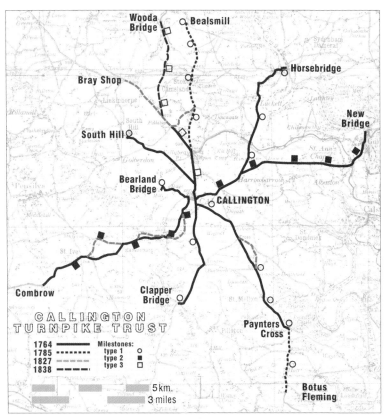

CALLINGTON
TURNPIKE TRUST

1764	———	Milestones:	
1785	····	type 1	○
1827	– – –	type 2	◇
1838	— —	type 3	□

5 km.
3 miles

* Thro St Ive to Combrow. (Coombe Row Bridge was the end of the Liskeard Turnpike.)
* From Seven Stones on Hingston Down to the West end of Horsebridge. (This was to bring Devon traffic crossing the Tamar at Horsebridge into Callington.)
* To Watergate in the parish of South Hill. (This road was used by local traffic from South Hill. A milestone north of Manaton Mill marks the end of this turnpike – **2Mls 6Fur** from Callington (SX331721).)
* To Bearland Bridge, (This little lane due west of Callington has a milestone near the bridge giving the distance to Callington as **6 Furlos 25 Poles** (SX346700).)
* Over Hingston Downs to Calmady's Shop. (This is the road north-west from Callington. The toll house at Calmady's Shop is now called Camelot (SX351724).)
* By Brendon Tree over Viverdon Down thro' St Mellion to Penters Cross in Pillaton parish. (This road south-east from Callington was to become the main road to Saltash. It was considerably re-aligned in the 1990s.)
* To Clapper Bridge. (This was the road due south from Callington. It is still called St Germans Road. Two of its original three milestones survive.)

1785 IMPROVEMENTS
The main traffic was on the east to west route, from Tavistock to Liskeard, but the north to south route, parallel with the Devon border had problems because it did not link with the neighbouring Turnpike Trusts. The renewal Act of 1785 (25 GIII c.cvi) extended the road   south

Toll Cottage, Bealsmill, Callington Trust, undergoing renovation in 2010. SX358769

passed over the river Tamar a very good stone bridge into the County of Devon to a place called Horsebridge though big enough for Coaches or any other Carriage to pass over Conveniently.'[13]

Note that the road Wynne followed by-passed Callington completely. He misunderstands the derivation of Horsebridge. It does not mean a bridge suitable for horses, but is a corruption of 'Hautes Brygge', the name used in an Indulgence of 1437, possibly from the French 'haute' for high.[14]

BCT - Boundary of Callington Trust, Bealsmill.SX359769

CALLINGTON TURNPIKE TRUST
It was in 1764 that an Act enabling the Callington Turnpike Trust to be set up was passed (4 GIII c.xlviii). The Trustees decided to go for every road leading out of the town:
* Over Hingston Down to the West end of Tavistock New Bridge. (This was the road east to Devon. New Bridge, across the Tamar at Gunnislake, was built by Sir Piers Edgcumbe in about 1520. Hingston Down was unenclosed in the mid-eighteenth Century, though there was considerable mineral extraction.)

from Paynters Cross to Fighting Cocks, Botus Fleming to meet the Saltash turnpike, and north through Stoke Climlsland to meet the Launceston turnpike at Beals Mill. A hundred yards south of the bridge at Beals Mill is the Callington Trust Boundary stone (SX359769). The bridge and its approaches were maintained by the County, so this stone marked the limit of the Trust's responsibility. A similar distance to the north of Beals Mill Bridge is a stone inscribed with the letter **C** for County, marking the division of responsibility between Cornwall County and the Launceston Turnpike Trust. The Callington toll keeper's cottage is south of the boundary stone on the west side of the road (SX358769).

PUT-ON AND TAKE-OFF STONES

On the Liskeard road the hills were so steep that vehicles would hire an extra horse to help them climb up. The horse was only added for the climb and was not subject to a toll. Travelling away from Callington, the worst climb was from New Bridge. A stone beside the original road, by the entrance to Cadson Farm (SX340679) is inscribed **TAKE OFF**. Here, horses hired from the toll gate keeper at New Bridge would be unhitched and sent back.

A **PUT ON** stone stands at the end of the parapet over the stream east of Coombegate Cottage (SX321672) on the line of the original Callington to Liskeard road. This allowed an extra horse to be put on when tackling the long steep climb towards Callington. The climb

Newbridge, Callington

westwards to St Ive Cross and Liskeard was also long, but not quite as steep. The climbs in both directions at Newbridge and at Coombegate made this a hard road to travel.

IMPROVEMENTS 1827 (7&8 GIV C.CI)

The renewal Act passed on 14th June 1827 proposed twenty 'new pieces of road'. Most of these were minor alterations to improve the gradient. For example, on the road north towards Launceston there was to be a 'New Piece of Road passing through part of Dighouse Farm near Beal's Mill Turnpike Gate in the Parish of Stokeclimsland.' The new road cuts across the corner of a field.

Some of the new sections were more major:

*   A new route was proposed to climb the hill from 'Tavistock New Bridge' which passed between the existing road and the River Tamar and 'through Gunnis Lake Mining Ground' to the Cornish Inn.
*   On the Saltash road a new line 'diverging from Mewsland Green through Tipwell Farm and along the edge of Viverdon Common to join the present road at Kiln Lane End' skirted the side of Viverdon Hill rather than climbing straight over the top.
*   There were to be nine 'New Pieces of Road' on the Liskeard road under the 1827 Act, including the approaches to both sides of New Bridge and a major diversion to Keason to avoid the steep hills on either side of Coombegate. This left both the **TAKE OFF** and the **PUT ON** stones on narrow, quiet lanes, as reminders of the challenges of the original route.

New Bridge on the Tamar,
CYRUS REDDING 1842

TAKE OFF SX340679
St Ive 61355

PUT ON SX321672
Coombegate, St Ive

WHEEL ROAD TO CALLN SX347679
Callington 61241

The old road from Liskeard down the hill to New Bridge survives as a green lane designated a public footpath.[15] It starts near the milestone by the junction of Werrington Drive and Liskeard Road (SX355688), inscribed **4? Furlongs to Callington Market Gate L 8**. In New Bridge hamlet, the new road ran downstream in front of the original toll house before turning to climb the hill towards Callington by the county bridge stone. Its route 'through an orchard at the back of Jasper's House near New Bridge Toll Gate' is marked by a stone against the wall of what is now called 'Cobbledick's Cottage'. The stone is inscribed **WHEEL ROAD TO CALLN** (SX347679).

The shorter, steeper route, along the green lane, was still used by pedestrians, while wheeled traffic took advantage of the new easier gradient. The old turnpike road from Newbridge to Callington is now a footpath

- Two existing roads were made turnpikes in 1827: the road 'at or near the Toll Gate at Calmady's Shop to a certain place called Bray's Shop' on B3257 towards the Launceston to Bodmin turnpike, and 'from Calmady's Shop to Shutta Green on the Turnpike Road from Launceston to Callington', a link to the road north through Stoke Climsland. There is no evidence of turnpike improvements on either of these roads.

NEW ROUTE TO LAUNCESTON, 1838

The Launceston Trust built a new road southwards under an Act of 1835 (see Chapter 6 Launceston and North Cornwall) and a new

bridge over the River Inny at Wooda Bridge. In 1838, the Callington Trust built a new road, the current A388, to meet the Launceston turnpike at Wooda Bridge, by-passing the Stoke Climsland and Beal's Mill road. The road has gentle gradients and sweeping bends, but is narrow in places, squeezing the milestones to the very edge of the carriageway, where modern traffic races past. The toll house just south of Wooda Bridge, built to service the new road, is now a two-storey roofless ruin (SX347768). It too is at the very edge of the high speed A388.

MILESTONES

Milestones of the Callington Turnpike Trust can be sorted into three groups: 18th Century, after 1827, and after 1838.

The first group have a single letter **C** for Callington and a number showing distance. The three examples on the road through Stoke Climsland to Bealsmill use Roman numerals – **II+C** (SX360729), **III+C** (SX360745) and **IV+C** (SX360760). The two survivors of the original three stones on the road south to Clapper Bridge, the St Germans road, have Arabic numerals – **C 1** (SX360679) and **C 3** (SX352653). The three milestones on the road over Kit Hill to Horsebridge have Arabic numerals – **C 2** (SX383713), **C 3** (SX388728) and **C 4¾ Miles** (SX398748). The last one at 4¾ miles marks the end of the turnpike and is the only one with the word **Miles**. Two other terminal milestones can be placed in this group, with a single letter **C** – marking the end of the turnpike to Bearland Bridge at 6 Furlongs 25 Poles (SX346700), and to Watergate, South Hill at 2 Miles 6 Furlongs (SX331721). The milestones on the road south are measured from Saltash, giving odd half miles to Callington. Only the most southerly of these has an S for Saltash. This milestone, south of Paynter's Cross is on the section of road added in 1785 to meet the Saltash Trust's turnpike at Fighting Cocks (SX398626). On this milestone the **C** is above the distance **5½**. All the others on this road have the distance above the **C**. The **1½ C** stone is missing. On the town side of the toll house which stood at the Dupath turn (SX375685) is the ½ mile stone, which is an elaborately inscribed triangular design (SX365692), giving distances to **Saltash Passage**, **Callington Town Hall** and **Callington Gate** in three different styles on three different faces. Unfortunately the third inscription, to the turnpike south gate, is obscured by a modern garden wall at present.

Toll House south of Wooda Bridge A388 SX347768

SX360729
Stoke Climsland
394455

SX360745
Stoke Climsland
394401

SX360760
Stoke Climsland
393994

SX360679
Callington 503275

SX352653
St Mellion 503274

SX383713
Stoke Climsland
394128

SX388728
Stoke Climsland
393995

SX398748
Stoke Climsland
394156

SX346700 Callington
6 Furlongs 25 Poles.
Callington 61209

SX331721 Callington
2 Miles 6 Furlongs.
South Hill 61438

SX365691 right face.
To Callington Town
Hall Half Mile.
Callington 61211

SX365691 left face. To
Saltash Passage 9 miles

SX386669 old A388
Viverdon, St Mellion
503278

SX389653 A388
St Mellion 61433

SX399642 old A388
Paynter's Cross,
Pillaton 503276

SX398626 A388
Botus Fleming 503279

Callington from the
north. SX362706
A388

SX372700 A390
Callington 503495

SX380705 A390
Hingston Down,
Calstock

SX386708 A390
Calstock 60801

SX402709 A390
Calstock 503497

SX418708 A390
St Anne's Chapel

SX431714 A390
Calstock 503500

A second group of stones, on the roads east and west of Callington, have sloping front faces, and rounded tops. Those on the A390 road to Gunnislake New Bridge give distances to **C** for Callington and **T** for Tavistock with a distinctive square full stop after the initial letter. Those on the A390 road to Liskeard have a more elaborate **C** for Callington and an **L** for Liskeard with distances measured from Liskeard. These stones are on the post 1827 route through Keason. The last stone at Coombe Row (SX294661) is the only one to give destinations in full – **LISKEARD 3 CALLINGTON 5½**.

The third group on the road north to Wooda Bridge are rectangular with a pyramid top, set with one edge to the road, with writing painted but not carved on two adjacent faces. Neglected and largely buried, standing at the very edge of the road, it is surprising that all five of these milestones survive. Distances are measured from **L** for Launceston, so that the **C** for Callington distance has an odd ½ mile.

Neglected and almost buried milestone south of Wooda Bridge SX348765 A388 Stoke Climsland

SX355688
Callington 61210

SX348680 A390
Callington 61244

SX335678 A390
St Ive 61351

SX318679 A390
St Ive 61360

SX307670 A390
St Ive 61352

SX294661 A390
Menheniot 61279

SX360706 A388
Callington 503492

SX354721 A388
Stoke Climsland
394058

SX346734 A388
Stoke Climsland

SX348750 A388
Stoke Climsland

SX348765 A388
Stoke Climsland

THE END OF THE TURNPIKE

On 9 November 1874 the *West Briton* reported

The good people of Callington are in ecstasies at the turnpikes being done away with in the neighbourhood.

...not being connected by rail or steamboat with other places, as most towns are, travelling by road is, therefore, indispensable, and even this luxury (if such it is) has been denied the inhabitants of and visitors to the town, unless they consent to the levy of blackmail from gates, which are studded around the town like so many forts around a castle...

An advertisement in 1866 shows that there was an inner and an outer ring of toll gates, as well as some intermediate gates on the roads from Callington:

East Gate
South Gate
North Gate
West Gate
(were all within the town.)

Calmady's Shop
Wooda Bridge
Horse Bridge
New Bridge
Beal's Mill
Brendon Tree
(were an outer ring, most with toll houses.)

Meaders
Stoke Climsland village
Seven Stones
Saint Ann's Chapel
The Four Crossroads
Hingston Common
Haye Road
(were additional gates, bars or chains.)

No wonder the Callington folk rejoiced when all these were done away with.

NO TRACTION ENGINES

In the last quarter of the 19th Century, heavy steam locomotives were used in increasing numbers, both on farms and for heavy haulage. Roads and especially bridges were not strong enough for such heavy loads. Rather than raise the very large sums needed to strengthen roads and bridges, the Justices of the Peace, and from 1889 Cornwall County Council, put up notices effectively banning traction engines from many of the county's weaker bridges. An example

Clapper Bridge

survives on Clapper Bridge (SX351652) on the road to St Germans. It reads:

COUNTY OF CORNWALL

Take notice that this bridge (which is a County Bridge) is insufficient to carry weights beyond the ordinary traffic of the district and that the owners, drivers and persons in charge of Locomotives are warned against attempting the passage of the bridge without the consent of the County Surveyor.

By order of the County Justices
Silvanus W. Jenkin, Surveyor

The reference to the County Justices of the Peace and the absence of any reference to the County Council shows that this is a notice put up before 1889. Silvanus Jenkin was Bridge Surveyor for the Eastern Division from 1856 until his death in 1911.

*No Traction Engines!
notice on Clapper Bridge*

159

SX280709 B3254
Linkinhorne 62170

SX279725 B3254
Linkinhorne 62154

SX278734 B3254
Linkinhorne 62153

SX338739 B3257
Stoke Climsland
394060

SX324745 B3257
Linkinhorne 62156

SX309752 B3257
Linkinhorne 62155

POST TURNPIKE MILESTONES

The Callington District Highway Board was set up in 1863 to maintain the parish roads in the eleven parishes around Callington, namely Menheniot, Calstock, Quethiock, St Ive, Southill, St Dominick, Callington, St Mellion, Pillaton, Linkinhorne, Stokeclimlsand.[16] Money from the parish rate was used for repair work, supervised by a Surveyor for the District Highway Board and either one or two Waywardens in each parish.

When the Turnpike Trust was wound up, the old turnpike roads became the responsibility of the District Highway Board as Main Roads (41 & 42 V c.LXXVII) and half the cost of maintenance was paid from the county rate.[17] The Callington District Highway Board co-operated with the neighbouring Launceston District Highway Board and Liskeard District Highway Board to have the whole of two roads, which are now called B3254 and B3257, made Main Roads, although only short lengths of the ends of each of these had ever been turnpike roads.

The Callington District Highway Board applied for the road between Tokenbury Corner and Botternell (B3254) to be made Main.[18] Three milestones were erected on this road by the Callington District Highway Board – LISKEARD 5, 6 and 7 (SX280709, SX 279724 and SX278735), before the road was taken over by the County and funds from the county rate could be used for maintenance. These milestones give distances to Liskeard, and match the milestones erected by the Liskeard District Highway Board milestones south of Tokenbury Corner. The bridge at Botternell marks the boundary between Linkinhorne and North Hill parishes and between Callington and Launceston District Highway Boards. Less than a mile to the north is the last of the Launceston District Highway Board milestones (SX278745) which gives distances to both Launceston (8) and Liskeard (7¾).

The milestone at Tokenbury Corner is not a roadside milestone. It refers to the mineral railway and gives the distance along the railway to the coast at Looe. B3254

The road from Taylor's Shop to Ashwell (B3257) was also to be made Main.[19] Three milestones were erected by the Callington District Highway Board giving distances to Callington and Plymouth (SX338739, SX324745 and SX309752). Here the milestones match the Launceston District Highway Board milestones to the west of Ashwell as far as the junction with the Bodmin Trust's turnpike at Plusha.

A POST-TURNPIKE DIRECTION STONE

There is one granite pillar in the Y of the junction at Pillatonmill (SX366633) with the inscriptions running vertically up and down two adjacent sides. The style of this stone looks similar to some parish boundary stones, for example the one in the middle of Wooda Bridge on A388 north of Callington. At Pillatonmill the

Mineral railway milestone, Tokenbury Corner. Liskeard & Caradon Railway 1861. 15 miles from Looe. SX280699

SX366633 Pillaton 60912

*SX368759
Stoke Climsland 393942*

*SX371762
Stoke Climsland 393943*

*SX375748 Stoke Climsland
393941*

stone gives **CALLINGTON 4M, PILLATON 1½M** to the left and **BOTUS FLEMING 3M, LANDULPH 4½M** to the right. The condition of the stone and the crisp sans-serif lettering suggests a late 19th century date.

EAST CORNWALL FINGERSTONES

Direction stones with elaborately carved pointing hands were a feature of the mining district of West Penwith at the extreme west of Cornwall (See Chapter 1).

A group of direction stones with elaborately carved pointing hands is also to be found to the north of Callington. Three stones at a group of junctions on minor lanes have two dressed faces with one or two hands on each face, giving destinations in three or four directions with no distances. All three stones have similar style carving, unlike the West Penwith stones where each stone was distinctly different. All three stones are within the parish of Stoke Climsland (SX368759, SX373748 and SX371762).

Are these three stones the survivors of a much larger collection of similar stones or are they the only examples of stone direction posts in an area where direction posts were made of wood and have subsequently rotted away?

*The old turnpike road
from Newbridge to
Callington is now a
footpath*

An advertisement for the Vivid Coach reveals the end of the era of long distance coach travel. Promising to transport the traveller from Launceston to London in a day, the small print reveals that the coach only went as far as Exeter, taking seven hours for the journey, where it linked with the railway for onward travel to London.
This poster for the 'new and well appointed coach' was printed in May 1862, but Launceston railway station opened on 1 June 1865, making the coach redundant.
LAWRENCE HOUSE MUSEUM, LAUNCESTON

CONCLUSION

Road development and vehicle development have gone hand in hand throughout history. Increased traffic in the 17th century wore out the roads faster than the parish system could hope to repair them. The solution attempted by successive governments was to adapt the vehicle to suit the road, not to adapt the road to suit the vehicle. Road surfaces which turned to mud in wet weather would be kept free of ruts by fitting wagons with wheels like garden rollers. A minimum width was specified for each class of vehicle and narrow wheels were penalised by excessive toll charges throughout much of the turnpike period. This policy was being advocated in the early 19th century when John Loudon McAdam presented his paper on his new method of road construction to a Parliamentary Committee.

Roads filled with potholes could only be used by sturdy and therefore heavy vehicles. Early carriages were made of massive timbers and wheels were constantly breaking through a combination of the poor roads and the heavy structure the wheels had to carry. As roads became smoother, vehicles could be made lighter. Technology transformed passenger vehicles. New materials allowed the leather suspension of the first stage coaches to be replaced by the steel springs of the 'flying' coaches. By the later 19th century, vehicle design and manufacture

Horse Power - a dog cart sits on a Cornish bow wagon in the Carriage Museum, Treskillard, Redruth

Royal Albert Railway Bridge at Saltash. 1855, in construction.
Height 100 ft above high water — *Span of each opening 455 feet*

Royal Albert Bridge, 1855 in construction, HISTORY OF BOROUGH OF LISKEARD BY JOHN ALLEN, 1856

whether for goods or passengers was a large scale, highly skilled industry.

The steam railway outclassed horse drawn road transport in speed and price. Once Cornwall was joined to England's railways by the Royal Albert Bridge in 1859, the horse could offer no competition to steam except at local level. If only steam power had been applied to road transport more successfully!

Richard Trevithick led the way with steam road vehicles in 1801 and 1803. Goldsworthy Gurney tried hard to make a commercial success of steam road power, with his famous journey from London to Bath and back in 1829. Despite these successes by Cornish inventors, steam on the road was not popular. Excessive tolls were charged by some turnpike trusts in an effort to drive steam off the road. In evidence before a Parliamentary Committee in 1832 it was stated that on the road between Liverpool and Prescot, a horse drawn coach would pay a 4s toll, but a steam coach would pay £2 8s.[1]

The 'Red Flag' Act of 1865 was aimed at controlling the ever increasing number of steam traction engines used for heavy haulage by road. Imposing a maximum speed of four miles an hour on all mechanically propelled vehicles, this Act handed any development for passenger road transport to Britain's foreign rivals in Europe and America. The first motor cars in Britain had to be imported from France or Germany by

First Brighton Run The Emancipation Run 14 November 1896

Ordinary bicycles were fast but difficult to ride

Safety bicycle advertisement in THE RAMBLER *1898*

Milepost on A30, Cornwall

the cyclist. By the mid 1870s it was estimated that there were nearly 50,000 'ordinaries' by various makers on the road. The 'ordinary' was fast but difficult and potentially dangerous to ride. The next decade produced the 'safety' bicycle with chain drive to the rear wheel, which is the basis of bicycles today. Cyclists in cycle clubs travelled far and wide. They wanted to know how far and how fast they travelled and brought a new emphasis to the accuracy of milestones.

The great days of the turnpike trusts were two centuries ago, but some people see their return as the best way to pay for modern motoring. Tolls on motorways have spread to Britain from the Continent and number plate recognition systems make road pricing much easier to set up on any road. Today, the busiest toll gates in the west of England are on the Tamar Bridge at Saltash. Turnpike gates rise and fall continually as the traffic heads out of Cornwall. Few vehicles going west will stop to visit Saltash as they cross the road bridge built in 1961 and enter the road tunnel built under the town in 1987, heading off into Cornwall on the dual carriageway. None would want to attempt the original, narrow, steep road from the banks of the Tamar up through the town.

In 2000, milestones in Britain were declared to be no longer useful 'highway furniture' – an essential feature of the highway. They were reclassified as 'historic roadside features'. This called into question their survival and gave rise to the formation of the Milestone Society, a national charity dedicated to their preservation and celebration.

Milestones may be part of road history, but distance markers on modern roads are still important. They stand at 100 metres intervals along the verges of our trunk roads, helping highway engineers and others with location and identification. In France, the kilometre marker (*borne routiere*) is a national institution. Today they are made in plastic, but remain an important item of road furniture.

Will milestones come back to British roads? With satellite navigation systems do we need roadside direction posts? As times change and technology rolls forward, our past recedes and can easily be forgotten. Cornwall is fortunate that so many of its milestones have survived so far. They need to be cared for, protected and celebrated as solid reminders of the history of our roads.

people like Charles Jarrott and S. F. Edge. Slow moving traction engines survived with some 8,000 on the road when the motor car became a distinct legal vehicle for the first time in Britain with the Emancipation Act of 1896.

It was not the motor car, but the bicycle which brought the public back to Britain's roads from the railways. James Starley's development of the 'penny farthing' or 'ordinary' bicycle in 1871 achieved instant popularity. The large front wheel and gear drive gave unheard of speed to

ROMAN MILESTONES
IN CORNWALL

The Romans are famed for building monuments as well as roads, so it is no surprise that they lined their roads with monuments. The roadsides into Rome itself were crammed with tombs and monumental sculptures as well as simpler memorial stones. Historians can date these accurately since almost invariably they give the name of the current emperor when they were carved.

Away from the Empire's capital, memorial stones were less frequent, but there seems to have been one every mile on the important roads in every Province within the Roman Empire. In some cases these stones carry the distance to the nearest Roman town.

Roman milestones have been found and studied throughout what was the Roman Empire, from Spain in the west to Turkey in the east, in all the countries bordering the Mediterranean Sea, and in Britain. While there may have been a Roman milestone every Roman mile along the main Roman roads of the Roman Empire, there were also Roman milestones at crossroads, bridges, fords, frontiers, monuments and centres of population.

A Roman pace was a double step, a left and a right, and was equivalent to 1.48 metres, so a Roman mile ('millia passum' – a thousand paces) was 1,480 metres, which is 0.92 statute miles. The Roman mile, inscribed as **M P**, was used within the Roman Provinces, but in the border territories of 'long-haired' Gaul and Germany, a Roman league of 2,220 metres (1.5 Roman miles) or a Gallic league of 2'415 metres was indicated by an **L** or the word **LEUGA** on the milestone.

In France, Roman milestones are called 'bornes milliaires'. 'Borne' is the French word for a boundary stone or landmark, and 'milliaire' refers to the thousand paces of a Roman mile.

Detailed records were made in France in the 19th century under Emperor Napoleon III, but the 20th century has not been kind to Roman milestones, and while the descriptions of the 19th century were accurate, the locations given were much less clear.

It is thought that over 500 Roman milestones survive in France. These are listed on an internet website. A detailed modern record, including photographs, has been started and is available on the internet (http://archeolyon.araire.org). Of the 197 Roman milestones described in detail, only four are rectangular and one is described as a monolith. The rest are all cylindrical or parts of cylinders. This has special significance in Cornwall, where all five 'Roman milestones' are rectangular. Cylindrical milestones are typically 0.45 to 0.60metres in diameter and 1.80 to 2.50 metres tall on a square base. More slender cylindrical milestones may be re-cycled columns from buildings.

Distances were usually measured from the nearest town, though sometimes from the provincial capital. The distance was invariably at the base of the milestone, below the dedication to the current Emperor, which made the distance the most vulnerable to damage over the centuries.

With rare exceptions in the South of France, no Roman milestones in France are in their original location.

In Britain 95 Roman milestones have been identified and are still known to survive.[1] In 1956, the Ordnance Survey identified 63 locations of Roman Milestones, though some of these contain more than one milestone (Map of Roman Britain, Third Edition, 1956, Ordnance Survey). The milestones are scattered all over England and Wales, with the greatest concentration in the North, near Hadrian's Wall. No Roman milestones have been found in Britain that can be dated before the reign of Hadrian (120 A.D.). Approximately two thirds (65 out of 95) of the milestones have dates from between 235 and 337 A.D. This late period of the Roman Empire in Britain was particularly turbulent. From 100 to 200 A.D. there were 13 emperors, but between 200 and 300 A.D. there were 85 emperors.[2]

Of the 95 Roman milestones surviving, only 8 give a distance, which may call into question their definition as milestones.

The Roman presence in Britain ended officially in 395 A.D.

In Cornwall, 5 Roman milestones have been

identified. None gives a distance. Unlike most Roman milestones, the Cornish stones are basically rectangular in cross section, not cylindrical. A study of the sources of stone for Britain's Roman milestones showed that the materials used for the Cornish milestones were unique. Where the material was identified, only one milestone was slate, and only four were granite. These are the five Cornish milestones.[3] This may explain their unusual shape, first because slate shears to give a flat surface and is very difficult to cut into a cylinder, and second because granite is very hard and difficult to carve compared with the other types of stone used for cylindrical milestones.

The Imperial dedications of the Cornish milestones seem a random selection from the large number of emperors of the 3rd and early 4th century A.D.

1. SW719418 Menheer Farm, Redruth. AD 238-244. Found during ploughing in 1942, it is now in the (private) garden of Menheer Farm. Granite slab, roughly rectangular 100cm high by 20cm wide (EH66917), it is described as illegible in the English Heritage listing notes. **IMP CAES ANT GORDIANO PIO FEL**

Attributed to the child emperor Gordian III who was proclaimed emperor at the age of 13 and who ruled for five and a half years before being defeated and dying in Persia.

2. SX076891 St Piran's Chapel, Trethevey, Tintagel. AD 251-253. It was discovered in 1909 being used as a gatepost. It is a squared granite pillar. **IMP C DOMI N GALLO ET VOLVS...**

Emperor Trebonianus Gallus was proclaimed emperor by his troops while fighting the Goths and made his son Gaius Vibius Volusianus co-emperor when he returned to Rome. The joint emperors failed to fend off incursions from the Persians in the east or the Goths in the north and were murdered by their own troops.

3. SW618284 Breage, Helston AD 260-268. Discovered in 1924 being used as a gatepost, it is now inside the church of St Breaca and listed with the church (EH65731). It is a rectangular granite pillar. **IMP C DO NO MARC CASSI ANIO...**

This refers to Marcus Cassianus Latinus Postumus who was declared emperor by his troops on the Rhine and established a separate Gallic Empire, which in 261 included Britain. He evaded the central Emperor Gallienus and co-

SW618284 Breage Church 65731

existed with the main empire for several years, before an internal rebellion led to him being murdered by his own troops.

4. SW550313 St Hilary AD 306-337. This is described as a restored granite milestone. It is listed as part of the contents of the church of St Hilary (EH70042). **IMP CAES FLAV VAL CONSTANTINO PIO NOB CAES DIVI CONSTANTINI PII FEL AUGUSTI FILIO**

Constantine I was born in Serbia. His father was a soldier called Constantinus who rose to high rank. When his father died on 25 July 306 while campaigning in Britain against the Picts, the soldiers proclaimed Constantine emperor. Constantine defeated Maxentius at the battle of the Milvian Bridge in 312 to become sole ruler of the Western Empire. Believing that the Christian god had aided his victory, Constantine became a Christian.

In 324 Constantine defeated Emperor Licinius to become the sole ruler of the Roman Empire. Constantine died of natural causes in 337.

5.SX050884 Tintagel. AD 308-324. This was found in the wall of the churchyard of St Materiana in 1888 and is a rectangular slate pillar. It is the only known slate Roman milestone in Britain and now stands inside the church

(EH68846). **IMP C G VAL LIC LICIN...** or **MPCQ VA LIC IIV** (or **LICIN**) [4]

Valerius Licinianus Licinius came from a Dacian family. He rose to become Emperor of Thrace Illyricum and Pannonia in 308. Following his marriage to Constantine's daughter, Licinius was attacked at Byzantium and driven from the city by Emperor Maximinus Daia in 313. However, Licinius then defeated Daia to become ruler of the Eastern Empire. Licinius was defeated and killed by Constantine in 324.

There seems very little to connect these inscribed stones except their reference to a Roman emperor. The emperors mentioned are an odd selection.

The teenage emperor Gordian III who

SW550313 St Hilary Church 70042

fought and died in Persia, would seem to have no connection with Cornwall.

There is no evidence that Gallus ever visited Cornwall, though he spent his time in Europe rather than in the East.

Postumus established an independent Gallic empire, including Britain. When this empire finally collapsed and rejoined the main Roman Empire, why was not this memorial stone to Postumus destroyed or re-carved?

Constantine the Great was proclaimed emperor in York and ruled the Western Empire for many years, so this dedication seems appropriate.

The slate stone to Licinius is the most unusual. Although he was not always at war with Constantine, he ruled the Eastern Empire from Byzantium. Not only did he never visit Cornwall, but Cornwall was never ruled by him.

None of these 'Roman milestones' in Cornwall gives a distance, either in Roman miles (MP) or in Leagues (L). Nor do any have a place name, such as the Roman fortress town at Exeter (ISCA DVUMONIORVM). In that sense they are not truly 'milestones' at all. It seems likely that these are a handful of surviving commemorative stones erected by someone, or to the memory of someone who had a connection to a particular emperor, perhaps during their military career before they retired to Cornwall.

Commemorative stones continued to be erected in Cornwall after the Romans had left. Pevsner records 22 post-Roman inscribed stones from the 5th to the 10th century A.D.[5] Thirteen of these stones date from the 4th to the 7th century. Dating seems to be by the language used in the inscription as it changed from Latin on the earlier stones to Hiberno-Saxon, as the ruling peoples of Britain changed during these six centuries. Without expert knowledge it is impossible to tell some of these post-Roman stones from the 'Roman milestones', except for the lack of an emperor's name, yet these have never been referred to as "post-Roman milestones".

BIBLIOGRAPHY

Albert, W. *The Turnpike Road System in England*, Cambridge University Press 1972

Allen, J. *The History of the Borough of Liskeard*. J. Philp, Liskeard 1856

Balejka-Hoffmann, A. A *History of Angarrack*. Angarrack 1977

Besley, H. *The Route Book of Cornwall*. Exeter 1850

Bird, S. *The Book of Cornish Villages*. Dovecote Press 1980

Black, A. & C. *Guide to Cornwall*. London 1895

Britton, J. & E. W .Brayley, E. W. Fisher *Cornwall Illustrated*. Fisher, Son & Co 1831

Browne, A. L. *Looe Corporation Chronicles*. Looe 1904

Bunn, C. *The Book of St Austell*. Barracuda 1978

Burrows, J. *Hayle, Cornwall, The Official Guide Book*. Hayle Town Guide Committee 1965

Carter, C. 'If It's Metal Take it to Holman's' *Archive* Issue 3, September 1994

Cary, G. & J. *Six Sheet Map of England and Wales, Sheet 1*. 1832

Collins, W. W. *Rambles Beyond Railways*. Richard Bentley, London 1851

Defoe, D. *A Tour Through England and Wales 1724*. Dent, London 1959

Fiennes C., Ed. Morris, C. *The Journeys of Celia Fiennes*. The Cresset Press 1947

Forbes, J. 'Tour into Cornwall to the Land's End in 1794' *Journal of the Royal Institution of Cornwall*. 1983

Gascoyne, J. *A Map of the County of Cornwall Newly Surveyed* reprinted in facsimile, Devon and Cornwall Record Society, 1991

Gilbert, D. *The Parochial History of Cornwall, Vol. IV.* J. B. Nicholls 1838

Glen, R. C. *Glen's Highway Surveyor*. Second Edition, Knight & Co 1888

Gordon, A. *An Historical and Practical Treatise upon Elemental Locomotion by Means of Steam Carriages on Common Roads*. London 1832

Heligan A Brief Guide to The Lost Gardens of Heligan 1994

Henderson, C. *Essays in Cornish History*. reprinted D. Bradford Barton 1963

Henderson, C. & Coates, H. *Old Cornish Bridges*. 1928 reprinted Barton 1972

Henderson, C. 'A History of the Parish of Constantine in Cornwall' *Journal of the Royal Institution of Cornwall*. 1937

Jenkins, S. C. & Langley, R. C. *The West Cornwall Railway*. Oakwood Press 2002

Jiggins, J. 'Roman Milestones in Britain' *Milestones & Waymarkers Vol. 5* 2012 p 11

Hosier F. A. 'The Measured Mile' *Federation of Old Cornwall Societies Journal*. 1983

Hunt, B. E. *The Saltash Ferry 2011* (published as a website)

Jenkinson, T. & Taylor, P. *The Toll-houses of South Devon*. Polystar Press 2009

Jusserand, J. J. *English Wayfaring Life in the Middle Ages*. Fisher Unwin 1889

Kelly's Directory of Cornwall 1889

Langdon, A. G. *Wade-Bridge*. Federation of Old Cornwall Societies 2012

Lavelle, J. 'Penryn Swing Bridge' *Cornwall Association of Local Historians Journal*. Autumn 2004

Lowe, M. C. 'Devon Turnpike Trusts: 1753 – 1889' *Devonshire Association Vol. 122.* 1980

Luck, E. *Green Lane Walks in South-East Cornwall*. The Green Lane Project, Liskeard 1985

Lysons, D. & S. *Magna Britannia, Volume 3 – Cornwall*. Cadell & Davies 1814

McAdam, J. L. *Observations on the Highways of the Kingdom*. London 1811

Macpherson, D. *Annals of Commerce*. London 1805

Messenger, M. J. *Caradon & Looe; the canal, railways and mines*. Twelveheads Press 2001

Munn, P. *Introducing Bodmin – The Cornish Capital*. Bodmin Books 1977

National Benzole Famous Milestones. circa 1935

Noall, C. *A History of Cornish mail and Stage Coaches*. Barton 1963

Noall, C. *The Book of Penzance*. Barracuda Books 1983

Ogilby, J. *Britannia Volume the First*. London 1675

Palmer, J. *Penryn in the Eighteenth Century*. Truro 1991

Pevsner, N. *The Buildings of England – Cornwall*. Penguin 1970

Pool, P. A. S. *The History of the Town and Borough of Penzance*. Corporation of Penzance 1974

Rabey, Ivan *The Silver Ball*. St Columb 1984

Reader, W. J. *Macadam*. Heinemann 1980

Redding, C. *An Illustrated Itinerary of the County of Cornwall*. How & Parsons 1842

Rice, Matthew *Village Buildings of Britain*. Time Warner 1991

Sedgley, J. *The Roman Milestones of Britain*. British Archaeological Report number 18, 1975

Smith, J. R. *Cornwall's China Clay Heritage* Twelveheads Press 1992

Spreadbury, I. D. ed. *Through Cornwall by Coach*. Kingston, Mevagissey 1971

Stockdale, F. W. L. *Excursions through Cornwall*. Simpkin & Marshall 1824

Taylor, P. *The Toll-houses of Cornwall*. Polystar Press 2001

Thorn, Caroline & Frank (Eds.) *Domesday Book, Cornwall*. Philimore & Co. 1979

Vale, E. *The Harveys of Hayle*. Barton 1966

White, P. *The South West Highway Atlas for 1675*. Tamar Books, Launceston 2005

Wynne, W. 'A Journey into Cornwall in the Year 1755' *Journal of the Royal Institution of Cornwall*. 1981

ACKNOWLEDGEMENTS

This book is a tribute to the highway workers of the eighteenth and nineteenth centuries who built the roads and erected the milestones. It could not have been written if the highway workers of the twentieth century had not been so diligent in maintaining the old milestones. This book is a plea to highway engineers of the twenty first century to safeguard the roadside features they have inherited for the future.

I am indebted to librarian Angela Broome for allowing me to use the notes of the late Miss M. E. Philbrick and many other treasures deposited at the Courtney Library of the Royal Institution of Cornwall in Truro, which formed the foundation on which this book is constructed. My research was greatly assisted by Kim Cooper and her staff at the Cornish Studies Centre and by the staff at the Cornwall Record Office.

Veryan Heal introduced me to Jane Powning who worked with me for six years to prepare two hundred and thirty six milestone listing applications to be submitted to English Heritage. This is where much of the real work was done for the book.

I thank the Quiller Couch Memorial Fund which gave me the confidence to try to publish my book.

Jeremy Edwards saw the possibilities of a partnership between Cornwall Council and the Milestone Society to maintain the milestones in his care. It is thanks to Jeremy and his colleagues Paul Allen and Peter Tatlow that I was able to paint so many of the milestones illustrated here.

David Viner, Jan Scrine, Alan Rosevear, the late Terry Keegan and other members of the national Milestone Society, a charity set up in 2001 to promote and preserve our roadside heritage, have been a source of inspiration. Andrew Langdon, Pete Goodchild and other local milestone enthusiasts have offered encouragement and practical help at critical times.

Michael, John and Alan at Twelveheads Press have somehow turned my words and pictures into a book.

My wife deserves the biggest thanks for putting up with my obsession for the last twenty years.

REFERENCES

ABBREVIATIONS:

CRO   Cornwall Record Office
OS   Ordnance Survey
Philbrick   Philbrick Archive, Royal
            Institution of Cornwall,
            Courtney Library
RCG   *Royal Cornwall Gazette*
WB   *West Briton*

NOTES:

Introduction
1. Henderson & Coates 1928
2. Assize Rolls Crown Pleas No. III.
3. Jusserand 1889
4. Macpherson 1805
5. Albert 1972
6. Henderson & Coates 1928
7. McAdam 1811

Chapter 1 : West Penwith
1. Collins 1851
2. Wynne 1981
3 Carter 1994
4. Redding 1842

Chapter 2 : Penzance, Redruth and Hayle
1. Ogilby 1675

2. Henderson & Coates 1928
3. Stockdale 1824
4. Fiennes 1947
5. Henderson & Coates 1928
6. Vale 1966
7. Henderson & Coates 1928, p. 103
8. CRO QS/PDT/4/1 Turnpike Road from Hayle Causeway to Ponjou Lane
9. Pool 1974
10. Noall 1983
11. Besley 1850
12. Burrows 1965.
13. Balejka-Hoffmann 1977
14. Jenkins & Langley 2002
15. Noall 1963
16. RCG 6 November 1890
17. Henderson & Coates 1928
18. Lavelle 2004
19. CRO TP/RED/104, Redruth Turnpike Minute Book 21 March 1836
20. CRO TP/RED/104, Redruth Turnpike Minute Book 25 March 1840
21. Philbrick PHIL/A/22
22. Philbrick PHIL/A/22

Chapter 3 : Helston and the Lizard
1. Noall 1983
2. CRO FS/2/2 Cornish Road Acts 1759-1785

3. Gascoyne 19914. Henderson & Coates 1928
5. Palmer 1991
6. Philbrick PHIL/A/23
7. Henderson & Coates 1928
8. Bird 1980
9. Henderson 1937
10. Interview by the author with Sir Ferrers Vyvyan at Trelowarren, 21 May 2009
11. Redding 1842
12. Britton & Brayley 1831
13. Glen 1888
14. Glen 1888
15. RCG 9 October 1863
16. RCG 12 February 1864
17. RCG 6 November 1890
18. RCG 4 February 1892
19. RCG 6 November 1890
20. RCG 16 June 1892
21. Lavelle 2004

Chapter 4 : Truro
1. Thorn 1979
2. Henderson 1963
3. Henderson & Coates 1928
4. Ogilby 1675
5. Fiennes 1947
6. Defoe 1724-26

7. Wynne 1981
8. Forbes 1983
9. Cary 1832
10. CRO DD/RH Helston Turnpike Minute Book 1834
11. Reader 1980
12. CRO TP/TRU/106 Truro Turnpike Order Book
13. CRO DD/RH Helston Turnpike Minute Book 1834
14. Lysons 1814
15. Taylor 2001
16. Ogilby 1675
17. Kelly's Directory of Cornwall 1889
18. CRO P197/8/1 Redruth Vestry Book

Chapter 5 : The Haleworthy Trust, Colan, Newquay and St Columb

1. Gilbert 1838
2. Gilbert 1838
3. Noall 1963
4. Parliamentary Select Committee on State of Roads 1840
5. Ogilby 1675
6. Fiennes 1947
7. CRO QS/PDT 2/3 Camelford, Wadebridge & St Columb Trust Plans
8. Langdon 2012
9. Taylor 2001, p.52
10. RCG 8 May 1824
11. Report by William Fillis Pierce of Camelford, clerk to the trust, to the Select Committee on the State of Roads, 1840
12. Taylor 2001
13. RCG 6 November 1890
14. WB 16 September 1864
15. Rabey 1984

Chapter 6 : Launceston and North Cornwall

1. Ogilby 1675
2. Black 1895
3. Wynne 1981
4. Philbrick PHIL/A/30/1
5. Lowe 1980
6. CRO TP/LAUS/31Launceston Trust Minute Books
7. Philbrick PHIL A30/1
8. Report to Secretary of State, 1866 for 1867 Acts 30 & 31 V c.xii
9. RCG 9 October 1863
10. Glen 1888
11. Glen 1888
12. Glen 1888.
13. RCG 9 January 1880
14. RCG 17 July 1890

15. RCG 2 April 1880
16. RCG 6 November 1890
17. RCG 4 February 1892

Chapter 7 : Bodmin

1. *Newquay Express* 5 July 1907
2. Ogilby 1675
3. Philbrick PHIL/A/37/1 XVII p24
4. Philbrick PHIL/A/37
5. The Western Flying Post or Sherborne and Yeovil Mercury, 7 October 1754)
6. Munn 1977
7. Henderson & Coates 1928
8. Talk by John Woods, Altarnun Local History Group, 2010
9. Henderson & Coates 1928
10. Greenwood county map 1827
11. Taylor 2001
12. Spreadbury 1971
13. Henderson & Coates 1928
14. O.S. 1:50,000 First Series Sheet 200 Newquay and Bodmin 1977
15. CRO QS/PDT/4/1 Bodmin Turnpike Proposed New Road
16. RCG 6 November 1890
17. RCG 9 October 1863; 12 February 1864
18. National Benzole 1935
19. Ken Dymond Collection, The Milestone Society
20. Old Cornwall Vol VII No.7 50th Anniversary Edition, Autumn 1970
21. WB 16 September 1864
22. Philbrick PHIL/A/28

Chapter 8 : St Austell, Lostwithiel, Luxulyan and Roseland

1. Henderson & Coates 1928
2. Taylor 2001
3. CRO AD105/1 St Austell Minute Book
4. CRO AD105/1 St Austell Minute Book
5. Bunn 1978
6. Smith 1992
7. CRO FS/2/2 Cornish Road Acts 1759-1785
8. Henderson & Coates 1928
9. WB 24 July 1863
10. Philbrick PHIL/A/25
11. Bird 1980
12. Heligan 1994
13. Letter from David Stark, March 2002.
14. Stockdale 1824
15. Redding 1842
16. Fiennes 1947
17. Black 1895
18. RCG 9 October 1863
19. RCG 6 November 1890
20. Rice 1991 page 25

Chapter 9 : Liskeard and Looe

1. Redding 1842
2. Ogilby 1675
3. Fiennes 1947
4. Ogilby 1675
5. Allen 1856
6. Spreadbury 1971
7. House of Commons Reports 19 January 1761; Crafthole Road
8. Messenger 2001
9. Allen 1856
10. Allen 1856
11. Henderson & Coates 1928
12. Fiennes 1947
13. Redding 1842
14. Browne 1904
15. Allen 1856
16. RCG 6 November 1890
17. OS Second Edition 6 inch map 1907
18. White 2005

Chapter 10 : Saltash and Callington

1. Hunt 2011
2. Defoe 1724
3. Hosier 1983
4. Notes from C.J.Squires, Saltash local historian, 2002
5. OS 25-inch to 1 mile map 1890
6. Jenkinson & Taylor 2009
7. Jenkinson & Taylor 2009
8. Hunt 2011
9. Jenkinson & Taylor 2009
10. OS 25-inch to 1 mile map 1889
11. OS 25-inch to 1 mile map 1953
12. Redding 1842
13. Wynne 1981
14. Henderson & Coates 1928
15. Luck 1985
16. RCG 9 October 1863
17. Glen 1888
18. RCG 6 November 1890
19. RCG 16 June 1892

Chapter 11 : Conclusion

1. Gordon 1832

Chapter 12: Roman Milestones

1. http://archeolyon.araire.org
2. Higgins 2012
3. Ordnance Survey, Map of Roman Britain, Third Edition, 1956
4. Long, J. De Imperatoribus Romanis, 2012   http://www.roman-emperors.org
5. Sedgley 1975
6. Pevsner 1970
7. Pevsner 1970

West Penwith milestones

Grid Ref	Road	Parish	Left Face	Front Face	Right Face	Listed
SW355248	B3315	Sennen		1		1407760
SW362260	A30	Sennen		2		69855
SW364261	A30	Sennen	TO PENZANCE 1834		TP BURYAN and PAUL	69854
SW376237	B3315	St Leven	LAND'S END 2½ MILES		LOGAN ROCK 1¾ MILES	69748
SW372271	A30	Sennen		3		1406869
SW376273	A30	St Just	TO PENZANCE 7 MILES		TO ST JUST 3 MILES	69227
			TO LANDS END 2¾ MILES			
SW379286	B3306	St Just	TO ST BURYAN 3 MILES		TO LANDS END 4 MILES	69220
			AD1836		TO ST JUST 2 MILES	
SW387272	A30	St Buryan		4		69611
SW398241	B3315	St Buryan	ST BURYAN PENZANCE		LAMORNA NEWLYN MOUSEHOLE	69607
SW395276	A30	St Buryan	TO PENZANCE 5½ MILES		TO SAINT JUST 3 MILES	69652
			TO LANDS END 4½ MILES			
SW374309	A3071	St Just	TO PENZANCE 6 MILES		TO ST BURYAN 5 MILES	69222
			AD1836		TO LANDS END 6 MILES	
SW379309	A3071	St Just		FROM PENZ 6		69225
SW370318	B3306	St Just	BOTALLACK 1 MILE		MORVAH 4 MILES	
SW381309	A3071	St Just	PENZANCE DIRECT ROAD		TO SANCREED CHURCH TOWN	69224
			AD1835		AND PAUL	
SW386334	B3318	St Just		6		1406916
SW388344	B3306	St Just	PENZANCE 6 MILES		ST JUST 3 MILES	1405974
			PENDEEN 1 MILE		MORVAH ZENNOR 1836	
SW389340	B3318	St Just		6		1405968
SW395311	A3071	St Just		FROM PENZ 5		1405977
SW397326	B3318	Sancreed		5		69815
SW393333	B3318	St Just	TREWELLARD 1 MILE		PENDEEN COVE 2 MILES	69228
			ST JUST 3 MILES		MORVAH 2 MILES	
SW400246	B3283	St Buryan	LOGAN ROCK		ST LEVAN	69608
SW401248	B3283	St Buryan	ST LEVAN		TO SENNEN	69609
SW402275	A30	St Buryan		5		69610
SW417280	A30	St Buryan		6		
SW431280	A30	Sancreed		7		1406886
SW443288	A30	Paul		8		69564
SW455295	A30	Penzance	PENZANCE 1		LANDS END 9	0
SW406317	A3071	Sancreed	ST. JUST		PENDEEN	69811
SW407318	A3071	Sancreed	SAINT JUST NORTH ROAD		SAINT JUST CHURCH TOWN	69812
			and MORVAH		1819	
SW403353	B3306	Morvah		4		1406889
SW414348		Morvah	MORVAH AND ST JUST		ZENNOR AND ST IVES	1410391
SW416345		Madron		3		1406892
SW426315	A3071	Madron		3		1405971
SW438373	B3306	Zennor	STIVS 6M (S's reversed)		PENZANCE 6M	70570
SW451380	B3306	Zennor	PENZANCE 6M		MORVAH 4M	426214

Penzance, Redruth and Hayle milestones

Grid Ref	Road	Parish	Left Face	Front Face	Right Face	Listed
SW474317	B3311	Gulval	illegible		illegible	0
SW485311	A30	Penzance	PENZANCE 1 MILE		HAYLE 7 MILES CAMBORNE 13	1405965
			LANDS END 11		REDRUTH 16 TRURO 25	
SW494347	B3311	Ludgvan		PENZANCE ROAD 1812		70366
SW501314	Old A30	Ludgvan	PENZANCE 2 MILES		HAYLE 6 MILES CAMBORNE 12	70385
			LANDS END 12		REDRUTH 15 TRURO 24	
SW511325	A30	Ludgvan	PENZANCE 3 MILES		HAYLE 5 MILES CAMBORNE 11	70367
			LANDS END 13		REDRUTH 14 TRURO 23	
SW521338	A30	Ludgvan	PENZANCE 4 MILES		HAYLE 4 MILES CAMBORNE 10	70368
			LANDS END 14		REDRUTH 13 TRURO 22	
SW536344	Tredrea Lane	Ludgvan	ST ERTH		ST HILARY	70414
SW531350	A30	Ludgvan	PENZANCE 5 MILES		HAYLE 3 MILES CAMBORNE 9	70379
			LANDS END 15		REDRUTH 12 TRURO 21	
SW530382	A3074	St Ives	PENZANCE 8 HAYLE 4		ST IVES 2	0
SW543360	A30	Ludgvan	PENZANCE 6 MILES		HAYLE 2 MILES CAMBORNE 8	426203
			LAND'S END 16		REDRUTH 11 TRURO 20	
SW543373	A3074	St Ives	PENZANCE 7 HAYLE 3		ST IVES 3	0
SW553371	B3301	Hayle	PENZANCE 7 MILES		HAYLE 1 MILE CAMBORNE 7	70151
			LANDS END 17		REDRUTH 10 TRURO 19	
SW559370	B3301	Hayle	8 P (Hidden)	18 L		70246
SW564378	B3301	Hayle	HAYLE PENZANCE 8 MILES		HAYLE CAMBORNE 6 MILES	70185
			LANDS END 18		REDRUTH 9 TRURO 18	
SW573376	High Lanes	Hayle	9P	19 L		1408993
SW577386	Old A30	Hayle	HAYLE 1 MILE PENZANCE 9		CAMBORNE 5 MILES	70152
			LANDS END 19		REDRUTH 8 TRURO 17	
SW587384	Steamers Hill	Hayle	10P	20 L		70164
SW592392	Old A30	Gwinnear	HAYLE 2 MILES PENZANCE 10		CAMBORNE 4 MILES	1409024
			LANDS END 20		REDRUTH 7 TRURO 16	
SW601391	Angarrack Lane	Gwinnear	11P	21 L		70107
SW608394	Old A30	Gwinnear	HAYLE 3 MILES PENZANCE 11		CAMBORNE 3 MILES	1410449
			LANDS END 21		REDRUTH 6 TRURO 15	
SW622399	Old A30	Camborne	HAYLE 4 MILES PENZANCE 12		CAMBORNE 2 MILES	1410393
			LANDS END 22		REDRUTH 5 TRURO 14	
SW637404	Old A30	Camborne	HAYLE 5 MILES PENZANCE 13		CAMBORNE 1 MILE	66650
			LANDS END 23		REDRUTH 4 TRURO 13	
SW649403		Camborne		14 P	24 L	66638
SW656442	Cot Road	Illogan	POOL 2 MILES		PORTREATH I MILE	66752
SW659452	B3300	Portreath	POOL 3		REDRUTH 4	66791
SW663412	Old A30	Carn Brea	CAMBORNE 1 PENZANCE 15		REDRUTH 2 TRURO 11	66732
SW665429	Cot Road	Illogan	POOL 1 MILE		PORTREATH 2 MILES	66756
SW671415	Old A30	Carn Brea		16 P	26 L	508046
SW679415	Old A30	Carn Brea	CAMBORNE 2 MILES HAYLE 6		REDRUTH 1 MILE	490344
			PENZANCE 16 LANDS END 26		TRURO 10	
SW675448	B3300	Camborne	PORTREATH 1.MILE		REDRUTH 3.MILES	1409062
SW688446	B3300	Redruth	PORTREATH 2.MILES		REDRUTH 2.MILES	66836
SW695419	Old A30	Redruth	CAMBORNE 3 PENZANCE 17		TRURO 9	1409467
SW690430	B3300	Redruth	PORTREATH 3.MILES		REDRUTH T.C. 1.MILE	66841
SW736397	A393	Gwennap	(PENRYN 5 MILES		(REDRUTH 3 MILES	0
			FALMOUTH 7 MILES)		CAMBORNE 6 MILES	
SW749388	A393	Gwennap	(PENRYN 4 MILES		(REDRUTH 4 MILES	0
			FALMOUTH 6 MILES)		CAMBORNE 7 MILES)	
SW758377	A393	St Gluvias	REDRUTH 5 MILES		PENRYN 3 MILES	66532
			CAMBORNE 8 MILES		FALMOUTH 5 MILES	
SW769365	A393	St Gluvias	PENRYN 2 MILES		REDRUTH 6 MILES	66513
			FALMOUTH 4 MILES		CAMBORNE 9 MILES	
SW702422	Old A30	Redruth	18 P	28 L		66816

Helston and the Lizard milestones

Grid Ref	Road	Parish	Left Face	Front Face	Right Face	Listed
SW560294	A394	Breage	PENZANCE 6 LANDS END 16		HELSTON 7 FALMOUTH 19	65700
SW576291	A394	Breage	PENZANCE 7 LANDS END 17		HELSTON 6 FALMOUTH 18	65701
SW592288	A394	Breage	PENZANCE 8 LANDS END 18		HELSTON 5 FALMOUTH 17	65702
SW516306		Marazion	PENZANCE 3 LANDS END 13		HELSTON 10FALMOUTH 22	69908
SW530305		Marazion	PENZANCE 4 LANDS END 14		HELSTON 9 FALMOUTH 21	69994
SW545300	A394	Perranuthnoe	PENZANCE 5 LANDS END 15		HELSTON 8 FALMOUTH 20	70009
SW575351	B3302	St Erth	HELSTON 8		HAYLE 2	0
SW697179	A3083	Mullion	LIZARD 3 ½		HELSTON 7	0
SW697195	A3083	Mullion	LIZARD 4 ½		HELSTON 6	0
SW607284	A394	Breage	PENZANCE 9 LANDS END 19		HELSTON 4 FALMOUTH 16	65703
SW621279	A394	Breage	PENZANCE 10 LANDS END 20		HELSTON 3 FALMOUTH 15	65704
SW632280	A394	Sithney	PENZANCE 11 LANDS END 21		HELSTON 2 FALMOUTH 14	65932
SW639283	A394	Sithney	HELSTON PENZANCE BREAGE		SITHNEY PENROSE	65926
SW639292	B3302	Sithney	HELSTON 2 MILES		CAMBORNE 8 MILES HAYLE 8 MILES	65933
SW641262	B3304	Helston				0
SW645265	B3304	Helston	PENROSE PORTHLEVEN HELSTON		SITHNEY	385560
SW648279	A394	Helston	PENZANCE 12 LANDS END22		HELSTON 1 FALMOUTH 13	385568
SW642280		Sithney	PENROSE PORTHLEVEN HELSTON		SITHNEY	511886
SW663261	A3083	Helston	GWEEK 2¾ MILES		HELSTON 1 MILE	0
SW671251	A3083	Mawgan	GWEEK 1¾ MILES		HELSTON 2	0
SW672283	A394	Wendron	HELSTON 1 PENZANCE 14		FALMOUTH 11 TRURO 15¾	511887
SW684235	A3083	Cury		FROM HELSTON III MILES		0
SW683293	A394	Wendron	HELSTON 2 PENZANCE 15		FALMOUTH 10 TRURO 14¾	511889
SW686299	A394	Wendron	WENDRON & REDRUTH 1845		GWEEK & CONSTANTINE	66311
SW694209	A3083	Cury		FROM HELSTON V MILES		0
SW693224	A3083	Mawgan		4 MILES FROM HELSTON		0
SW695246	B3293	Mawgan	ST KEVERNE 7½ MILES		HELSTON 3 MILES	0
SW695260	B3291	Mawgan	GWEEK ¾		HELSTON 3	0
SW604343	B3302	Crowan	HELSTON 6 MILES		HAYLE 4 MILES	0
SW622319	B3302	Breage	HELSTON 4		HAYLE 6	0
SW632307	B3302	Sithney	HELSTON 3 MILES		HAYLE 7 MILES	1142171
SW636307	B3303	Sithney	HELSTON 3 MILES		CAMBORNE 7 MILES	65979
SW638347	B3303	Crowan	HELSTON 5 ½ MILES		CAMBORNE 4 MILES	0
SW640376	B3303	Crowan	HELSTON 7 ½ MILES		CAMBORNE 2 MILES	0
SW643390	B3303	Camborne	HELSTON 9 MILES		CAMBORNE 1	0
SW674304	B3297	Wendron		H 2	L 25	66325
SW674304	B3297	Wendron	REDRUTH 8 MILES		HELSTON 2 MILES	66326
SW678332	B3297	Wendron	REDRUTH 6 MILES		HELSTON 4 MILES	66321
SW678348	B3297	Wendron	REDRUTH 5 MILES		HELSTON 5 MILES	66362
SW681317	B3297	Wendron	REDRUTH 7 MILES		HELSTON 3 MILES	66322
SW681317	B3297	Wendron		H 3	L 26	66323
SW681331		Wendron		HELSTON 4 CARN MENELLIS 2 ½ REDRUTH 6		66324
SW682364	B3297	Wendron	REDRUTH 4 MILES		HELSTON 6 MILES	66320
SW684379	B3297	Carn Brea	REDRUTH 3 MILES		HELSTON 7 MILES	66698
SW693305	A394	Wendron	HELSTON 3 PENZANCE 16		FALMOUTH 9 TRURO 13	66376
SW694334		Wendron		HELSTON 5 CARN MENELLIS 1 ½ REDRUTH 5		1410384
SW694391	B3297	Carn Brea	REDRUTH 2 MILES		HELSTON 8 MILES	66696
SW698398		Redruth		REDRUTH 1¼ CARN MENELLIS 3 HELSTON 9½		66800
SW699405	B3297	Redruth	HELSTON 9 MILES		REDRUTH 1 MILE	66799
SW703133	A3083	Landewednack	LIZARD ½		HELSTON 10	0
SW700148	A3083	Landewednack	LIZARD 1 ½		HELSTON 9	0
SW755198	B3293	St Keverne	ST KEVERNE 2 ½ MILES		HELSTON 8 MILES	0
SW771198	B3293	St Keverne	ST KEVERNE 1 ½ MILES		HELSTON 9 MILES	0
SW773198	B3293	St Keverne		COVERACK		0
SW706236	B3293	Mawgan	ST KEVERNE 6 ½ MILES		HELSTON 4 MILES	0
SW706242		Mawgan		FROM TRELOWARREN I MILE		65342
SW706266	B3291	Gweek		FROM TRELOWARREN III		66130
SW706281		Gweek		FROM TRELOWARREN IV		66106
SW710298		Constantine		FROM TRELOWARREN V		66028
SW718225	B3293	Mawgan	ST KEVERNE 5 ½ MILES		HELSTON 5 MILES	0
SW729213	B3293	Mawgan	ST KEVERNE 4 ½ MILES		HELSTON 6 MILES	0
SW740202	B3293	St Keverne	ST KEVERNE 3 ½ MILES		HELSTON 7 MILES	0
SW744218		St Keverne			ST MARTIN 1838 I.T	64686
SW775224		St Keverne	ST ANTHONY 1838 I.B		HELSTON ST KEVERNE I.P	64690
SW784206	B3293	St Keverne	HELSTON 10 MILES		ST KEVERNE ½ MILE	0
SW701347		Wendron		HELSTON 6 CARN MENELLIS ½ REDRUTH 4		66327
SW704364		Wendron		REDRUTH 3 CARN MENELLIS ½ HELSTON 7		427864
SW708371		Wendron		REDRUTH 3 ¼ CARN MENELLIS 1 HELSTON 7 ½		1400355
SW706384		Stithians		REDRUTH 2 ¼ CARN MENELLIS 2 HELSTON 8 ½		66229
SW714314		Constantine		FROM TRELOWARREN VI		66029
SW718328		Wendron		FROM TRELOWARREN VII		66329
SW726338	A394	Wendron	HELSTON 6 PENZANCE 19		FALMOUTH 6 TRURO 10¾	66390
SW727339	A394	Wendron	TO STITHIANS		TO PENRYN	66391
			GWENNAP REDRUTH		FALMOUTH TRURO	
SW728346		Wendron		H 7 T 10	H 7 (back face)	66328
SW742311	B3291	Constantine	PENRYN 4 M		GWEEK 4 M LIZARD 14 M	66030
SW740343	A394	Stithians	HELSTON 7 PENZANCE 20		FALMOUTH 5 TRURO 9 ¾	0
SW746340	A394	Mabe		erased		0
SW754316	B3291	Budock	PENRYN 3 M		GWEEK 5 M LIZARD 15 M	66427

Helston and the Lizard milestones continued

Grid Ref	Road	Parish	Left Face	Front Face	Right Face	Listed
SW754346	A394	Mabe	HELSTON 8 PENZANCE 21		FALMOUTH 4 TRURO 8 ¾	0
SW766322	B3291	Budock	PENRYN 2 M		GWEEK 6 M LIZARD 16M	66431
SW779330	B3291	Budock	PENRYN 1 M		GWEEK 7 M LIZARD 17 M	66432
SW783310		Budock	PENRYN	MAWNAN	FALMOUTH	66422
				1828		
SW784344	Lower St	Penryn	HELSTON 10 PENZANCE 23		FALMOUTH 2 TRURO 8	365854
SW797376	Old Road	Falmouth	HELSTON 11 PENZANCE 24		FALMOUTH 1 PENRYN 1	0

Truro milestones

Grid Ref	Road	Parish	Left Face	Front Face	Right Face	Listed
SW731363		Stithians		FROM TRURO 9 MILES		509235
SW741372		Stithians	KENNAL MILLS &c.		HELSTON	66227
SW741374		Stithians		FROM TRURO 8 MILES		427860
SW751384		Stithians		FROM TRURO 7 MILES		509239
SW766386		Perranarworthal		FROM TRURO 6 MILES		63583
SW770363	A39	St Gluvias		FROM TRURO 7 MILES		66514
SW777365		St Gluvias		FROM TRURO 7 MILES		428071
SW771379	A39	St Gluvias		FROM TRURO 6 MILES		443405
SW781350		Penryn		FROM TRURO 8 MILES		365685
SW782388	A39	Mylor		FROM TRURO 5 MILES		63584
SW796350		Mylor		I From Penryn		63579
SW794396	A39	Feock		FROM TRURO 4 MILES		63295
SW708428		Redruth		REDRUTH 1 TRURO 8		66835
SW719439	A3047	St Day		FROM TRURO 7 MILES		66896
SW719497	B3277	St Agnes	ST AGNES 1 MILE		REDRUTH 6½ MILES	0
					TRURO 8 MILES	
SW728438	B3298	St Day	SCORRIER STATION ½M		PENRYN 8M	66897
SW728452		St Agnes	REDRUTH 3 MILES		ST AGNES 4 MILES	0
SW727484	B3277	St Agnes		FROM TRURO 7 MILES		63750
SW730411	B3298	St Day	SCORRIER STATION 2½M		PENRYN 6M	66657
SW733426	B3298	St Day	SCORRIER STATION 1½M		PENRYN 7M	66898
SW734444		Chacewater		FROM TRURO 6 MILES		63104
SW733458		St Agnes				1406160
SW738473	B3277	St Agnes		FROM TRURO 6 MILES		63751
SW749443		Chacewater		FROM TRURO 5 MILES		63161
SW745468		Chacewater		5 R		63105
SW754466	A390	Chacewater		FROM TRURO 5 MILES		63272
SW757479	A30	Perranzabuloe				63680
SW755496	B3284	Perranzabuloe	(TO PERRANPORTH 3 MILES)		(TO TRURO 6 MILES)	0
SW764450		Kenwyn		FROM TRURO 4 MILES		63284
SW765457	A390	Kenwyn		FROM TRURO 4 MILES		63273
SW765488	B3284	Perranzabuloe		FROM TRURO 5 MILES		63681
SW771486	A30	Kenwyn	BODMIN 23M	34 L	PENZANCE 24M	63270
SW780450		Kenwyn		FROM TRURO 3 MILES		63286
SW783487	B3284	Kenwyn		FROM TRURO 4 MILES		63274
SW785492	A30	Perranzabuloe	BODMIN 22M	35 L	PENZANCE 25M	63271
SW796450	A390	Truro		FROM TRURO 2 MILES		162
SW798483	B3284	Kenwyn		FROM TRURO 3 MILES		63275
SW719503	B3277	St Agnes	ST AGNES ¼ MILE		REDRUTH 7 MILES	508475
					TRURO 8½ MILES	
SW727518		St Agnes		1 FROM MILESTONE		0
SW754511	B3284	Perranzabuloe	TO PERRANPORTH 2 MILES		TO TRURO 7 MILES	0
SW755527	B3284	Perranzabuloe	TO PERRANPORTH 1 MILE		TO TRURO 8 MILES	0
SW757540	B3284	Perranzabuloe	TO PERRANPORTH		TO TRURO 9 MILES	0
SW797502	A30	Perranzabuloe	BODMIN 21M	36 L	PENZANCE 26M	63714
SW807343		Mylor		II From Penryn		63472
SW818393		Feock		FROM TRURO 4 MILES		63296
SW823397	B3289	Feock		FROM TRURO 4 MILES		63297
SW838396	B3289	Feock		FROM TRURO 5 MILES		63328
SW805408	A39	Feock		FROM TRURO 3 MILES		63294
SW809472	B3284	Kenwyn		FROM TRURO 2 MILES		63276
SW809487		St Allen		FROM TRURO 3 MILES		63920
SW815409	B3289	Feock		FROM TRURO 3 MILES		63399
SW813421	A39	Kea		FROM TRURO 2 MILES		63398
SW813420		Kea		FROM TRURO 2 MILES		508971
SW819435	A39	Truro		FROM TRURO 1 MILE		508973
SW811446	A390	Truro		FROM TRURO 1 MILE		377396
SW816459	B3284	Kenwyn		FROM TRURO 1 MILE		508974
SW834437		Truro		FROM TRURO 1 MILE		377499
SW838457	A390	Truro	TRURO 1 FALMOUTH 11½		BODMIN 23¼ LONDON 249	508951
SW833462		Truro		FROM TRURO 1 MILE		508975
SW833477	A39	St Clement		FROM TRURO 2 MILES		508978
SW842425		St Clement		FROM TRURO 2 MILES		351276
SW840490		St Erme		FROM TRURO 3 MILES		63930
SW851460	A390	St Clement	TRURO 2 FALMOUTH 12½		BODMIN 22¼ LONDON 248	508982
SW876469	B3275	Probus	TRURO 4 FALMOUTH 14½		BODMIN 20¼ LONDON 246	508983
SW886479	B3275	Probus	TRURO 5 FALMOUTH 15½		BODMIN 19¼ LONDON 245	508984
SW888477		Probus		FROM TRURO 5 MILES		508950
SW890493	B3275	Probus	TRURO 6 FALMOUTH 16½		BODMIN 18¼ LONDON 244	508985
SW808502		St Allen		FROM TRURO 4 MILES		63919
SW807513		St Allen	PENZANCE 27M	9 R	BODMIN 20M	63912
SW816525	A30	St Allen	BODMIN 19M	10 R	PENZANCE 28M	63916
SW831532	A30	St Erme	BODMIN 18M		PENZANCE 29M	508472
SW842505		St Erme		FROM TRURO 4 MILES		63931
SW846520		St Erme		FROM TRURO 5 MILES		63932
SW845539	A30	St Erme	BODMIN 17M	R 12	PENZANCE 30M	508473

Truro milestones continued

Grid Ref	Road	Parish	Left Face	Front Face	Right Face	Listed
SW857544		St Newlyn East		FROM TRURO 7 MILES		63962
SW892508	B3275	Ladock	TRURO 7 FALMOUTH 17½		BODMIN 17¼ LONDON 243	508986
SW899522	B3275	Ladock	TRURO 8 FALMOUTH 18½		BODMIN 16¼ LONDON 242	508987
SW904478		Probus		FROM TRURO 6 MILES		508361
SW916486	A390	Probus		FROM TRURO 7 MILES		508362
SW931484	A390	Grampound		FROM TRURO 8 MILES		508363
SW906535	B3275	St Enoder	TRURO 9 FALMOUTH 19½		BODMIN 15¼ LONDON 241	507772
SW902551	B3275	Ladock	TRURO 10 FALMOUTH 20½		BODMIN 14¼ LONDON 240	507782
SW904567	B3275	St Enoder	TRURO 11 FALMOUTH 21½		BODMIN 13¼ LONDON 239	71307
SW911580		St Enoder	TRURO 12 FALMOUTH 22½		BODMIN 12¼ LONDON 238	507740

The Haleworthy Trust, Colan, Newquay and St Columb milestones

Grid Ref	Road	Parish	Left Face	Front Face	Right Face	Listed
SW803570	A3075	Cubert	NEWLYN / CUBERT	NEWQUAY / TREVEMPER BRIDGE		63652
SW820529	B3285	St Allen			TRURO	63917
SW852590	A3058	St Newlyn		NEWQUAY 4		508256
SW866548	A30	St Enoder		VII MILE To Saint COLUMB		71301
SW861550	A3076	St Newlyn		NEWQUAY 7		508258
SW861579	A3058	St Newlyn		NEWQUAY 5		63995
SW870580		St Newlyn	MITCHELL		ST COLUMB / NEWLYN	63993
SW878555	A30	St Enoder		VI MILE To Saint COLUMB		71303
SW874570	A3058	St Enoder		NEWQUAY 6		71302
SW887560	A3058	St Enoder		NEWQUAY 7		71304
SW897549	A3058	St Enoder		NEWQUAY 8		71306
SW891564		St Enoder		V MILE To Saint COLUMB		71305
SW893598	A392	St Enoder		NEWQUAY 6		508250
SW824620	A392	Newquay		NEWQUAY 1		508246
SW839617	A392	Newquay		NEWQUAY 2		71110
SW838621		Newquay	ST COLUMB 5¼ MILES		NEWQUAY 2 MILES	71119
SW849604	A392	Colan		NEWQUAY 3		508247
SW852623	A3059	Colan	NEWQUAY 3 MILES		ST COLUMB 4¼ MILES	71013
SW867629	A3059	Colan	NEWQUAY 4 MILES		ST COLUMB 3¾ MILES	71015
SW871602	A392	Colan	ST COLUMB 4		QUEENS 3¼	71016
			COLAN CHURCH 1		ST MICHAEL 4¼	
			FIR HILL 1½		TRURO 11¼	
SW878601	A392	Colan		NEWQUAY 5		508248
SW885623		St Columb	THE FIR HILL 1½ COLAN 2		ST COLUMB 2	508253
SW882634	A3059	St Columb	NEWQUAY 5 MILES		ST COLUMB 2¾ MILES	71158
SW896612		St Columb	NEWLYN		COLAN	71151
SW895612		St Columb	COLAN 2		ST COLUMB 2	508252
SW896613		St Columb		TREBUDANNON		
SW896634	A3059	St Columb	NEWQUAY 6 MILES		ST COLUMB 1¼ MILES	71159
SW899630		St Columb	COLAN CHURCH 3		ST COLUMB 1	508254
SW892676		St Ervan	ST ISSEY	ST ERVAN ST COLUMB ST MERRYN		396939
SW905573		St Enoder		IV MILE To Saint COLUMB		71308
SW907596		St Columb		NEWQUAY 7		507795
SW912587		St Enoder		III MILE To Saint COLUMB		71310
SW918590		St Enoder	BODMIN 11¾		NEWQUAY 7¾	71311
SW904623		St Columb	COLAN CHURCH 3		ST COLUMB 1	507800
SW907625		St Columb	NEWQUAY 7		ST COLUMB ½	71161
SW907624		St Columb		ST COLUMB 1m	TREBADANNON 1m	508477
			BODMIN		NEWLYN	
			TRURO		CRANTOCK 9m	
			ST AUSTLE		CUBERT 10	
SW901630	A3059	St Columb	ST COLUMB 1	MAWGAN 3	BODMIN 12	71160
			COLAN (face 3)	NEWQUAY 7	TRURO 16	
SW908647		St Columb	TALSKIDDY ST WENN		MAWGAN ST COLUMB	71153
SW911602		St Columb		II MILE To Saint COLUMB		507527
SW912618	A39	St Columb		I MILE To Saint COLUMB		71162
SW926632		St Columb	TREGANA TREWOLVES		BODMIN ST COLUMB	71155
SW922643		St Columb		I MILE To Saint COLUMB		71154
SW929665	A39	St Columb		II MILE To Saint COLUMB		71163
SW936680	A39	St Columb		III MILE To Saint COLUMB		71164
SW937683	A39	St Issey	ST ISSEY LITTLE PETHERICK			397126
SW942617		St Columb	ST COLUMB NEWQUAY		ST COLUMB	71156
			BODMIN ST AUSTLE		TRESADDRN	
SW943693	A39	St Issey		IV MILE To Saint COLUMB		397162
SW908732	A389	Padstow	PADSTOW 2		WADEBRIDGE 6	507529
SW909748	B3276	Padstow	PADSTOW 1		WADEBRIDGE 7	396035
SW911704	B3274	St Issey+St Ervan	ST MERRYN ST ERVAN		PADSTOW	397127+396940
			ST ISSEY		ST COLUMB	
SW914721	A389	St Issey	PADSTOW 3		WADEBRIDGE 5	397158
SW931718	A389	St Issey	PADSTOW 4		WADEBRIDGE 4	397190
SW947715	A389	St Issey	PADSTOW 5		WADEBRIDGE 3	397159
SW951707	A39	St Breock+St Issey		V MILE To Saint COLUMB		67679+397160
SW961718	A39	St Breock		VI MILE To Saint COLUMB		67678
SW975725		St Breock		VII MILE To Saint COLUMB		67677
SW999730		Egloshayle		10 CAM		505802
SX013738	A39	Wadebridge		9 CAM		0
SX025747	A39	St Kew		8 CAM		505713
SX047766	A39	St Kew		6 CAM		351507
SX055780	A39	St Kew		5 CAM		351506
SX066792	A39	St Teath		4 CAM		505711
SX072806	A39	Advent		C		68474
SX097823	A39	Camelford		1 CAM		68527
SX099824	A39	Camelford	CAMELFORD	WADEBRIDGE	BODMIN	68535
SX091876		Trevalga	TINTAGEL	CAMELFORD	LANSON	68885
SX108839		Lanteglos		1 Mile To Camelford 1752		0
SX109839	A39	Camelford		L 16		68544
SX132862	A39	Forrabury		L 14		68667
SX144870	A395	Davidstow		L 13		505706
SX159874	A395	Davidstow		L 12		67387
SX175877	A395	Davidstow		L 11		67388

Launceston and north Cornwall milestones

Grid Ref	Road	Parish	Left Face	Front Face	Right Face	Listed
SS239054	A3072	Stratton	HOLSY. 7		BUDE 2½ STRATTON 1	503533
SS230068		Stratton		BIDEFORD 23 BUDE 2		0
SS236082		Stratton		BIDEFORD 22 BUDE 3 STRATTON 1		0
SS242096	A39	Kilkhampton		BIDEFORD 21 BUDE 4 STRATTON 2		0
SS254049	A3072	Launcells	HOLSY. 6		BUDE 3½ STRATTON 2	503535
SS268002	B3254	Whitstone		LAUNCESTON 11 KILKHAMPTON 8 BUDE 8		0
SS265033	B3254	Launcells		LAUNCESTON 13 KILKHAMPTON 6 BUDE 6		0
SS264049	B3254	Launcells		LAUNCESTON 14 KILKHAMPTON 5 BUDE 5		0
SS269052	A3072	Launcells	HOLSY. 5		BUDE 4½ STRATTON 3	0
SS264064	B3254	Launcells		LAUNCESTON 15 KILKHAMPTON 4		0
SS260079	B3254	Launcells		LAUNCESTON 16 KILKHAMPTON 3		0
SS262095	B3254	Kilkhampton		LAUNCESTON 17 KILKHAMPTON 2		0
SS250109	A39	Kilkhampton		BIDEFORD 20 BUDE 5		0
SS256137	A39	Kilkhampton		BIDEFORD 18 BUDE 7 STRATTON 5		0
SS255153	A39	Morwenstow		BIDEFORD 17 BUDE 8 STRATTON 6		0
SS260110	B3254	Kilkhampton		LAUNCESTON 18 KILKHAMPTON 1		0
SS260122	A39	Kilkhampton		BIDEFORD 19 BUDE 6 STRATTON 4		0
SS262166	A39	Morwenstow		BIDEFORD 16 BUDE 9 STRATTON 7		0
SX180764	A30	Altarnun		LAUNCESTON 12 BODMIN 10		68301
SX191873	A395	Treneglos		L 10		68091
SX264776		North Hill	FIVE LANES 4		LAUNCESTON 7	432410
			BODMIN 18		CALLINGTON 9	
			CAMELFORD 13	LISKEARD 10	PLYMOUTH 22	
SX266770		North Hill		LISKEARD 9iii		431710
SX 266796	B3257	Lewannick		CALLINGTON 9 PLYMOUTH 22		1406859
SX278745	B3254	North Hill		LAUNCESTON 8 LISKEARD 7iii		431723
SX273756	B3254	North Hill		2 M		0
SX274759	B3254	North Hill		LAUNCESTON 7 LISKEARD 8iii		431720
SX277776		North Hill		LAUNCESTON 6 CALLINGTON 8		431715
SX278788	B3257	Lewannick		CALLINGTON 8 PLYMOUTH 21		430672
SX280773	B3254	North Hill		LAUNCESTON 6 LISKEARD 9iii		431719
SX281776	B3254	North Hill	LISKEARD		NORTH HILL AND TREBARTHA	431698
SX288776	B3257	North Hill		CALLINGTON 7 PLYMOUTH 20		431726
SX286788	B3254	North Hill		LAUNCESTON 5 LISKEARD 10iii		431718
SX299764	B3257	North Hill		CALLINGTON 6 PLYMOUTH 19		431729
SX298797	B3254	Lewannick		LAUNCESTON 4 LISKEARD 11iii		430669
SX204864	A395	Treneglos		L 9		68092
SX217854	A395	St Clether		L 8		68389
SX214864		Treneglos		VIII To Cam		0
SX224806		Altarnun		LAUNCESTON 8 BODMIN 14		68312
SX231848	A395	Laneast		L 7		68352
SX242803	A30	Altarnun		LAUNCESTON 7 BODMIN 15		68240
SX246843	A395	Laneast		L 6		68353
SX254801	B3257	Lewannick		CALLINGTON 10 PLYMOUTH 23		430670
SX256803		Lewannick		LAUNCESTON 6 BODMIN 16		430668
SX266812		Lewannick		LAUNCESTON 5 BODMIN 17		503128
SX262840	A395	Trewen		L 5		432429
SX265863		Egloskerry		XI To Cam		0
SX275831	A395	South Petherwin+St Thomas		L 4		68412+393844
SX276865		Egloskerry		L4		67933
SX288832	A395	St Thomas		LAUNCESTON 3 BODMIN 19 CAMELFORD 13		0
SX291861		St Stephen		L3		68034
SX269970	B3254	Whitstone		LAUNCESTON 9 KILKHAMPTON 10 BUDE 10		0
SX266986	B3254	Whitstone		LAUNCESTON 10 KILKHAMPTON 9 BUDE (9)		0
SX274955	B3254	North Tamerton		LAUNCESTON 8 KILKHAMPTON 11 BUDE 11		0
SX284943	B3254	Boyton		LAUNCESTON 7 BUDE 12 KILKHAMPTON 12		0
SX298915	B3254	Boyton		L5 BUDE 14 KILKHAMPTON 14		67895
SX291928	B3254	Boyton		LAUNCESTON 6 BUDE 13 KILKHAMPTON 13		67894
SX348779	A388	Lezant		LANSON 5 MILE CALL 5½ MILE		393597
SX347793	A388	Lezant		LANSON 4 MILE CALL 6½ MILE		393596
SX303811	B3254	South Petherwin		L 3		503129
SX304841		St Thomas		LAUNCESTON 2 BODMIN 20 CAMELFORD 14		393842
SX307861		St Stephen		L 2		68031
SX303899	B3254	North Petherwin		L 4		67973
SX320837		Launceston		LAUNCESTON 1 BODMIN 21 CAMELFORD 15		503131
SX321833	B3254	Launceston		L J		503130
SX323861	B3254	St Stephen		L J		68033
SX345808	A388	Lawhitton		LANSON 3 MILE CALL 7 MILE		68405
SX345823	A388	Lawhitton		LAUNCESTON 2 TAVISTOCK 11½ CALLINGTON 8½		503134
SX348866	A388	St Stephen		L 2		68030
SX358817	A384	Lawhitton		LAUNCESTON 3 TAVISTOCK 10½		68399
SX367804	A384	Lezant		LAUNCESTON 4 TAVISTOCK 9½		393587

Bodmin milestones

Grid Ref	Road	Parish	Left Face	Front Face	Right Face	Listed
SW913584		St Enoder	B 12			50776
SW918590		St Enoder	BODMIN 11¾		NEWQUAY 7¾	71311
SW925595		St Columb		B 11		507729
SW939602		St Columb		B 10		71165
SW970611		Roche	B 8		T 16	70967
SW997624		Roche		WITHIEL		70959
SW989797		St Endellion	PADSTOW	PORT ISAAC	ROSCAR ROCK	24282
			(4th side) PORT QUINN			
SX013624		Luxulyan		5 B		70910
SX046633		Lanivet	To ST COLUMB	To ST AUSTLE	LOSTWITHIEL 1776	428374
			(4th side) To BODMIN			
SX046633		Lanivet		LANIVT		67575
SX041688	A389	Lanivet		2 B		67579
SX068699		Helland	(Rectangular capstone missing)			0
SX076667	A389	Bodmin	LANSON		LISKEARD	368043
					TO STATION	
SX070686		Helland		B 1		507024
SX086617	B3269	Lanlivery	ST AUSTEL	LOSTWITHIEL	BODMYN	70759
			(4th side) ST COLUMB			
SX082624	B3268	Lostwithiel		3 B		70797
SX080639	B3268	Lanhydrock		2 B		67541
SX086662	A38	Bodmin	L 11½		B 1	504619
SX082673	A389	Bodmin		1 B		Replica
SX089688		Cardinham		B 2		0
SX090610	B3269	Lanlivery		4 B		70767
SX099655	A38	Cardinham	L 10½		B 2	504618
SX091697		Cardinham		2 B		507019
SX033701	A389	Egloshayle		3 B		67652
SX046705	B3266	Egloshayle		B 3		67653
SX055716	B3266	St Mabyn		B 4		67737
SX057721	B3266	St Mabyn	ST TUDY	ST MABYN	WASHAWAY	67753
			CAMELFORD	PORT ISAAC	BODMIN	
			(4th side) HELLAND			
SX065712		Helland		B 3		67533
SX065713		Helland	BODMIN	LISKEARD	WADEBRIDGE	67525
SX060733	B3266	St Mabyn	BLISLAND	ST TUDY	ST MABYN	67751
			LISKEARD	CAMELFORD	WADEBRIDGE	
			(4th side) BODMIN ST AUSTELL			
SX064744	B3266	St Tudy	ST TUDY	BODMIN	CAMELFORD	67771
SX064746		St Tudy		B 6		67782
SX065745	B3266	St Tudy		B 6		67783
SX065762		St Tudy		BODMIN 7		0
SX066774		St Tudy	CAMELFORD	ST TEATH	WADEBRIDGE	67770
			(4th side) BODMIN			
SX072759	B3266	St Tudy		B 7		67784
SX072759	B3266	St Tudy	LISKD	CAMELFO(RD)	(ST) TUDY	505709
			(4th side) BODMIN			
SX073774	B3266	Michaelstow	BODMIN	CAMELFORD	ST TEATH	68546
SX074774	B3266	Michaelstow		B 8		505710
SX088715		Helland		3 B		507021
SX089729		Blisland		B 4		67313
SX087738		St Breward	BODMIN	CAMELFORD	ST TUDY	67434
SX089731		Blisland	CAMELFORD	WADEBRIDGE	BODMIN	67361
			(4th side) BLISSLAND			
SX086743		St Breward		5 B		0
SX082757		St Breward		6 B		Replica
SX085751		St Breward	Cam Rod	Bodmin Rode		67431
SX082773		St Tudy		7 B		Replica
SX084787	B3266	Michaelstow		8 B		Replica
SX090704		Helland	BODMIN	LISKEARD	CAMELFORD	508685
			(4th side) WADEBRIDGE			
SX098701	A30	Cardinham	L XIX		B 3	507027
SX090802	B3266	Advent		B 9		68462
SX096816	B3266	Advent		B 10		68461
SX107646	A38	Cardinham	L 9½		B 3	0
SX116633		St Winnow		4 B		1409033
SX121648	A38	Cardinham	L 8½		B 4	504563
SX137651	A38	Broadoak	L 7½		B 5	504562
SX153652	A38	Broadoak	L 6½		B 6	504561
SX166649	A38	St Neot	L 5½		B 7	62251
SX195649	A38	Dobwalls	L 3½		B 9	504560
SX103704	A30	Cardinham		Blisland 2 B 3		507022
SX112709	A30	Blisland		B 4		67312
SX118724		Blisland		BODMIN		0
SX172750	A30	St Neot		B 9		504622
SX180764	A30	Altarnun		LAUNCESTON 12 BODMIN 10		68301
SX212800	A30	Altarnun		B 13		68241
SX253822		Altarnun	LAUNCESTON RODE	CAMELFORD	BODMY(N) RODE	68232

St Austell, Lostwithiel, Luxulyan and Roseland milestones

Grid Ref	Road	Parish	Left Face	Front Face	Right Face	Listed
SW878372	A3078	Gerrans		ST MAWES 4¼ TREGONY 6¼		509241
SW890382	A3078	Gerrans		ST MAWES V TREGONY V		509240
SW858428		St Michael Penkevil		FROM TREGOTHNAN 1 MILE		508989
SW868437		St Michael Penkevil		FROM TREGOTHNAN 2 MILES		508990
SW876452		St Michael Penkevil		FROM TREGOTHAN 3 MILES		508992
SW884464		St Michael Penkevil		FROM TREGOTHNAN 4 MILES		508993
SW892465		Probus	TRURO 5		TREGONY 2½	508988
SW909405	A3078	Veryan		ST MAWeS 7 TRegONy 3		508358
SW911456		Tregony	GRAMPOUND ROAD 3¼ MILES		TREGONY 1 MILE	0
SW917451		Tregony	TRURO 7		TREGONY ½	508365
SW918469		Probus	TREGONY 2 MILES		GRAMPOUND ROAD 2¾ MILES	0
SW915484		Probus	TREGONY 3 MILES		GRAMPOUND ROAD 1¾ MILES	0
SW924401		Veryan	illegible		illegible	0
SW920420	A3078	Veryan	ST MaWES 8 TReGONY 2		RUAN 2	508357
SW921432	A3078	Ruan Lanihorne		VeRyaN 3 TREGONEY 1		508359
SW932404		Veryan		illegible		0
SW932404		Veryan	illegible	illegible	illegible	0
SW932410		Veryan	illegible		S AUS....	0
SW953469	B3287	Cuby	TO.....NT....	TO....AND....	TO....	0
SW957473		Grampound		ST A USTELL	TO GRAMPOUND and TREG	71353
SW952489	A390	Grampound		ST AUSTEL IIIIi TRURO IX		71356
SW964497		Creed		ST AUSTEL IIIi TRURO X		71355
SW9724/3		St Ewe	GRAMP OUND		St AUSTE LL	71504
SW984471		St Ewe	ST EWE	GRAM POUND		71505
SW991471		St Ewe	GRAMPOUND AND TREGONY	MEVAGIS SEY	St AUSTE LL	71506
SW915504		Ladock	TREGONY 4¼ MILES		BLUE ANCHOR 5 MILES	0
SW917500		Probus	TREGONY 4 MILES		GRAMPOUND ROAD ¼ MILE	0
SW910576		St Enoder	GRAMPOUND ROAD		TRURO	71309
SW920518		Ladock	GRAMPOUND ROAD 1 MILE		BLUE ANCHOR 4 MILES	0
SW920534		Ladock	GRAMPOUND ROAD 2 MILES		BLUE ANCHOR 3 MILES	0
SW980502		St Mewen		ST AUSTEL Iii TRURO XI		71452
SW992512	A390	St Mewen		ST AUSTEL Ii TRURO XII		71426
SX008479	B3273	St Austell	ST A 3		HELIGAN 1	508306
SX011463		St Austell	TO GRAM POUND	TO MEVAG ISSEY	ST AUST ELL	478860
SX006520	A390	St Austell		ST AUSTEL i TRURO XIII		507031
SX005553	A391	Treverbyn	B 9		St A 2	478897
SX011509	B3273	St Austell		ST A 1		507524
SX018523		St Austell		STAUSTELL ½ MILE TRURO XIV MILES		1407574
SX012539	A391	Treverbyn	B 10		St A 1	478900
SX011566	A391	Treverbyn	B 8		St A 3	478899
SX014581	A391	St Austell	B 7		St A 4	507054
SX018597	A391	Treverbyn	B 6		St A 5	507030
SX028510		St Austell	PENRICE 1 MILE		ST AUSTLE 1¾	478835
SX025524		St Austell	PENRICE 2 MILES		ST AUSTEL ¾	507035
SX034524	A390	St Austell		ST AUSTEL Ii TRURO XV		507028
SX049531	A390	St Austell		ST AUSTEL Iii TRURO XVI		478839
SX044571		Luxulyan		LUXULYA N 1 MILE		70915
SX043593		Luxulyan		LUXULYAN 1 MILE		70914
SX056545		St Austell		LUXULYAN 3 MILES		506702
SX050558		Luxulyan		LUXULYAN 2 MILES		70916
SX061537	A390	St Austell		ST AUSTEL IIIi TRURO XVII		506699
SX069551	A390	St Austell		ST AUSTEL IIIIi TRURO XVIII		506700
SX078561	A390	St Austell		ST AUSTEL Vi TRURO XIX		506701
SX087582	B3269	Lanlivery	PAR		FOWEY	70760
SX089591	A390	Lostwithiel		ST AUSTEL VIIi TRURO XXI		70798
SX039609		Luxulyan		LUXULYAN 2 MILES		70913
SX035622		Luxulyan	B 4		St A 7	70911
SX036621		Luxulyan		LUXULYAN 3 MILES		70912
SX103597	A390	Lostwithiel		ST AUSTEL VIIIi TRURO XXII		70881
SX119602	A390	Lostwithiel		LOSTW L I TRURO XXIII		0
SX124617	A390	St Winnow		LOSTW L II TRURO XXIIII		60650
SX135628	A390	Broadoak		LOSTW L III TRURO XXV		60527
SX149632	A390	Broadoak		LOSTW L IIII TRURO XXVI		60528
SX162635	A390	Broadoak		LOSTW L V TRURO XXVII		60532

Liskeard and Looe milestones

Grid Ref	Road	Parish	Left Face	Front Face	Right Face	Listed
SX137527		Lanteglos	LOOE	FOWEY	POLPARrow	60594
SX137560		St Veep	MANALE	FOWEY	LOSTL	504621
				St VEEP		
SX146561		St Veep	LOOE	LISKD	LOSTL	60610
				4th side - FOY St VEE(P)		
SX157543		St Veep	LesK. d	St VEEP	Looe	505803
SX150568		Lerryn	St VEEP FOWE	LOSTL LISKD	FOY	60609
SX165545		Lanreath	FOY III	PELNT II	LOST VI	60542
				LOOE VI	LANTH II	
SX163564		Lanreath	FOY IV	LISK XI	LOS V	506697
SX162572		Lanreath	LISK. d	LOSTW I	FOWEY	60541
				4th side - LOOE		
SX174523		Lansallos	LOOE 6		FOWE 3	61472
SX178522		Lansallos	LANSA	POLPE 2	LOOE 5	61467
				4th side - FOWE 3½		
SX171543		Lansallos	POLPERRO III	LOOE 6	FOWEY 3	61473
SX172571		Lanreath	LISK LOOE	LOS V	FOWEY V	60540
SX185530		Lansallos	LeRy(n)	LAnsallos	LooE	508369
				4th face - LISKd		
SX186545		Pelynt	LANREATH II	FOWEY IV	POLPERO III	508368
				4th face - LOOE V		
SX184569		Lanreath		BODMIN XII		0
SX196562		Pelynt	LISKd IX	LANREATH I	LANSALLOS III	61619
				4th face - LOOE V PELYNT I		
SX178633	A390	St Pinnock	LISKEARD 5½		LOSTWITHL 6	60599
SX191642	A390	Dobwalls	LISKEARD 4½		LOSTWITHL 7	504558
SX200525		Lansallos	FOWE 4½	POLPERRO 1	LOOE 4	61474
SX203540		Pelynt	LOOE III	PELYИT I	FOWEY V	61618
				4th face - POLPERO II		
SX236579	B3254	Duloe		LISKD 5 M		60685
SX265558	B3253	St Martin		TORPT 14		60746
SX288576	B5253	Morval		TORPT 12		60703
SX205648		Dobwalls	LISKEARD 3½		LOSTWITHL 8	504559
SX220649		Dobwalls		LISKD 2½ LOSTW 9		61257
SX244619		St Keyne		L H		0
SX244632		Liskeard		LISKEARD 1 MILE FROM CENTRE OF PARADE		382257
SX244642		Liskeard	LISKEARD ½ MILE TO THE CROSS IN CHURCH STREEET			382221
			TORPOINT 17 MILES		LOSTWITHOL 11 MILES	
SX244659		Liskeard		LISKEARD 1 MILE FROM CENTRE OF PARADE		382095
SX237668	SX240666	Liskeard	CANAL	LISKEARD	St CLEER	382108
SX261640		Liskeard	TORPOINT 16		LISKEARD ½ MILE	503127
					TO THE CHURCH GATES	
SX263655	A390	Liskeard		LISKEARD 1 MILE FROM CENTRE OF PARADE		382128
				CALLINGTON 7½		
SX265670	B3254	Liskeard		L 2		382241
SX275679	B3254	St Cleer		LISKEARD 3		503493
SX303574	A387	St Martin		TORPT 11		60745
SX319574	A387	St Germans		TORPOINT 10 MILES		62060
SX316595	A38	St Germans	LISKEARD 6 MILES		TORPOINT 10 MILES	62059
SX332570	A387	St Germans		TORPT 9		62063
SX334575	A374	St Germans	TORPOINT 9		LISKEARD 7½	62064
SX331589	A374	St Germans	TORPOINT 10		LISKEARD 6½	62062
SX347569	A374	St Germans	TORPOINT 8		LISKEARD 8½	62111
SX365543	B3247	Sheviock		7 Miles From Mount Edgcumbe		61952
SX360554	A374	Sheviock	TORPOINT 6		LISKEARD 10 ½	61942
SX362565	A374	Sheviock	TORPOINT 7		LISKEARD 9½	61943
SX378535	B3247	Sheviock		6 Miles From Mount Edgcumbe		61945
SX375548	A374	Sheviock	TORPOINT 5		LISKEARD 11 ½	61944
SX389550	A374	Antony	TORPOINT 4		LISKEARD 12 ½	61664
SX392529	B3247	Antony		5 Miles From Mount Edgcumbe		61665
SX301600	A38	Menheniot	LISKEARD 5 MILES		TORPOINT 11 MILES	0
SX408528	B3247	Millbrook		4 Mile From Mot Edgcumbe		61913
SX419519	B3247	Millbrook		3 Mile From Mot Edgcumbe		61924
SX416555	A374	Antony	TORPOINT 2		LISKEARD 14 ½	61667
SX430559	A374	Torpoint	TORPOINT 1 FERRY		LISKEARD 15 ½	0
SX430515	B3247	Maker with Rame		2 Mile From Mot Edgcumbe		61725
SX437518	B3247	Maker with Rame		1½ Mile From Mot Edgcumbe		61726
SX444520	B3247	Maker with Rame		1 Mile From Mot Edgcumbe		61727
SX447527	B3247	Maker with Rame		½ Mile From Mot Edgcumbe House		61774

Saltash and Callington milestones

Grid Ref	Road	Parish	Left Face	Front Face	Right Face	Listed
SX294661	A390	Menheniot		LISKEARD 3 CALLINGTON 5½		61279
SX279724	B3254	Linkinhorne		LISKEARD 6		62154
SX278734	B3254	Linkinhorne		LISKEARD 7		62153
SX280709	B3254	Linkinhorne		LISKEARD 5		62170
SX328588		St Germans		7 M 22 P 1 Y S B		62061
SX343595	A38	St Germans		6 miles To S		430028
SX398598	A38	Saltash		2 M S		60450
SX307670	A390	St Ive		C 4½ L 4		61352
SX304687		St Ive	RED GATE	S GERMANS	LANCESTON	61345
SX308682		St Ive	CALLINGTON	LAUNCESTON	S GERMANS	503453
SX301698		St Ive	LISKEARD	S GERMANS	CALLINGTON	61346
			4th side LAUNCESTON			
SX318679	A390	St Ive	LAUNCESTON	LISKEARD	CALLINGTON	61359
SX318679	A390	St Ive		C 3½ L 5		61360
SX321672		St Ive		Put on		61354
SX335678	A390	St Ive		C 2½ L 6		61351
SX340679		St Ive		TAKE OFF		61355
SX347678		Callington		WHEEL ROAD TO CALLN		61241
SX348680	A390	Callington		C 1½ L 7		61244
SX347699		Callington		C / 6 Furlos / 25 Poles		61209
SX354600		Landrake		L 1½		61999
SX357600	A38	Landrake		V miles To S		503273
SX352653		St Mellion		C 3		503274
SX355688		Callington		4⅓ Furlongs to Callington market gate L 8		61210
SX366633		Pillaton	CALLINGTON 4M		BOTUSFLEMING 3M	60912
			PILLATON 1½M		LANDULPH 4½M	
SX360679		Callington		C 1		503275
SX365691	A388	Callington	TO SALTASH	TO CALLING	TO CALLINGTON	61211
			PASSAGE	TON TOWN	(east) GATE	
			9 MILES	HALL	FUS 3 POLES 8	
				HALF MILE		
SX372604		Landrake		4 M S		62034
SX389653	A388	St Mellion		3½ C		61433
SX386669		St Mellion		2½ C		503278
SX398611	A388	Saltash		3 miles To S		60414
SX398626	A388	Botus Fleming		C 5½ S 4		503279
SX399642		Pillaton		4½ C		503276
SX302740		Linkinhorne	REDGATE	LISKEARD	LAUNCESTON	62148
			4th side CAMELFORDE			
SX309752	B3257	Linkinhorne		CALLINGTON 5 PLYMOUTH 18		62155
SX324745	B3257	Linkinhorne		CALLINGTON 4 PLYMOUTH 17		62156
SX331721		South Hill		C 2Mls 6 Fur		61438
SX338739	B3257	Stoke Climsland		CALLINGTON 3 PLYMOUTH 16		394060
SX346700		Callington		C 6 Furlos 25 Poles		61209
SX346734	A388	Stoke Climsland	L 8		C 2½	0
SX348750	A388	Stoke Climsland	L 7		C 3½	0
SX348765	A388	Stoke Climsland	L 6		C 4½	0
SX354721	A388	Stoke Climsland	C 1½		L 9	394058
SX359769		Stoke Climsland		B C T		394064
SX360706	A388	Callington	C ½		L 10	503492
SX360729		Stoke Climsland	II + C	II + C		394455
SX360745		Stoke Climsland		III + C		394401
SX368759		Stoke Climsland	BEALSMILL CALSTOCK		BRAYSHOP STOKE	393942
SX360760		Stoke Climsland		IV + C		393994
SX372700	A390	Callington		C.1 T.8½		503495
SX373748		Stoke Climsland	HORSEBRIDGE BRAY SHOP		BEALSMILL LUCKET	393941
SX371762		Stoke Climsland	STOKE		HORSE BRIDGE LANSON	393943
SX380705	A390	Calstock	HORSE.BRIDGE		TAVISTOCK	0
SX386708	A390	Calstock		C.2 T.7½		60801
SX383713		Stoke Climsland		C 2		394128
SX388728		Stoke Climsland		C 3		393995
SX398748		Stoke Climsland		C 4¾ MILES		394156
SX412594		Saltash		1 mile To S 1765		60447
SX421594		Saltash		1 mile To S		503135
SX431586		Saltash		B S T		0
SX412603	A388	Saltash		II miles To S		60413
SX402709	A390	Calstock		C.3 T.6½		503497
SX418708	A390	Calstock		C.4 T.5½		0
SX431714	A390	Calstock		C.5 T.4½		503500
SX453572		Plymouth		2 / MILES / FROM / PLYMOUTH		
SX465563		Plymouth		1 / MILE / FROM / PLYMOUTH		

INDEX